What Are the Sacred Roots of Islam?

And the Planned Modern Islamic Society

Jamil Effarah

authorHOUSE®

AuthorHouse™
1663 Liberty Drive
Bloomington, IN 47403
www.authorhouse.com
Phone: 1 (800) 839-8640

Published by AuthorHouse 06/15/2016

ISBN: 978-1-5246-1450-8 (sc)
ISBN: 978-1-5246-1449-2 (e)

Print information available on the last page.

Scripture quotations marked KJV are from the Holy Bible, King James Version
(Authorized Version). First published in 1611. Quoted from the KJV Classic
Reference Bible, Copyright © 1983 by The Zondervan Corporation.

TABLE OF CONTENTS

DEDICATED TO

The New Arab American Generations and to the elite of the world community who are eager to learn more about the crucial facts as bases to Arab history, culture, civilization, identity and common heritage of a background that should make the Arab new generations understand how their monolithic believes and their monotheistic doctrine that their ancestors brought to the world despite current events of the new tactic of "creative anarchy in politics," Messianic Judaism and Islamic State in Syria and Levant" are all involved in destroying the Arab World.

PREFACE

I was uprooted from my home in Haifa, Palestine, in 1948, along with my community; such change in my life caused me to be involved in the politics of the Middle East for over half of a century. Most Palestinians were thrown to the winds to live in tents, and to roam from one Arab country to another waiting for a form of a peaceful settlement. With my family, I was 13 years old when we settled in Lebanon and reinstate our original Lebanese nationality; I pursued my education at the American University of Beirut (AUB). But after years of struggle for survival, working in different Arab countries, such as the Sudan, Saudi Arabia and Kuwait, and back into Lebanon to establish an educational enterprise "Kfarshima College", in Kfarshima, Lebanon, I was given the opportunities to visit the United States and decided to stay for my post graduate studies. The civil war in Lebanon prevented my return. I found refuge in California, and became a U.S. Citizen.

As a proud American citizen, I kept in mind the sincere words that the presiding judge uttered during the naturalization ceremony. He encouraged those who took the oath of allegiance not to forget their roots, their heritage and the people in their old country. Becoming an American citizen gave me the strength to enjoy freedom and tell the truth about my feelings and thoughts. I learned the value of time spent in thorough research that permitted me to express my own opinions openly, based on experience, and learned the importance of not being afraid from stating my viewpoints without hesitation. I became convinced that discussing sensitive issues in history about religions should not create intimidation, and should not be treated as "taboo" subject suppressed by the censorship of the powerful.

I learned that social studies and religious researches compete in favor of understanding and explaining the concept of faith in the human race. And through investigating the realities, I will become able to find the answer for the question: *what is the truth?* Man work, his thinking, his revisions are neither complete nor perfected, but man's effort should be respected for his endeavors.

In this book *"What Are the Sacred Roots of Islam"*, I attempt to provide historical evidence, in-depth knowledge and perception to what is supposed to be religious sacred revelation for the roots of Islam and to what the Arab Prophet established, through the Noble Qur'an, in building a nation, a religion and a state, or how the Umayyad Regime needed a new religion to serve the basis for its expansion. After searching for spiritual roots, I try to show how the Prophet Muhammad's Message was heard, contemplated, and believed in, based on the Nazarene teachings. Today Islam is spread all over the world.

I believe that religion gives a service to the human race, and is incorporated into man's daily living and constitutes an integral part of human cultural heritage. To understand the "Islamic Revelation" is to accept and understand the traditions to which early Nazarene Arab and Hebrew tribes in the Arabian Peninsula and the Levant believed in and not the pretended Islam of the current brutal plan to create an "Islamic State" in Iraq, Syria or the Levant.

It is important for the reader to understand that the common name for Christians as "Nazarenes" is confusing and misused. Christianity is well known in Syria and the Arabian Peninsula. "Christians" by name was not mentioned in the Noble Qur'an; the reference was to the "Nazarenes" only. "Nazarenes" is another religion for the Hebrew-Christian sect believed in Jesus Christ as a prophet and kept their adherence to the Law of Moses. Today such teachings are presented in a group known as "Messianic Judaism".

The Nazarenes or Nazoreans or Nassarah are those who were mentioned in the Acts of the Apostles 15:5 *"But some of the Pharisees' sect who had accepted the faith, got up and said, 'They must be circumcised and also told to observe the Law of Moses.'"* While the "Christians" are those who were referenced in the Acts 21:21 *"Now, they have heard about thee that thou dost teach the Jews who live among the Gentiles to depart from Moses, telling them they should not circumcise their children or observe the customs."*

To serve the purpose for writing this book that deals to answer what are the sacred roots of Islam, there is a need to demonstrate the basic concepts and convictions in Islam that spread in the traditional tribal environment in the land Syria and in the Najd and Hijaz of the Arabia Peninsula.

I will introduce the ancestry of Islam and how Islam is deeply entrenched in the history of the Nazarenes and their theology, religious life, social traditions that was spread in Syria and the Arabian Peninsula and integrated and unified under the leadership of a Prophet Muhammad. A vivid review for the development and growth of the early Christian belief as represented in the five Ecumenical Councils of the Orthodox Catholic Church during the first 600 hundred years after Christ, and how the natives interpreted them before the Birth of Islam. Followed by presenting the Birth of Islam among the pre-Islamic Arab Christians, Nazarenes and Jewish tribes; and that the Qur'an as a Holy Book and how the Qur'anic verse difference between those supposed to reveal in Mecca and those in Al-Medina.

I will explain the divine qualities and signs that describe Jesus Christ in the Holy Qur'an at Birth, during His Early Life, His Message, End of His Life, the Judgment Day, and as the Word and Spirit of God.

I will introduce the political environment of the Prophet, the phases of change in the life of the Prophet, the genius personality of the Prophet and whether he was victorious in the wars; and discuss the difference between Christianity, Nazarenes and Islam as having one source of origin.

The intellectual Arabs – Muslims, Christians and Jews - should be interested in the history of religion, its growth and be ready to pursue the major goals of the true religious message that is based on love and justice, without holding of radical religious views or taking of extreme actions on the basis of these views that call for "Jewish state" and for an "Islamic state".

But as an Arab American citizen who earned his understanding of his past and remembering that the illegal British Balfour Declaration of 1917 promised a "national home for the Jewish people" in Palestine, where Arabs and Jews they were to peacefully coexist with all other communities currently living in Palestine (CITE). The Balfour Declaration also stated that the rights of all Palestinians, Jewish or not, were to be protected, yet we now find in Palestine a Jewish military state that has been neglecting the rights of non-Jewish Palestinians. Since 1948, Palestinians have been being uprooted from their homes and forced into tent communities in surrounding countries while Jewish immigrants, hailing from over one-hundred countries and speaking eighty-four different languages, have been replacing them.

Over sixty-eight years of bloodshed and dispute later, American presidents still act as brokers trying to fix the Palestinian dilemma that is causing a major crisis in the Middle East. They have called for meetings in Camp David, bringing Palestinian and Israeli Leaders to sit at a round table to negotiate peace. A peace that ends up a scribble on a piece of paper, and an argument on how to divide the piece of land that seems to always come short of the needs of Palestinians. Failed negotiations and an increasingly infuriated Palestinian people have led to Palestinian Intifadas (uprisings). This has created new rounds of Palestinian-Israeli bloodshed. More Palestinian uprisings are still expected to come in their attempts to end the struggle.

Diplomatically, those leaders are very smart in metamorphosing the vital issues of human rights into a game named peace, and interchanging the concept of "peace" for "pieces". It is a creative and original technique to produce more tragedies, more bloodshed, and more death to innocent human beings; the solution would be very simple if it were based on justice, the international law, and the UN resolutions. It is important to end the occupation of the Palestinian territories that took place after the 1967 war and to dismantle the illegally built colonies in these occupied territories. This would be a courageous step in establishing the Palestinian State that can peacefully coexist with the introduced Jewish immigrants.

As an Arab American citizen, I feel the need to talk more freely about the urgent desires of the people in the Arab World. As an American, I have a moral obligation to show the rest of the world the greatness and the values of the American democracy.

American honesty and partiality must teach the oppressed people how to face their current problems with strength and courage. I have an obligation to help the oppressed build a real democratic life for their new generation, based on the concepts of justice, freedom, and equality for all.

In order to enjoy life, I think that American leaders should develop a new approach in dealing with their allies and friends. They should not allow those allies to take advantage of their mutual relationship with the United States and use it to abuse and prosecute those with differing ideologies. Americans need to analyze their foreign policy when they look for their national interests. Arab Americans are living in a great American nation; they should not build their greatness on force, retaliation and revenge. Americans should not build greatness on diplomacy of exceptionalism that carries the ingredients of corruption and causes real obstacles to progress and to world democratic ideals.

The delay in the progress to reach peaceful solutions to the Middle Eastern problems will continue drugging along as long as the American Administration does not allow justice to prevail equally to all the people of the Middle East.

As a scientific educator by profession, I also have the impulse to keep writing more articles and books to help develop better ways of communication among Arab American citizens, especially through an increased understanding of Islam by learning more about its historical and religious roots.

When I decided to tackle hidden religious issues that are treated as taboos not to be discussed in writings, but only to whisper about them in the ear of a friend, I decided to bridge that gap by talking about these issues that will minimize the religious conflicts among the Arab Americans themselves. I need to go back in history to pave the way toward understanding the historic pre-Islamic growth of the Arab tribal societies in the Arabian Peninsula. This approach gives the readers the knowledge and the understandings that will allow them comprehend the current relations of the Jewish-Christian-Muslim Arab companionship.

I started this uphill road by conveying my message in articles written in Arabic. I felt the tension of the old taboo still creating grudges among some of the misinformed Arab Americans (Muslims and Christians) and noticed that they are still carrying false grudges between them. They brought such fuzzy and ugly superstitions with them to the United States of America instead of burying them there where they belonged.

I have spent the last thirty years writing articles in a local Arabic newspaper urging readers to "think Palestine". I keep trying to help the readers understand the Palestinian calamity and the needed approach to overcome the well-disguised Zionist conspiracy to control the Middle East.

I decided to publish my articles in English. It is important to spread the knowledge among the new Arab American generations who do not read Arabic to learn the truth about their history and culture, to reject fallacies, and to start their own research. I published my researched English articles in two volumes, on-line, under the title **"THINK PALESTINE"**[1]. Volume one included articles written from 2001 to 2006, and volume two from 2007 to 2012, and volume three for my unpublished articles from 2013 to 2015.

I hoped the educated and the elite of the new generation would contemplate while reading the articles and I now hope they will use their inquisitive minds to comprehend and tolerate the rarely referenced and neglected parts of their heritage, culture, and history in this book questioning "What Are *the Sacred Roots of Islam*".

The current research deals with hidden historical facts that have nothing to do with politics. It is an intellectual attempt to clarify and verify the approach to create an honest dialogue among Arabs - Muslims and Christians - and the world population if possible. I try to present a lesson from history to learn and comprehend, and to reach a conclusion that Islam and Christianity are the product of one religion, and that the Arabs are one Middle Eastern nation, contrary to the overwhelming belief in the existing diversities and misconceptions by calling Muslims terrorists. Judaism, Christianity and Islam are religions developed from one founding set of beliefs in One and Only One God, and no appeal to any deity except Him. Jews, Christians and Muslims are brothers in faith, whether they know it or not.

The twenty-first century is expected to recognize an Arab awakening based on the acceptance of a mutual understanding among Arabs, a consensus needed to enrich their Christian-Muslim culture, and strengthen their Arab patriotism and belief in their Arab unity. Arabs are going through crucial times to prevent a foreign coalition from swallowing them and their

---

[1] www.AuthorHouse.com

countries. Arabs need a leader of Muhammad's caliber to reunify them and wake them up to understand their modern reality.

The open-minded readers, who are reading *"What are the Sacred Roots of Islam"*, are requested to keep in mind that if they read a "fact," they should consider the source. And if they hear a news story, they must check that it is true. Once the readers get the facts straight, they will be ready to acquire knowledge, and have a better understanding to begin a dialog and transmit their knowledge faithfully to others, despite the doubt whether mythology has referred in history or whether mythology has become the basis of history.

Recently, I read for a contemporary Muslim writer Shabbir Akhtar[2], the followings: "Most Muslims, including educated ones, know next to nothing about Christology. Few Muslims can distinguish clearly between the view that a man claims to be divine – a blasphemy – and the entirely different view according to which God volunteers to become human – the orthodox Christian conviction. And both of these views are routinely confused with the heretical doctrine that God 'adopted' a son... A Muslim cannot reasonably claim to be seriously engaged in dialogue with Christians unless he can possess a thorough knowledge of the Christian faith. ..."

I agree that the same charge can be applied towards Christians and their ignorance of the Islamic faith, and the many stereotyped images that Christians have developed against Muslims.

Most Muslims never read the Gospels of Jesus Christ, and the same is true that many Christians never read the Holy Qur'an. But if Muslims and Christians attempt to read intelligently and become able to know each other's Holy Book, no war, no conflict and no violence will take place among themselves. Christians and Muslims believe in Only One God and the Last day judgment. Therefore, the understanding of their beliefs allows them to live in peace and give rise for love to triumph over their differences.

The Arabs in the Arabian Peninsula, Jews, Muslims and Christians, have a completely different background than the people in the West. In spite of all confusions, the three main monotheistic religions came from the land of Palestine in the region known by Syria and is part of the Arabian Peninsula. The people of that region have authentic characteristics, a common history and common traditions and behaviors not easy to understand if the person did not live there as participant observer.

Pre-Islamic complex perception of the Arabic culture and civilizations were vital and well established in trade, in literature and in religious ideas molded together to pave the way for the coming of Islam. Islam did not change the Arab traditions and behaviors, but it modified and ratified them

---

[2] Akhtar, Shabbir, *"A Faith For All Seasons,"* Ivan R. Dee Publication, Chicago, 1990, p. 182.

into laws. To be a participant observer to the life in the Middle East, a person should be very close to the Middle East.

While researching references for this book, an interesting story attracted my attention; it was traced back to the third Century AD. It says that the Church fathers who spent time in the East: such as Bishop Epiphanies [3] of the Melkite Church who was born and raised in Palestine, and The Catholic scholar Jerome, who wrote "The Latin Fathers". Both wrote about the synagogue curse because they knew about it, and agreed that the Western Fathers did never know it. The curse had never been uttered in the synagogue of the West. Epiphanies refers to the curse (three times a day they say: 'May God curse the Nazarenes').

Jerome, who lived in the East found it necessary to explain the whole matter to his younger western contemporary Augustine so he described it and referred to it more than five times in his "Epistles to Augustine."

In 1948, Marcel Simon published his book *"Verus Israel"* in Paris. He speaks in details about the Jewish curse, which was placed on the Nazarenes and the Christians who, according to the faithful Jews, are people of no worth to deal with. There is no other explanation for the curse except that it was totally based on fear and grudge.

Again, Julius Scott [4] summarizes the curse in the synagogue in the East as follows: "It was fear of these dangers that must have prompted Rabbi Gamaliel and his associates, sometime before the end of the first century, to alter the Jewish synagogue liturgy. This involved a change in the twelfth benediction of the Shemonesh 'Esreh (The Eighteenth Benediction [berakhoth] of the Daily Prayer) to contain a condemnation of Jewish Christians. This effectively excluded them from synagogue worship and continuing participation in Jewish life – their enthusiasm for corporate prayer would be understandably dampened if in doing so they prayed for their own damnation. From that time onward the break between Judaism and Christianity was final; as far as the synagogue was concerned, the Church was banned."

Interestingly, this curse-prayer exists in many different forms. The modern version has effectively been censored (as were forms in the Ashkenazi liturgies – but the Sephardi rites do preserve the term minim). [Minim is a term used in the rabbinic to denote Jews who reckon themselves, to be Jews, but the Rabbis excluded them from Judaism.] Of the older versions of this curse, the two best ones are the Palestinian Talmud, and that of

---

[3] Epiphanius, Bishop of Salamis, *Refutation of All Hersies –Panarion"*, translated by Philip R. Amidon, New York, Oxford University Press, 1990, section 29.9.2

[4] Scott, Julius, *Glimpses of Jewish Christianity from the End of Acts to Justin Martyr"*, unpublished paper presented at ETS meeting, November 1997

the Babylonian: The Babylonian version says: "And for informers let there be no hope, and let all who do wickedness quickly perish; and let them all be speedily destroyed; and root and crush and hurl down and humble the insolent, speedily in our days…"

The Palestinian version states: "And all apostates let there be no hope; and may the insolent kingdom be quickly uprooted, in our days. And may the Nazarenes and heretics (minim) perish quickly; and may they be erased from the Book of Life; and may they not be inscribed with the righteous."

The actual wording seems to vary according to the locality, with more direct references occurring as one gets closer to the East and mainly to Al-Quds Al-Sharif (Jerusalem), in Palestine. Of course, this course differs than what St. Paul, the Apostle, who tells us in his epistle to the Galatians about the concept related to the curse as practiced in the Law of Moses. He says that "… It is written, Cursed is everyone who does not hold to all things that are written in the book of the Law, to perform them. But that the Law justifies before no man God is evident, because 'he who is just lives by faith,' but the Law does not rest on faith….Christ redeemed us from the curse of the Law…" [5]

Is the curse used in the Mosaic Law still applicable? Is it reflected into the Arab-Israeli relationship? Is it not a reason that invites for more tension in the Middle East? Or, is it still part of the "Jewish" liturgies to carry on in a continuous bloody struggle, in the Middle East, for ages to come?

This book *"What are the Sacred Roots of Islam"* has no theme except to tell the story of the political, religious, social and economic environment of the Arabian Peninsula inhabitants before and after the coming of Islam. Before Islam is a period referred to in literature as the "Jahiliyah Era", (or a state of prevailing ignorance – paganism). Jahiliyah is a name that does not reflect the logical facts of the time. It is an emotional name set to meet the change that resulted out of spreading the new "Hanifa" Nazarene's message of Islam from that part of the Arabian Peninsula. The hidden truth is that Jahiliyah period was an age of enlightenment, full of knowledge of religion and is most effective in literature and mainly, poetry recitation.[6] Christian Arab poets were responsible for the most outstanding (suspended) poems that prospered and lived as monuments in the Arabic literature, up to this date. It was also a period of activities, in trade, that took place in Hijaz and the surrounding areas.

---

[5] St. Paul the Apostle, *Epistle to the Galatians*, Chapter 3 Verses 10-13

[6] To those who are interested in learning about poetry in the Arabic "Jahili" literature, Dr. Mustafa Naseff's book *"A Second Reading to Our Old Poetry"* is a worthy reference; published in Arabic by Dar Al-Andalus in Beirut, 1981.

When I started the writing about *"what are the Sacred Roots of Islam"*, I felt strongly quoting St. Matthew [7] on Jesus Christ's commission of His Apostles, before His Ascension to Heaven: "But the eleven disciples went into Galilee, to the mountain where Jesus had directed them to go. And when they saw him they worshipped him; but some doubted. And Jesus drew near and spoke to them saying, 'All power in heaven and on earth has been given to me.' Go, therefore, and make disciples of all nations, baptizing them in the name of the Father, and of the Son, and of the Holy Spirit, teaching them to observe all that I have commanded you; and behold, I am with you all days, even unto the consummation of the world." Again, we hear St. Mark [8] says: "And he said to them, "Go into the whole world and preach the gospel to every creature."

It becomes obvious that the message of Christianity is universal to all nations in the whole world. It does not call for Jewish nationhood, as expected by the Jews from "their Savior" to act. But, the Disciples of Christ and His followers left Jerusalem and Palestine and followed Christ's teachings to spread all over the whole world and preach the Gospel of Christ and the Evangelical Monotheism concept to every creature. The Disciples, Apostles and Followers of Christ were calling for monotheism among the atheistic environments, before preaching the Gospel. St. Paul [9] took the expression of the "Unknown God" and applied it to the true God whom in fact they did not know.

It is also natural and more obvious to start preaching in the neighborhood of Palestine, in Syria and the Arab countries, in the Arabian Peninsula before spreading to the outside world. We are told by St. Paul that his first epistle, after he received the miraculous call from Christ "to preach His name among all nations" or "to the unlearned or ignorant." [10] It was carried by the Nazarenes to Arabia and revealed in the Qur'an, when referring to the Jews in Mecca and Medina describing the Arab inhabitants in the verse, "They say; there is no call on us with these ignorant." [11] "And say to the People of

---

[7] From the Holy Gospel of Jesus Christ according to St. Matthew, Chapter 28, verses 16-19.

[8] From the Holy Gospel of Jesus Christ according to St. Mark, Chapter 16, verse 5.

[9] From St. Paul's *"Discourse in Areopagus of Athens"* as recorded in the (Acts of the Apostles 17: 22-32)

[10] [The term "**Umam** or **Ummy**", used for the people who do not write or read (unlettered, unlearned or ignorant), is Hebrew in origin. While "Ummy" in the Qur'an is intended to be "an Arab" as in Sura Al-Jumua (the congregation), Friday, verse 2.

[11] The Noble Qur'an, Sura Al-Imran - the House of Imran) 3: verse 75

the Book, and to those who are unlearned: Do you submit yourselves? If they do, they are in right guidance." [12]

Six hundred years before Islam, St. Paul spoke about himself, he says: [13] "...And without going up to Jerusalem to those appointed apostles before me, I retired into Arabia, and again returned to Damascus." Arabia, or the land (diyar) of the Arabs, extends from the North of Syria and Palestine up to Hijaz. We learn from the epistles of St. Paul, his eagerness to spread Christianity among the unlearned people. It does not hurt us to conclude that he left his impact and influence among the people of Arabia.

The followers of Christ who went to preach in India went along the communication route that passes from the East of the Arabian Peninsula to its West, through Hijaz, Yemen, Hadramout, and Oman to India. In reading the events that took place during the early spread of Nazarenes that the apostles Yose and Jude, the brothers of Jacob, preached in Dir'aa, Syria, and became martyrs there; Taymoun, one of the seven deacons of Busra or Basra, became a bishop there too. Famous Arab Muslim historians [14] agree that the apostle of Jesus Christ who preached his religion in Hijaz was "Ibn Thalma". The Gospel calls this apostle "Bar-thalma-ous", an Aramaic name where Bar means Ibn, and Thalma, the lineage, and the ous at the end is from the Greek.

According to the Arab Muslim historians, Christianity monotheism had been introduced into Arabia and Hijaz through the "Nazarenes" since the early days of the apostles of Christ.[15] And according to the Noble Qur'an the Jews and the Nazarenes, are those God referred to in "Those are the ones to whom We have given the Book, along with Discretion and Prophet hood" ... and "Such are the ones whom God has guided, so copy their guidance..." [16]

To a Muslim, based on such verses of the Qur'an, the Nazarenes are mistakably considered "Christians", and to most of them the Nazarenes are the "true Hebrew Christians". That conclusion is the most confusing when a small group of Jewish faith accepted Jesus as a Prophet are the sect called "Nazarenes" is assumed to present Christendom or is considered to be an expression of Christology.

In the following study, I try my best to clarify certain concepts about the Nazarenes who do not represent Christianity. Those concepts are still misinterpreted, misunderstood and confusing in the Middle East, mainly among the Arabs, Christians and Muslims.

---

[12] Ibid. 3: verse 20

[13] From St. Paul's epistle to the Galatians Chapter 1 verse17

[14] In Ibn Hisham book "*Al-Sira*" (4:255), and in Al-Tabari (1:738), and Ibn Khaldun's "*History*" book (2:150).

[15] Ibid.

[16] Noble Qur'an Sura Al-Ena'am – (Livestock) 6: verses 89-90

The Nazarenes are known by the Arabic term "Nusraaniah" in relation to the City of Nasseerah or Nazareth in Palestine. (Nassarah is the plural of Nusraani in Arabic). By researching the origin of the Nazarenes, it was confirmed for us that the name "Nazarenes" was confined to those who followed Christ from "Beni Israel" and kept their allegiance to Moses. This is also confirmed in the Qur'an too, in Sura Al-Suff "You who believe, act as God's supporters just as 'Isa Bin Mariam told the disciples: "Who will be my supporters [along the way] towards God?" The disciples said: "We are God's supporters." A faction from Beni (the Children) of Israel believed, while another faction disbelieved. We assisted the ones who believed against their enemy, till they held the upper hand." [17]

The Nazarenes, mainly a Jewish sect accepted Jesus as a Prophet, were completely different from the followers of Jesus Christ, the Christians of all the nations of the world, who were known everywhere, since the establishment of Christianity, by the name "Christians." [18]

Tertullus, the lawyer of the high priest Ananias, accused Paul by saying "We have found this man a pest, and a promoter of sedition among all the Jews throughout the world, and a ringleader of the sedition of the Nazarene sect." [19] This is the first time the Nazarenes are named in the Gospel. It does not apply to a sect within followers of Jesus, but to a trouble-making sect within Hebraism itself.

It is also confirmed to us from reading the Acts of the Apostles and from the epistles of St. Paul that the Nazarenes from Beni Israel were a denomination, a sect, or a "Shiite" in relations to the convention or "the Sunni" of Christianity.

They adhered to the Laws of Moses and, later on, they accepted the imamate or leadership of the "kindred of the House" over them. In order to show the right of "the people of the House" in their leadership over the Apostles, the Disciples of Christ, they used to call themselves "the Cousins of Christ" or "the Brothers of the Lord" or "the Chiefs". They used to consider Jacob, St. James, the head of the people of the House, and the first Bishop in Jerusalem, as the Caliph of Christ, according to the eastern traditions.

It was also confirmed for us from "the Seven Catholic Epistles" that the Nazarenes' adherence to Moses' Law and to Jesus. Their belief took them

---

[17] Sura Al-Suff – (The row or the Rank) 61: verse 14

[18] See (the Acts of the Apostles 11:26) "it was in Antioch that the disciples were first called "Christians". In (Acts 26:28) "Agrippa said to Paul: 'In a short while thou wouldst persuade me to become a Christian'". As well as it is mentioned in (1 St. Peter 4:16) "But if he suffered as a Christian, let him not be ashamed, but let him glorify God under this name."

[19] Acts of the Apostle, Chapter 24, verses 4-5

at the end of the period of the Arabian Prophet to become "a heresy and an apostasy", in comparison to the main stream of Christians' belief.

In the first chapter, I talk about the history of the Nazarenes and present their history as the history of the early Jewish Christians of Palestine who may have left Palestine to all parts of the Arabian Peninsula between the time of the Gospel of Jesus and the Qur'an. Then on how I found out the different "Jewish" sects who believed in Jesus, the Messiah, and kept their adherence to the Mosaic Law had dragged themselves slowly to become a heresy and an apostasy to the Christians' creed, and cannot be called a true representation of Christianity.

Most historians agreed that diverse forms of Christianity flourished in the early years of the Christian movement. They considered the "Nazarenes", as a sect or a religion, and was one of the earliest Christian's movement.

As mentioned before, this book tells the story of the political, religious, social and economic environment during the "Jahiliyah Era," that was interpreted as a state of prevailing ignorance in the Arabian Peninsula before the coming of Islam. But to most historians that age was nothing more than a dynamic historic era preceded the spread of Islamic Nazarenes.

Once more, Nazarenes or Nassarah is a term related to definite Israelite groups who accept Jesus as a prophet and adhered to Moses' Law while the Hebrews of the Israelites rejected Jesus Christ completely. The same confusion is still going on.

Since the spread of Islam, Muslims through history and even up to this day have strange views about Christians. They misunderstood Christianity. They accused Christians and called them "associators". Muslims did not understand the concept of "Trinity" and the divinity of Jesus as Christians do. Muslims are under the impression that Christians do not believe in One God alone and that their Gospel is not a revealed book and is based on falsified origin. To such accusation, Muslims have nothing to rely on because they do not know or have the Christians' original Book to compare with and to show any forgery. The only Book true Christians have is God Himself as He chose to reveal Himself as human in Jesus Christ; while some current western historians shed doubt on whether Prophet Muhammad and the Qur'an are really true as Muslims believe.

Again, the belief of Christians in Trinity is the belief in the Oneness of God - One God Only. God, His Word and His wisdom in the way He presents Himself to the world as One God only. Jesus explain to Nicodemus, one of the Pharisees, that "For God (the Father) so loved the world that he gave his only Son (the Son), that whoever believes in him (through the Holy Spirit) should not perish but have eternal life. For God who sent the Son into the world, not to condemn the world, but that the world might be saved through him." [20]

To Christians, just as the "Son" Jesus is a true presentation for the Wisdom and Power by which God is wise and powerful, so the Spirit is the Holiness by which He is Holy representing the oneness in God. It is as simple as the fresh water is the same whether at the source (Father), the spring (Son) and the stream (Holy Spirit). Similarly, it is also true when we identify the heat of the sun (Father), the light (Son) and the ray (Holy Spirit).

Jesus Christ revealed the trinity doctrine in explicit terms, by bidding His Apostles to "go and teach all nations, baptizing them in the name of the Father, and of the Son, and of the Holy Ghost." [21] The force of this passage is decisive. That "the Father" and "the Son" are distinct Persons follow the terms themselves, which are mutually exclusive. The mention of the Holy Spirit in the same series connected to the others with the conjunctions "and . . . and" is evident that we have here a Third Person coordinate with the Father and the Son, and excludes together the supposition that the Apostles understood the Holy Spirit not as a distinct Person, but as God viewed in His action on creatures.

My forceful achievement is to understand the Arab culture and wake up the new Arab generations to preserve their heritage and their Holy Lands. To understand the controversy between the Christian dogma and what revealed in the Qur'an, the readers will understand the Nazarenes' doctrine.

I also present some quick historic events that coexisted with the Islamic period, and endeavor to show that if the believers read the Noble Book carefully, they will learn the Nazarenes' doctrines thoroughly. They will reach the same conclusion I call for; that is, the unification of the Book of God into the religious concepts, and that the Jews, Christians and Muslims of the Middle East are brothers in faith and belong to one family.

Every time Christians profess their belief, they pray "in the name of one God the Father Almighty, Creator of heaven and earth . . . and in one Lord Jesus Christ . . . by whom all things were made . . . and in the Holy Spirit."

Judaism does not believe in Jesus Christ even as one of the prophets. Judaism rejects Christianity and rejects Christ completely. Today, a group of Jews calling themselves "Messianic Judaism" proclaim that they accept Jesus as a Jewish prophet.

Nazarenes as a Jewish sect adhered to the Law of Moses and accepted Jesus as a prophet. They denied the divine nature of Jesus Christ. They were active in Syria and the Arabian Peninsula and they were known as Muslims (Nazarenes) before the coming of Islam.

---

[20] The Gospel according to St. John 3:15-17
[21] The Gospel according to St. Matthew 28:18

Christianity believes in Jesus Christ as the Only God incarnated, God revealed Himself as a Human Being to teach humanity the meaning of love, justice and charity and to praise Himself in the highest. God incarnated in Jesus Christ put an end to prophesy after Him.

Christianity does not believe in any prophet after Christ, because they already have God Himself. The only truth that Christians accept is based on the belief that Jesus Christ is the Only God Himself Who revealed/ incarnated Himself as a Man, while the Gospels are nothing more than guides, as interpreted by His Apostles, to His message of love. A message that God Jesus has for humanity is to follow and adhere. True Christianity accepts any Call, any time that reveals the presence of Almighty God and spreads spiritual and moral values and all teachings based on justice, love and peace on earth. Christianity accepts the call of Islam because it reveals the presence of God Almighty to those who do not believe in Him. Muslims believe in the Qur'an as the Holy Book revealed by God.

To Christian historians, the Noble Qur'an reflected the Nazarenes teachings as it refers to events and quotes from the Holy Book. The Call of the Noble Qur'an interprets the Nazarenes and the Ebonite's doctrines by "Revelation." The doctrines of early Christian Jewish sects (Nazarenes) adhered to Moses' Law and accepted Jesus Christ (Isa) as a prophet of God to save them.

As we are starting the third millennium, and in 2016, it is time to start a new approach of tolerance and create an honest "meeting of minds and hearts" among Arabs – Muslims and Christians to understand each other as the people of one nation, in order to understand and rebut the western interpretation. Such interpretations are based on accusation and falsified information that they consider as a matter of principle. But, those principles are still "vague and undefined," therefore; they do not constitute a basis for an intelligent "dialogue."

Currently the created an assumed "Islamic State" by foreign power forces in Syria and Iraq add to the confusion in understanding Islam as terrorists, killers and heart eater monsters.

History did not preserve for us much of the truth about the real conditions of "Al-Jahiliyah Era or pre-Islamic Era." Most of these conditions went away with the attacks, revolutions, and invasions, occupations and conquests that took place as a result of the spread of Islam.

In early Christian heresiology, Panarion was and still is a treaty on heresies written during the period 374- 376 AD. It is an important source of information on the Nazarenes-Jewish Gospels, Gospel of the Ebionites and the Gospel according to the Hebrews; and where Nazarene was used as a term to identify the Jewish sect that believed Jesus was the Messiah while adhering to the Law of Moses.

Early Christianity as presented by the Nazarenes' movement and that of the Israeli/Nazarenes Ebionites held that Jesus is a man and the Mosaic Law was binding. They spread in Syria and the Arabian Peninsula and helped in transferring most of the Hijaz region from pageantry to monotheism. That environment contributed to a certain extent to the fast spreading of Islam between the Arab tribes and the rest of the Middle Eastern region, North Africa and Asia.

Prophet Muhammad, the outstanding Arab leader, led the Nazarenes' faith as represented and fought victoriously in spreading Islam beyond Syria and the Arabian Peninsula. The Arab Prophet set the foundations for the Arab tribes in the "Arabian Peninsula" to unite and to spread out into an "Islamic Empire."

While recently some American historians, such as Robert Spenser [22] wrote books on Islam and questions the existence of the prophet of Islam who lived and led in seventh-century Arabia. Spencer revealed the shocking contents of the earliest Islamic biographical material about the prophet of Islam in his book *"Did Muhammad Exist?"* He uncovers that material's surprisingly shaky historical foundations. Spencer meticulously examines historical records, archaeological findings, and pioneering new scholarship to reconstruct what we can know about Muhammad, the Qur'an, and the early days of Islam.

The evidence he presents challenges the most fundamental assumptions about Islam's origins. His book reveals the followings:

- How the earliest biographical material about Muhammad dates from at least 125 years after his reported death,
- How six decades passed before the Arabian conquerors—or the people they conquered—even mentioned Muhammad, the Qur'an, or Islam.
- How he comes with startling evidence that the Qur'an was constructed from existing materials—including pre-Islamic Christian texts.
- How he wonders why a famous mosque inscription may referred not to Muhammad but, astonishingly, to Jesus. And
- How the oldest records referring to a man named Muhammad bear little resemblance to the now-standard Islamic account of the life of the prophet. While Judaism and Christianity have been subjected to

---

[22] Spencer, Robert, "Did Muhammad Really Exist? An Inquiry into Islam's Obscure Origins," Kindle Edition, Wilmington, Delaware, 2012

searching historical criticism for more than two centuries, Islam has never received the same treatment on any significant scale.

It seems that the real story of Muhammad and early Islam has long remained in the shadows according to Robert Spencer.

But, in this book, I give a quick review to the phases of growth in the Christians' faith as compared to that of the Nazarenes and the Ebionites before the spread of their teachings in Islam, the message of Muhammad, the Arab unity and the spread of Islam. I also give a historic background that eastern historians consider to the growth of Islam; to most of them, their interpretations show that Islam is a true combination and a real reflection of the early Christianity of the Nazarenes and Ebionites understanding of monotheism.

Currently, the Jewish Ebionites Community that was organized in 1985 and the current Zionist "born-again Christian" or a Judeo-Christianity philosophy and the Messianic Judaism do not represent the true Christian Spirit and Belief. What they are trying to proof is nothing more than a failing attempt to change the divinity of God Jesus Christ to another G-d YHWA. [23]

This book is written mainly to the young Arab and American intellectuals who believe in renewal, innovation and knowledge production that make the contemporary Arab elites' mentality open to global intellectual, psychological, social and human interactions. To those who believe that Arab intellectual heritage is the beginning of the Islamic period, Arab mentality relies upon a set of knowledge, scientific and cultural foundations and formations, and open to knowledge, action and creativity.

This book is written to those who believe that the Islamic "Revelation", based on the Arabic culture, is addressed to the human mind to comprehend, and therefore it addressed itself to the human reason. The "Revelation" was the starting point of the School that favored the acceptance of the tradition to which early Arab religious scholars, traditionalists, and the masses of believers adhered. With the spread of Islam across other nations and cultures, the position of "reason" was elevated. But after the collapse of the Abbasid Caliphate, a tendency toward asceticism was produced abandoning worldly life to immerse in the teaching of Sufism and ecstatic communion with God and the Absolute. The traces of that move toward mystical and its supernatural have remained to the present day and are thriving in most popular environments. It is my job as an Arab American citizen intellectual to help uprooting such extreme subcultures by grasping the approach to understanding the true message of religions.

---

[23] Ebionite.org website

I hope that Arab (Jews, Muslims and Christians) intellectuals prevail over all obstacles that will prevent them from pursuing the major goal of the religious message, based on love and justice, to help people correct misconceptions and foment greater understanding among them.

This book has no main theme except to provide a better understanding for what are supposed to be the sacred roots of Islam based on the "Nazarene-Judaism" or "Hebrew-Christians" teaching as was practiced in the land of Hijaz, and not be led astray by how modernism versus Islamic extremism such as what is called "Islamic State" in Syria and Iraq (ISIS) or "Daesh" the "ISIL" in the Levant that muddied the waters of modern and moderate Islamic religion into acts of terrorism.

I ask my readers for comments; if any one disagrees with me, he is requested to correct me. I ask the reader's permission to borrow from the Holy Qur'an the following verse, "SAY: This is my way. I and any one, who follows me, appeal to God through insight. Glory is to God! I am no associate." [24]

- Jamil Effarah, Ph.D.

---

[24] Sura Yusuf – (Joseph) 12: verse 108

CHAPTER ONE

A Summary of the Nazarenes' History

The objective from writing a summary of Nazarenes' history in the "Middle East" is to allow readers who are acquainted with the Noble Qur'an to familiarize them with what religions took place before it, mainly the Nazarenes teachings that was included in it with an "Ebionites" approach. It covers what Nazarenes believed in based primarily on the Hebrew Bible, Talmud, Mathews' Gospel and some of the writings of falsified origins and what traditions they practiced during the first 600 years before Islam. The history of the Nazarenes went through three major phases. The first phase started from the Ascension of Christ to the War of the Seventies. The second passed through both catastrophic crises of the year 70 to 135 AD. The third was started from the dispersion of the Nazarenes in the Roman Empire, until Christianity was announced as the official religion of the Empire in the mid of the fifth century.

1. The Nazarenes from the Ascension of Christ to the first Jewish catastrophe in the year 70 AD

This period of forty years is also known by the "Apostolic Period"; the Nazarenes followed the "straight way" in the evangelical belief by adhering to both the Hebrew Bible and to Jesus under the leadership of Jacob, St. James, and head of the people of the House.

Two events took place that caused the conflict and the split among the followers of Jesus of Nazareth into two "sects": "Nusraaniah or Nazarenes" and "Christianity".

The first event was St. Paul international appeal of Christ to all the nations. St. Paul appeal was based on complete independence of Christianity from Moses' Hebraism.

1

The second event was the Pharisees who came into the evangelical faith to change it into Hebraism, and force Moses' Law upon the faithful "Gentiles" of all nations. "But some of the Pharisee's sect, who had accepted the faith, got up and said; they must be circumcised and also told to observe the Law of Moses."[25] St. Paul sees the Pharisees' acceptance of the new faith as a dubious movement.

At the conference of the apostles and presbyters in Jerusalem in 49 AD, St. Paul reports, "But not even Titus, who was with me, Gentile (Hellenistic) though he was, was compelled to be circumcised. Although it was urged on account of false brethren who were brought in secretly, who slipped in to spy upon our liberty which we have in Christ Jesus, that they might bring us into slavery. Now to these we did not yield in submission, no, not for an hour, that the truth of the gospel might continue with you." [26] As Antioch was the center of the evangelical appeal to all the nations, some of the Pharisees who accepted Jesus used to come down from Jerusalem to Antioch to cause conflict among Christians to accept the Law of Moses. "But some came down from Judea and began to teach the brethren, saying, 'Unless you be circumcised after the manner of Moses, you cannot be saved.' And when no little objection was made against them by Paul and Barnabas, they decided that Paul and Barnabas and certain others of them should go up to the apostles and presbyters at Jerusalem about this question." [27]

a. Council of Jerusalem in 49 AD

The first Christian Church conference took place in Jerusalem in 49 AD known as "Council of Jerusalem" in the presence of apostles and presbyters or the elders "about this question" whether to force the Gentiles to go after the manner of Moses! So the apostles and presbyters had a meeting to look into this matter. And after a long debate, Peter got up and said to them, "Brethren, you know that in early days God made choice among us, that through my mouth the Gentiles should hear the word of the gospel and believe. And God, who knew the heart, bore witness by giving them the Holy Spirit just as he did to us; and he made no distinction between them and us but cleansed their hearts by faith. Why then do you now try to test God by putting on the neck of the disciples a yoke, which neither our fathers nor we have been able to bear? But we believe we are saved through the grace of the Lord Jesus, just as they are." Then the whole meeting quieted down

---

[25] Acts chapter 15 verse 5
[26] The Epistle of St. Paul to the Galatians, Chapter 2, verses 3-5.
[27] Acts chapter 15 verses 1-2

and listened. ..." [28] So Peter, the leader of the apostles blocked the argument by liberating the Christians of all nations from the Law of Moses and from being circumcised.

James supported Peter's attitude. The conference left those who followed Jesus from "the people of the Book" (the Judeans), in Jerusalem, free to accept Christ and the Hebrew Bible together. They were led by James, who was according to the believe of being a Caliph of Christ, who kept his belief in rebuilding the Temple of David, "...I will return and will rebuild the tabernacle of David which has fallen down..."[29] But by keeping to their old traditions and accepting Jesus Christ, James' followers have set the stage for the conflict between those "Nazarenes" and Christianity all over the world. No one can deny the creed of those Nazarenes as clearly stated in the Epistle of St. James "to the twelve tribes that are in the Dispersion." It is interpreted as an evangelical inspiration in a biblical format.

Who is James to be called "Caliph of Christ"? St. James the Less, the author of the first Epistle, in the "Catholic Epistles" that we read written in the New Testament, was the son of Alpheus or Cleophas. [30] His mother Mary was a sister, or a close relative of the Blessed Virgin, and for that reason, according to Jewish custom, he was sometimes called the brother of the Lord.[31] James or (Jacob) held a distinguished position among the early "Jewish Christians" or Nazarenes in Jerusalem. St. Paul tells us that James was a witness of the Resurrection of Christ; [32] he was called a "pillar" of the Church whom St. Paul consulted about the gospel. Although James was greatly esteemed by the Pharisees, and was called "James the Just", James was not saved from the Pharisees' persecution.

It is important to note that most "Gentiles" were pagan and did not have any relationship with Judaism, but they became Christians and accepted the "New Testament" and Jesus Christ teaching without considering the Hebrews traditions as they are not theirs. So they rejected the Hebrew Bible way of life of circumcision and adhering to Moses Law as St. Peter expected.

b. The Nazarene Pharisees Killing James

In 59 AD, when St. Paul was a captive in Caesarea of Palestine, he appealed his case, to be tried in Rome, as a Roman citizen. St. Paul escaped from the hands of the "Jews", and the news spread about his innocence,

---

[28] Acts of the Apostles, 15: 6-12

[29] *Ibid.* 15:16.

[30] The Holy Gospel of Jesus Christ according to St. Matthew 10:3

[31] Referenced in (Gal. 1:19, Math. 13:55 and Mark 6:3).

[32] St. Paul's First Epistle to the Corinthians 15:7.

and his success in converting the "gentiles" Romans into Christianity. The "Pharisees/Jews" reflected their rage upon St. James, the Bishop of Jerusalem, accusing him helping St. Paul's survival and running away from their hands. They started planning for revenge from St. James; the opportunity took place after the death of Phestus, the Roman governor in Palestine, who sent St. Peter to the court in Rome, with good recommendation, and before the appointment of Albinos, the new Roman governor. The supreme rabbi of the Pharisee sect, or "Jews", Hanan the Second, called for a meeting of the Sanhedrin, the Highest Jews Council of the elders, and decreed to kill James for his faith in Jesus as the Christ. They carried James to the top of the walls of the Temple and threw him into the valley, and stoned him to death. The historians Eusebius and Hegesippus relate that the Jews martyred St. James for the faith in the spring of the year 62 AD.

By the death of James in 62 AD, and the captive of St. Paul in Rome, the "Nazarenes Pharisees Party" moved to the second level in their adherence to the Law. They considered Jesus as equal to Moses, as another promised prophet. We have seen, in the epistles of Paul and the Catholic Epistles, and in the epistle to the Hebrews, direct answers to their deflected beliefs.

The Pharisee or Jewish Revolt against the Roman Imperialism took place in the year 66 AD up to 70 AD, and at that time early Christianity had already split into "Sunni" and Shiite" sects: the Sunni "gentile" Christians of all the nations, and the Shiite Nazarenes of the House of Beni Israel.

2. The Nazarenes between two catastrophes (70 –135 AD.)

In 66 AD, the "Pharisees/Jews" in Jerusalem, revolted against the Roman Empire, and the Roman Army came and besieged Jerusalem led by Phesbianus and his son Titus, to teach the Jews the lesson they deserved for their mutiny.

But before the blockade of Jerusalem took place, the Nazarenes in Jerusalem were warned of the coming siege, and remembered the words of Jesus and his recommendation to leave Jerusalem when besieged from the invading army, because its destruction gets near.[33] The Nazarenes run away from Jerusalem and Judea to an Arab-Aramaic non-Jewish community in Trans-Jordan (crossing the Jordan River to the eastern part of Palestine), and lived in Pella, and in Cochaba, and in Coele-Syria. They were saved from the blockade and from destruction. The siege was very severe, and people

---

[33] (As reported by the historian Eusebius in his book *"The History of the Church"*.)

ate each other as Eusebius reported by quoting what the Jewish historian Josephus wrote in his book "The Jewish War".

The Roman Army obliterated Jerusalem completely; they did not leave a stone rising above the other. The prophecy of Christ in the destruction of Jerusalem was carried out. It happened in the year 70 AD, approximately forty years after the prophecy of Christ.

After crushing the Jewish upheaval, then, the destruction of the Holy City and its Temple, the Roman peace prevailed.

Construction of the City was allowed, but not to rebuild the Jewish Temple that was the last stronghold to fall during the siege. So, the Roman built their Temple of Jupiter on the ruins of what supposed to be the Jewish Temple. Once the Temple had gone, the sacrificial system had disappeared, since it was forbidden according to the Pharisees and the priestly legislation to offer sacrifice other than in the central sanctuary, and together with the system, the Jewish priestly caste lost its overall domination. So, Jews failed to practice religion, as their influence in the City of Jerusalem withered away and vanished.

During the war against the Jews, the Romans destroyed the monasteries of Qumran for the Essenes Jewish priests who hid their books in caves underneath their monastery, but fire had eaten a big shank of, and what had been saved was recently discovered. [34]

In the year 76 AD, most of the "Nazarenes" went back to Jerusalem and to Judea, led by Simon, brother of Jacob (James). They also got isolated from the rest of the international Christianity because they adhered to the Law of Moses and to Jesus, in-spite of the warning that they received, during the blockade and the immigration, stated in "the Epistle to the Hebrews" from deflecting and becoming heretical.

The priests of Qumran were stunned by the fulfillment of Christ's prophecy in the destruction of Jerusalem and the Temple. They joined the "Nazarenes" in Jerusalem, but they accepted Jesus in a very strict biblical concept and in their priestly rigidity. They added more to the adherence of the Nazarenes to the Hebrew Bible over the "Truth of the Gospel". That new Nusraniah Essences' of Qumran movement, a "Jewish Christian sect" or "Hebrew Christian sect" had a new name "Ebionites", as they took their name from the words of Jesus: "Blessed are the poor in spirit" or "blessed to the Ebionites for theirs is the kingdom of heaven". They accepted the Aramaic gospel of Matthew, but reduced it to the first two chapters, not to mention the miraculous birth of Jesus from a Virgin (the Nazarenes believe

---

[34] [Another example for hiding books in jars, since the fourth century, for rival teachers who claimed to teach "the true doctrine of Christ", is reflected in the discovery that took place in 1945, in Upper Egypt, at Hag Hammadi.]

in the miraculous birth); that is why the Ebionites called their gospel, "the Gospel of the Hebrews".

With such variable theological currents, with time and interaction, the Ebionites managed to shape the Nazarenes movement completely. Fliche and Martin reported, [35] "The name Ebionites became a quality name, or a replacement for the name "Nazarenes" to denote the group of Christ's followers from the Jews." It seems that some contemporary researchers may be for political reasons; try to keep the history of the Nazarenes sect completely and clearly distinguished from that of the Ebionites. They accepted the Nazarenes as "Christians", and rejected the Ebionites as heretics. But those scholars who were there, such as Ireneaus, Justin Martyr, Origen and Eusebius who were closer to where the events took place and observed the gradual influence of the Ebionites on the Nazarenes should not be accused of being confused and confusing.

Eusebius[36], the Bishop of Caesarea of Palestine, as a historian, had the bishop library that grew with the time to contain all the writings of all earlier authors. He describes the influence of the Ebionites on the Jewish Nazarenes as such:

"From the beginning, they were called rightfully Ebionites (or poor), because they used to have in Christ low and poor opinion. They consider Christ, a normal human being only, got holy through grace. He was born from a man and Mary. They adhered to the Law, as they claimed that faith in Christ alone was not enough to be saved, there was a need to obey the Law of Moses too."

"Besides those, there were others who carried their name, but did not go along with their stupidity. Those did not deny the birth of Christ from a Virgin by a miracle from the Holy Spirit. But they were like them; they deny that of Christ's everlasting Life, in-spite of the fact that He is God, the Word, and the Wisdom. Then why did they surrender to the deflection and heresy of the previous ones? Similar to them, those others were eager to follow the material Law according to the manner of Moses. They rejected the epistles of St. Paul, the Apostle, and they called him "The Apostate". They never accepted any gospel except the gospel according to the Hebrews or (the Gospel of the Nazarenes), and nothing else. They observed the Sabbath, and followed the Jewish traditions, even though they observe Sunday too in memory of the Resurrection of Christ the Savior."

---

[35] Fliche and Martin, "The History of the Church" page 394.

[36] Eusebius, "The History of the Church from Christ to Constantine", translated by G.A. Williams, Miniapolis: Augsburg Press, 1975.

"They deserved the name "Ebionites" as it shows their weak minds. That is exactly what the Hebrew means by the word poor." This is a satisfactory definition for the "Nusraniah or Nazarenes"

According the Archimandrite Reverent Father Al-Haddad, [37] "this is the most correct historic abstract written about the development of the "Nazarenes" denomination creed up to the fourth century. That was the time when the Church Historian Bishop Eusebius wrote about them. He lived among them and we consider his words an authentic certificate coming from a respected eyewitness."

With the effect of the Essenes who followed Christ (They became Nazarenes), with their Qumran priests, were called "Ebionites", the biblical spirit overruled the Nusraniah and deflected from the truth of the Gospel. St. Paul noticed what was going on since the Pharisees became Nazarenes as hinted in "Now to these we did not yield in submission, no, not for an hour, that the truth of the gospel might continue with you." [38]

The common followers of the Essenes Pharisees Ebionites believed that the Lord Christ was born from a Virgin not touched by man. But Christ is not God, and the expressive names, they gave to Christ as "Son of God" and "Word of God" and "Wisdom of God", are used metaphorically. And in their growing "scientific" theological interpretation of the evangelical events, they describe the "Spirit" as representing the chief of the Angels.

This "Ebionites" approach in the Nusraniah is what St. Jude, the brother of James and Simon, intended when he spoke out before their bishops in his Epistle accusing them as those who were not sincere in embracing Christ, he said in the introduction: "For certain men have stealthily entered in, who long ago where marked out for this condemnation, ungodly men who turn the grace of God into one wantonness and disown our only Master and Lord, Jesus Christ." [39]

Around the year 80 AD, the Jewish Sanhedrin prohibited the Nazarenes from sharing the prayers with the Jews, under the influence of the rabbi Gamaleil the Second, as we mentioned in the Preface. Therefore, the Nazarenes and consequently including Christians were representing the

---

[37] The Archimandrite, Father Yusuf Durrah Al-Haddad (1913-1979), is one of the most famous contemporary Melkite Greek Catholic scholars and thinkers, in the Middle East. His writings have enriched the Arabic Literature with an educational and religious library of in-depth studies and analytical researches. His main collections of studies deal with Evangelical studies, Qur'anic studies and a series of Islamic-Christian dialogues. Father Al-Haddad encyclopedic knowledge is our inspiration in presenting his approach to the Nazarenes History.

[38] The Epistle of St. paul the Apostle to the Galatians, chapter 2, verse 5

[39] The Epistle of St. Jude the Apostle, Introduction, verse 4

atheist heterodoxy, from the Jewish point of view. That is why they must be cursed among the kind of the polytheists every day in their prayers "The Eighteenth Benediction". Their twelfth benediction says: "There should be no hope for the apostates! And let the State of Tyranny be uprooted in a hurry, and during our times! And let the Nazarenes and the polytheists vanished instantly! And be wiped out totally from existence! And have no luck with the faithful. Thanks to you, Adonai, for humiliating the despots!"

This Jewish anathema, from one side, and the independence of the Nazarenes from the Christians by holding to the Laws of Moses and the Gospel, on the other side, made the "Nusraniah" have its own status and creed. By the end of the first century AD, the "Nusraniah" became "an intermediate nation – Ummat Al-Wasat - (political body)" between Hebraism (Judaism) and Christianity, (later on, by the end of the second century AD, Hebraism was revived and modernized into Judaism).

All the endeavors of St. Peter he included in his first epistle, and specially the second; which was gathered after him. With the epistle of Jude, taken together With St. Peter's two epistle bring back to the straightway in Christianity. They insisted that they have seen in "being Nazarenes" the straightway and the right religion.

The Apostle St. John, was the last of Christ Disciple alive until the end of the first century AD, he wrote his first Epistle to the Christians describing those who call themselves the speakers for the Nazarenes as dissenters. During that period, Simon, the Nazarenes Bishop in Jerusalem, was leading the Nazarene Church following the steps of his brother and ancestor Jacob (James), by keeping to the Hebrew Bible and the Gospel together. Simon lived in the era of Trayanus Caesar. In Aktus, Simon was betrayed and the ruler of Aktus ordered him to die on the cross. Simon suffered painfully in his martyrdom, of which the ruler was astonished and said: "How can a person of 120 years old endure all these tormenting pains!" As reported by the church historian Eusebius (260-340 A.D.), who reported also that Yustus, or Yusa, a brother of James and Simon took the caliphate of the Nazarenes after Simon' death, with the help of a council of 15 bishops.

During the days of Trayanus Caesar, "the Chiefs" who belong to the House of Christ were betrayed, and were accused that they are claiming the Israeli throne. They were taken to Rome, but when Caesar saw them no more than commoners, he left them alone. So they were considered militants who took care of their own churches. "The Chiefs" kept their leadership to the House of Christ as caliphs of the Nazarenes, until the second Jewish revolt against the Roman Empire took place in the year 132 AD, during the rule of Hedrianus Caesar. The person who led the mutiny was from Kuzbat, who was called by the rabbi 'Akabat: "Ben Kaokab" – Barkokaba – he called himself, the promised Christ, and came to deliver Israel from the internationals. The Nazarenes refused to support him for his claim and for their allegiance to the Empire, of what the Jews got furious and made the Nazarenes target for the Jewish persecution on both religious and national levels. It is also reported by Eusebius that Jews performed massacres in manslaughter and killing the Nazarenes.

This time the Roman attack was a devastating and final blow and got rid of what could be called a Jewish nation, a Jewish State or a Holy City. In 135 AD, The Romans wiped the name of Jerusalem, and renamed the new city "'Eliya'" from the name of "Elianus Hedrianus Caesar". They prevented the Jews from entering the City, and such prevention touched the Nazarenes too. An International Christian Church was erected instead that of the Nazarenes under a Roman Archbishop. It is still surviving until this day.

In this second devastating catastrophe, the Nazarenes from the Israelites were spread thin in the Fertile Crescent of Syria and in Egypt; they lived in groups on the margin of the Christian churches.

3. The Nazarenes from the establishment of 'Eliya' until Christianity became the Religion of the Empire (135- 425 AD)

From the time the Nazarenes exodus from Jerusalem in 135 AD, and their disperse in the Eastern States of the Roman Empire, until the Roman Empire has made known its way into Christianity in the year 313 AD. Christianity became the official religion of the Roman Empire during the rule of Theodosius the Great and his sons in 425 AD; in that period rarely we find any historical resources to tell us more about the Nazarenes' creed, gospel or their presence.

This is Justin Martyr, the Catholic Philosopher, from Nablus, Palestine, and owner of a school in Rome, who wrote, at the beginning of the immigration of the Nazarenes to the Emperor and the Senators defending Christianity. He wrote his famous book "Dialogue with Trypho the Jew"[40]. To Justin, he answered all the inquiries of Trypho, and defended the Nazarenes as "they are going in a straight way." Being Nazarenes himself, he confirms that they are keeping up with the observation of the Mosaic institution, and accepting Jesus as the Christ. "They do not force their belief on others, in order not to make Christianity obligated to become Jews."

---

[40] Trypho was a Jewish theologian, attacking Christianity, and considering the Nazarenes as conservatives, and that Justin belongs to them.

Again, by the end of the second century, the famous Bishop Irenaeus gave a similar testimonial and pointed out that the Ebionites Nazarenes had a definite Gnostic background. During 182-188 AD, Irenaeus [41] wrote the "Ebionites agree that the world was made by God; but their opinions with respect to the Lord are similar to those of Cerinthus and Carpocrates. They use the gospel according to Matthew only, and repudiate the Apostle Paul, maintaining that he was an apostate from the law. As to the prophetical writings, they endeavor to expound in a somewhat singular manner. They practice circumcision, persevere in the observance of those customs which are enjoined by the law, and are so Judaic in their style of life, that they even adore Jerusalem as if it were the house of God."

In 230 AD, Hippolytus [42] of Rome wrote the Ebionites with a linkage to the Gnostics dogma. He said: "The Ebionites, however, acknowledge that the world was made by Him who is in reality God, but they propound legends concerning the Christ similarly with Cerinthus and Carpocrates. They live comfortably to the customs of the Jews, alleging that they are justified according to the law, and saying that Jesus was justified by fulfilling the law. And therefore it was, according to the Ebionites, that the Savior was named the Christ of God and Jesus, since not one of the rests of mankind had observed completely the law. For even if any other had fulfilled the commandments contained in the law he would have been that Christ. And the Ebionites allege that they themselves also, when in like manner they fulfill the law, are able to become Christ(s), for they assert that our Lord Himself was a man in a like sense with all (the rest of the human family)"

In the third century, the Scholar Origen stated that the "Ebionites" drift had prevailed over the Nazarenes, until the name "Ebionites" became interchangeable with "Nazarenes". In answering Calssus, Origen says: "It seems that Calssus does not know that those who believed in Christ from the Jews, they did not leave the Laws of their fathers, but they are still following its rules up to date. And their name is "Ebionites" derived from the poor quality of their Laws: In the language of the Jews, the word poor means "Ebion"; and the Jews who believed in Jesus to be the Christ have chosen for themselves the name "Ebionites" [43]

Another testimony from Origen tells us that the number of the Nazarenes was decreasing in the third century. In his previous reference he also says: "the translation of the verse (7:4) of the Apocalypse that the

[41] Irenaeus, *"Against The Heresies"*, translated by Dominic J. Unger & Rev. John J. Dilllen, Ancient Christina writers 55. New York: Paulist Press, 1992, Chapter XXVI, paragraph 2.

[42] Hippolytus, *"Refutation of All Heresies"*, 7:22

[43] Origen, "the Collection of the Greek Fathers", 7:4

number of 124,000 does not apply to the number of the Nazarenes because their number never reached the 124,000. But such a number applies to us, we, the Christians." The number of the Nazarenes started to decrease because of their introversion; they were hated by the Jews, and were alienated by the Christians. Origen distinguishes between the conservative Nazarenes and the aberrant Ebionites, he says: "Some of the Nazarenes are orthodox, and some knows that Jesus was born as any other human being." He also adds: "the Nazarenes Ebionites are two groups: one says in the inimitable birth of Christ, and the other says in his natural birth. And both groups deny His Everlasting Presence and so they deny His Deity." The Nazarenes creed reached the Holy Qur'an, at that level of rivalry and growth.

More testimonials reach us, from the fourth century. First, let us look at the Scholar Jerome [44] who gave special care for the Nazarenes, and translated their gospel to the Greek and to the Latin. He wrote to St. Augustine questioning, "What do you want me to say about the Ebionites? ... They are those whom the people call Nazarenes". From this message we predict that their popular name is Nazarenes and their "scientific" name is Ebionites. He also wrote that in their creed: "they believe in Christ that He is the Son of the Virgin Marie. They say that He was sacrificed under Pontius Pilate, buried and rose again. We do believe so. But because they want to be both Jews and Christians, they are not Jews and they are not Christians. "The words in Latin are as follows: *"qui credunt in Christum, Filium Dei, natum de Virgine Maria, et Eum dicunt esse qui sub Pontio passus est et resrrexit, in quem et nos credimus. Sed dum volunt et Judei esse et Christiani, non Judei sunt nec Christiani"*.

In another word, Nazarenes who are not Jews and are not Christians, they comprise by themselves a "people" that we can call a "Go-between (Intermediary) Nation" that fits between the Jews and the Christians.

By comparing the testimony of Origen with that of Jerome, it becomes clear that the Nazarenes calling Christ "Son of God" is an allegory; this figurative expression melted away by itself. Jerome also indicates that the Nazarenes used the Gospel called according to the Hebrew and the Ebionites is the same one when he translated, he says that: "This is the same Gospel that both the Nazarenes and the Ebionites accept."

Bishop Epiphanius, of the Melkite Greek fathers wrote, in the fourth century, about the Nazarenes and about the Ebionites. He says: "the Nazarenes Jews and their Jewish inclination have one common issue that distinguishes them from Christians and from the Jews. They are different from the Jews by their belief in Christ; and they are different from the Christians by adhering to the biblical traditions, Moses' Law, circumcision, and keeping up with Saturday. They are not Christians; they are Jews, nothing more than that." He

---

[44] Jerome, "Collection of the Latin Fathers", message 89:13

also adds that: "they use the Hebrew language in their prayers", the language that was expressed in the Aramaic Syrians. These successive definitions of their beliefs make them "an intermediate (go-between) nation" between Judaism and Christianity.

Archimandrite Al-Haddad, in discussing the Nazarenes issue, ends up by reintroducing the testimony of the greatest scholars of Christianity, Bishop Eusebius. Eusebius is the author of *"The History of the Church"* where he emphasizes that the Nazarenes followed the Hebrew Bible and the Gospel that they believe in the miraculous birth of Christ from a Virgin and that Christ is the Son of God, His Word, and His Wisdom. But they deny His Everlasting presence (preexistence) and His Deity. They used "Son of God" metaphorically. We also know that the Ebionites teachings controlled the Nazarenes, yet they denied such metaphoric description due to their "angelic" interpretation of their belief in Trinity. Such belief led them to deny the Deity of Christ, the Word of God. [45]

The references of the Evangelical Revelation warn us against the Nazarenes' heresy and apostasy through the early stages of their history. Christianity became the religion of influence in the Roman Empire during the realm of Constantine the Great. And from the First Ecumenical Assembly in 325 AD to the Third in 431 AD, and the Fourth, in 451 AD, the Nazarenes had fallen between fires: fires from their Jewish original background, and fires from the people of their religion, the Christians. Their umber grew less by getting more introverted.

In the middle of the fourth century AD, the Theodorian Constitution was published forcing Christianity as the State Religion. Since then, according to Archimandrite Al-Haddad, "the pressure to follow the Christian faith grew tremendously against infidelity. The Jews immigrated to Persia and became Persian spies and the fifth column against the Arabs and the Romans." [46] After that period, no outstanding source of reference to the Nazarenes could be traced in Christianity.

What Happened to the Nazarenes?

The question that puzzled historians up to this day is "what happened to the Nazarenes?" Did the Nazarenes vanish suddenly? Were they dissolved in Christianity or were they dissolved in Judaism? Some historians reached

---

[45] Archimandrite Yusuf Durrah Al-Haddad, "The Qur'an – a "Nazarene" Call", Al-maktabat Al-bulusiah, Beirut, 1986 [In Arabic]

[46] Archimandrite Al-Haddad, "Al-Qur'an wa Al-Kitab",(Al-maktabat Al-bulusiah), Beirut 1982, p. 32.

such suspicious conclusions. For example the scholar Jacques Zeiller shows that he relies on what the historian Duchesne stated in his Book, *"The Ancient History of the Church"*. He repeats, "It seems that a certain understanding had taken place between the Nazarenes and the Christian Church, individually, but not in groups. It also seems possible that some of Nazarenes went back to Judaism. And that the Jewish Nazarenes denomination was left defiled in the shade with degradation. With the growth of the Christian Church in the Roman Empire, Christians gradually went away from their cradle, by liberating themselves from the Jewish Nazarenes, in the same way they liberate themselves from Judaism." [47]

A contemporary American writer, Ray A. Pritz, wrote about the Nazarenes and considered their disappearance in the end of the fourth century AD.[48] While another contemporary priest from the Middle East, Archimandrite Al-Haddad finds out in his research and analysis that the Nazarenes did not disappear or dissolve in either Christianity or Judaism. To Al-Haddad, they never were left in the shade to defile with degradation and die. The Nazarenes and the Jews of the Middle East had a second immigration that took place from Persia to Hijaz; an area in the Arabian Peninsula surrounded by desert. The desert acted as barriers preventing Persians or Romans occupation. The move to Hijaz took place influenced by the fact that the tribes in the surrounding desert accepted different forms of faiths in Christianity before the Nazarenes migration. The presence of the Nazarenes in Hijaz and in Mecca (the mother of all Cities) helped to accelerate the coming of the Islamic movement.

The Nazarenes brought a new enlightenment into the "Jahiliyah" era in the fields of trade, commerce, literature, and religion. This information we receive from the Qur'an, the Sira and the Hadith (Qur'anic tradition), as it will be reflected in the coming chapters. [49] It is also important to mention that according to archeologists, surprising as it may seem, not one map before 900 AD even mentions to locate Mecca.

---

[47] Fliche and Martin, "The History of the Church"

[48] Pritz, A. Ray, "Nazarene Jewish Christians: From the End of the New Testament Period until its Disappearance in the Fourth Century." 1990. [We failed to order this book, not even from out of print books, to learn more about the book and the author; but from the title, the author assumes the disappearance of the Nazarenes in the fourth century AD.]

[49] Archimandrite Al-Haddad, "Al-Qur'an wa ... pp. 41-2.

Where is Mecca Located?

It is difficult for me to present conclusive evidence to demonstrate the discrepancies between ancient descriptions of Mecca and what archeology and historians have learned about the current location of Mecca and its associations with Abraham. If Islamic sources are correct in saying that Abraham journeyed to Mecca, it is surprising that there is no reference to this event in the biblical history. It would have required many months of difficult travel. If the Bible is correct, then it is surprising that Islam gives such a different view. Is there a possibility that the divergence is narrower than it appears?

But, if archeologists and historians can discover the original location of the Holy City of Islam and the location of the first Ka'ba, that it might also answer the questions and objections that historians have raised for years about associating Abraham with the Holy City of Islam.

To give more clarification to such situation, I intend to present some of what has been researched in Dan Gibson's book: *"Qur'anic Geography"* [50] which examines many geographical issues in the Qur'an. He presents a comprehensive study of every geographic reference in the Qur'an in light of its historic context. The book provides an outline of the entire history of the ancient tribes that lived in Arabia, in which references to peoples of 'Ad, Midian, and Thamud are identified with ancient civilizations.

Gibson argues that Qur'anic geographic references are concentrated in North Arabia. The original "Holy City" of Islam is not Mecca but another major prosperous ancient center of trade located in modern Jordan (Petra). Gibson shows how all prior civilizations in Arabia were connected with this area. He finds evidence that the original Holy City was in northern Arabia in the city of Petra; and theorizes that during an Islamic civil war one hundred years after Muhammad, the Ka'ba was destroyed and the Black Rock was moved to its present location. Gibson examines archaeological, historical and literary evidence that support this theory and addresses many questions and objections that readers may have. He explains why this location fits Qur'an and early Islamic history much better than Mecca and why references to this location were partially and ineffectively censored by later historians.

To support his argument, he provides ample evidence through an eye-opening study of ancient architecture, art and literature in light of the available geographic and archeological data. He relies heavily on the best early Muslim biographers of Mohammad and archivists of Sunna.

---

[50] Gibson, Dan "Qur'anic Geography", Published by Independent Scholars Press, 2011: ISBN: 978-0-9733642-8-6

In Part 6 of Qur'anic Geography, Gibson gives a detailed study of references to the "Holy City" near which Qur'an was first received by Mohammad and mentions that the city of Mecca which is mentioned once in Sūra 48-The Victory (Al-Fathh) verse 24. Qur'ānic commentators have traditionally linked the *location of Bekka* (…"the first place of worship…" as found in (Sūra 3-Al-Imran verse 96) Bekka is the one who weeps much, Arab historians related it to Mecca. There are numerous references in the Qur'ān to the sacred place, the Ka'ba, and the house; terms which are universally associated with Mecca today. Nevertheless, the Qur'an itself does not tell us in so many words that the Ka'ba was located in Mecca.

CHAPTER TWO

The Nazarenes' Theology

The (scholastic) theology is based on the persistence in the faith. The Right Way is the frugality in persistence. This is what distinguishes the Nazarenes of Beni Israel, in general, from the rest of the other sects, from going to extremes in Judaism, and going too far under the influence of the Hellenistic "Gnosticism", as a spiritual knowledge, to compete with Christianity.

Gnosticism

During the reign of Emperor Terayanus, (between the end of the first century and the beginning of the second AD), two opposite movements appeared in the Nusraniah (the Nasarenes). They were affected by the growing theology, which was based on, "Gnosticism" a Greek terms for "the people of science", the "scientific" interpretation to the evangelical dogma, and that the spiritual knowledge, rather than faith, was essential to salvation, they followed the style of the Apocalypse. They are: The "Cirenthusians", who were deeply affected by the "scientific" interpretation, they believed that a tangible paradise would come with the return of Christ, as reported by Eusebius in his "History of the Church". And the "Kasa'eeah" which was deeply involved with Hebraism, as reported by Epiphanius [51]. Bishop Epiphanius stated also that the "Kysa'ee" ordered the followers to direct their face towards Jerusalem when they pray, contrary to the Christians who pray with their face to the East.

The Nazarenes of Beni Israel theology was developed through historic stages. It is very important to understand the Nazarenes' theology by going

---

[51] Epiphanius, "The All-inclusive in History"

to that period of its growth between the times of Jesus up to the coming of Prophet Muhammad.

The Hellenistic Gnosticism penetrated Beni Israel, because they wanted to use wisdom with the sublimity of the written revelation that goes above it, through the Jewish Gnosticism. The Nazarenes of Beni Israel has inherited that approach.

Gnosticism was prosperous among the Essenes in Qumran, as their scripts show; and when most of them became Nazarenes, Gnosticism prevailed over the Nazarenes' theology.

In the beginning of the second century AD, the historian Eusebius reported [52] about Hajsyp testifying that the Gnosticism appeared by Zapotus "Who came from the Jewish sects that were spread among the Jewish people", during the time of Sime'an, (Simon), successor of his brother Jacob, as the Bishop of Jerusalem, in 62 AD.

From Palestine, came Simon who was called the father of the contingent Gnosticism upon Christianity, by the historians of the heresies in Christianity. Zapotus was, to them, the representative of the right "Nazarenes Gnosticism", while Simon represented the extremely deviated Gnosticism in Christianity. That group considered Gnosticism to be equivalent to theology, and the mystic knowledge in the revelation and in the vision. The Gnostic subjects were cosmology and cosmography, and the study of the beyond.

The Nazarenes' Gnosticism, in general, was the scholastic theology and the revelation in explaining the divinity, the cosmos and beyond. That infected Nazarenes phenomenon was also tainted toward Christianity.

To the Nazarenes, the greatest phenomenon of the persistence in their faith, was based on the "scientific Gnosticism", and was prevailing over the Hellenistic world at that time. In turn, it had affected the people of the Book. By the end of the apostolic era, the Apostle of Christ, Gnosticism was prevailing over the Nazarenes and they used it to attack Christianity, as Paul taught it in his established churches.

St. Paul epistles to the Romans, to the Corinthians and to the Galatians were of the same subject matter. After Paul learned that some of the Nazarene Pharisaic emissaries had arrived among his new converts were teachings contrary to his doctrines, that for salvation it was necessary to be circumcised and to observe the Mosaic rites. Those "Judaizers" Nazarenes sought to undermine the authority of the Apostle by questioning his divine commission. Paul asserted the divine origin of his teaching and of his authority.

He shows that justification is not through the Mosaic Law, but through faith in Jesus Christ, who was crucified and who raised from the dead. He concludes that consequently the Mosaic Law was something transient and

---

[52] Eusebius, "The History of....." (4:22:5)

17

not permanent, that it is not an essential part of Christianity. Nor does he fail to insist on the necessity of evangelical virtues, especially charity, the offspring of faith. [53]

Paul, in his epistles, defends "the scientific Gnosticism" as an absolute science in Christianity. While Christianity builds her theology on the Book of the New Testament and on the apostolic mission, the Nazarenes builds their theology, from the beginning, as dictated by the traditional Jewish scientific Gnosticism of knowledge. That manifested traditional knowledge became the emblem of the Nazarenes' theology.

The Nazarenes followed its teaching until the coming of the Qur'anic revelation. The Qur'an commends it and its people as it is stated in "Do they not have a sign since the scholars Children of Israel (Nazarenes) knew about it? [54] And in "SAY: "God suffices as a Witness between me and you (all), as well as anyone who has knowledge about the Book." [55] And in the verse, the Qur'an himself "exists as clear signs in the breasts of those who have been given knowledge ..." [56]

The Apostolic Dialogue Era, the Diligence in Faith

The Apostles, Disciples of Christ, were not theologians; they were the carriers of the Gospel and the Call. During the era of the Apostles, before the war of the year 70 AD, the evangelical faith was on the right track, according to St. Paul's previously stated epistle to the Galatians "that the truth of the gospel might continue with you." It was inevitable that the first tribulation would involve in the evangelical faith on whether the Mosaic rites are necessary to be followed by the people of the gospel?

Conflicting opinions took place between the Nazarenes of Beni Israel (Children of Israel) and the Christians from all the nations. The Nazarenes insisted on both the Mosaic Law and the Gospel. Christians called for the liberation of Christianity from the Mosaic Law. The conflict polarity was led by Jacob, the Bishop of Jerusalem, the leader of the House, and the Nazarenes of Beni Israel on one side; and by St. Paul, "the apostle of the nations" and the leader of the Christian faith in all nations, on the other side. This is

---

[53] The Holy Bible, St. Paul epistles to the Romans, to the Corinthians and to the Galatians, Confraternity and Douay Texts, Rembrandt Edition, Abradale Press Inc., 1959.

[54] Sura Al-Shu'araa' - (Poets) 26: verse 197

[55] Sura Al-Ra'ad - (Thunder) 13: verse

[56] Sura Al-'Ankabout - (Spider) 29: verse 49

clearly stated in the Acts of the Apostles and in St. Paul's Epistles of the New Testament.

Both groups appealed to the First General Council of the Church that took place in Jerusalem in 49 AD. After consultation, Peter, the head of the Apostles, decided to put an end to the conflict by giving his formal opinion to liberate Christians from Mosaic rites. He left the Nazarenes of Beni Israel to follow the Law and the gospel without comment.

Both Jacob and Paul supported Peter's decision; "then the whole meeting quieted down." [57] But some of the Pharisee's sect (or the Nazarenes of Beni Israel), who had accepted the faith, got up and said; "They must be circumcised and also told to observe the Law of Moses." [58] Those Nazarenes kept to what they believed in, and were after Paul to pervert his new converts. Paul had to defend his person and his doctrine against the "Jews" whom he called the people of mutilation, and the Nazarenes Pharisee's deceits.

The Battle for liberating Christianity from Hebraism

In researching the liberation of Christianity from Hebraism, the teaching of the Pharisees, four issues were taken under consideration: two of them were considered on either extreme, one to the extreme left and the other to the extreme right. And two were considered moderates sitting in between.

1. The Extreme Right Issue:

The first extreme issue was formed by the rightist Christians of the infant Church in Palestine led the first martyr Stephen and his colleagues the deacons of the Hellenistic of Beni Israel, and from the Christians all over, who complained against the Hebrews of Beni Israel, and the Palestinian Nazarenes. "There arose a murmuring among the Hellenists against the Hebrews…" [59] … then they [who were in dispute with Stephen] bribed men to say that they had heard him [Stephen] speaking blasphemous words against Moses and against God[60]. Clearly Stephen followers left the Temple (the motto of the Hebrews) and left the Mosaic rite (the basis of Hebraism and the Jewish nation). They had no reasons to follow the Mosaic rite or pray in a Pharisee Temple. The Holy Spirit and their faith in Jesus Christ were

---

[57] Acts chapter 15 verse 12

[58] Acts chapter 15 verse 5

[59] Acts chapter 6 verse 1

[60] Acts chapter 6 verse 11

their guidance. This extreme rightist Christians faded away after the death of Stephen.

2. The Extreme Left Issue:

The second extreme issue was to the extreme Left, those adhered to the Mosaic Law, and intended on forcing it on all Christians of all nations. Its obvious objective was to Judaize Christianity. The Apostles agreed, in their Council at Jerusalem in 49 AD, to liberate Christianity from the Mosaic Law, the Nazarenes of Beni Israel insisted on adhering to both the Law and the Gospel. The Nazarenes became stronger and more stubborn in their creed when the Essenes and their priests of Qumran joined them, creating more extreme theological Nazarenes methods.

3. The Moderate Issue of Jacob:

The third issue was moderate and led by Jacob, the Head of the House, and the Palestinian Nazarenes of Beni Israel, who believe in Christ and the Gospel and obey Law of Moses without forcing their believes on the Christians of all the nations. This moderate attitude qualified the Palestinian Nazarenes of Beni Israel during the period starting with Jesus to the time of Prophet Muhammad. So they represented the "Shiites" Nazarenes as compared to the Apostolic "Sunnis" Christians.

4. The Moderate Issue of Paul:

The fourth issue was the second moderate one led by St. Paul and his converts who were calling for the liberation of Christianity from the yoke of the Mosaic rites. They build their faith on the teachings of Jesus Christ of the New Testament.

"For in Christ Jesus neither circumcision nor un-circumcision but a new creation is of any account" [61] And "for in Christ Jesus neither circumcision is of any avail, nor un-circumcision, but faith which works through charity" [62]. They were the Christians of all nations and the "Hellenists" Hebrews who joined together to create one nation: the people of the Christianity, as compared to the Nazarenes of Beni Israel.

---

[61] Epistle of St. Paul the Apostle to the Galatians chapter 6, conclusion, verse 15
[62] Ibid. chapter 5 verse 6

A source for Discrepancy

Jesus Christ, in establishing the Kingdom of God, says, "Do not think that I have come to destroy the Law of the Prophets. I have not come to destroy but to fulfill... till all things have been accomplished." [63] The interpretation of "till all things have been accomplished" is obvious, once Jesus accomplishes "the Kingdom of God on earth", believers in Christ will adhere to His kingdom, and anything else will become of less value. In discussing what is meant by "to fulfill", we question the meaning whether it is to adjust or to change? Does "to fulfill" intend to mean a continuation of the biblical laws, or does it mean to fulfill the Book of a New Testament? "Christians" understood "to fulfill" in the Gospel to mean a change from the teaching of Old Testament to the new teachings of the Gospel--The New Testament. "...And Jesus said to them, Amen I say to you that you who had followed me, in the regeneration when the Son of Man shall sit on his throne of glory. ..." [64] "Therefore I say to you, that the kingdom of God will be taken away from you and will be given to a people yielding its fruits." [65] "Behold, your house is left to be desolate."[66] "...Amen I say to you, there will not be left here one stone upon another that will not be thrown down." [67] Jesus prophecy took place in 70 AD, and Jerusalem was occupied and the Temple was destroyed and not a stone left upon another. That was the sign of the regeneration of the kingdom of God and the beginning of the New Testament Era for spreading Charity and Love.

But the "Nazarenes" of Beni Israel, in Palestine, and those who followed them in different locations of Arabia, they understood "to fulfill" as "to adjust". So the Gospel came for verification of the Bible and for particularization. They reached to that conclusion because of their national and biblical precipitation. They mixed religion with nationhood, allowing for the Mosaic rites to prevail over the Gospel. So they followed both the Law and the Gospel; they accepted circumcision and baptism together, and gave respect to both Saturday and Sunday. Whenever they faced conflicting issues they referenced the Bible and not the Gospel.

The Nazarenes doctrines are transferred into the Qur'an as we see in "We had 'Isa Bin Mariam, follow in their footsteps in order to confirm what had come before him from the Torah ..." [68] And in "So 'Isa Bin Mariam said:

---

[63] The Holy Gospel of Jesus Christ according to St. Matthew chapter 5 verses 17-18.

[64] Ibid. Chapter 19 verse 28

[65] Ibid. Chapter 21 verse 43

[66] Ibid. Chapter 23 verse 38

[67] Ibid. 24:2

[68] Sura Al- Ma'ida - (The Table) 5: verse 46

"Children of Israel, I am God's messenger to you, confirming whatever came before me in the Torah…" [69] "Confirming what I have already [learned] from the Torah. I shall permit you some things that have been forbidden you…" [70] And "SAY: 'People of the Book, you will not make any point until you keep up the Torah and the Gospel …'" [71]

The Nazarenes' Creed Christ is a Prophet

It is important to differentiate between the Nazareth – Al-Nazareth- and the Christians. The Gospel of the Hebrews is the Gospel of the Nazarenes of Beni Israel. It is the main source for their creed, they believe in the unity of the prophecy and the Book from Adam to Jesus Christ. They all came with different names in different ages to call for One and Only One God - Yahweh. For every period, there is a Book; and for every nation, there is a Prophet. That was the theory of the "Right Prophet" that was written in the "Reports of Peter". "Reports of Peter" was one of the falsified attributed origins that the Christians do not believe in. To the Nazarenes, it talks about the "first Prophet" who was embodied in Noah, then descended upon the prophets, one by one, after him, and settled at last in the Greatest Prophet of all, Christ, in the form of the promised "Son of Man".

Since the first chapter of the reports, the world and humanity was described as a room full of smoke, everybody in it is looking for light and for knowledge. No one managed to get rid of the darkness except the "Right Prophet" himself who was able to open the door and the true light enters to clear away the darkness of the room. This "Right Prophet" is Christ, the one who first appeared in Adam and through ages in "Akhnoukh" (Idriss in Arabic), Noah, Abraham, Isaac, Jacob and Moses. Moses managed to renew the eternal law that descended on Adam, and allowed to slaughter animals as sacrifices. He preached of a prophet who will come after him at the end of time. The "Reports of Peter" copies Moses prophecy: "A prophet like me wills the LORD, your God, rise up for you from among your own kinsmen; to him you shall listen." [72] To them, this Greatest Prophet (the True Prophet) appeared, at last, in the person of Christ. He confirmed the prophecy and the Book, and gave the particularization of the Mosaic Law and abrogated the killing of animals as sacrifices.

---

[69] Sura Al-Suff - (Battle Array) 61: verse 6

[70] Sura of Al-Imran - (The House of Imran) 3: verse 50

[71] Sura Al-Ma'ida - (The Table) 5: verse 68

[72] The Old Testament, (Deuteronomy 18:15)

It is mentioned in the Gospel of the Hebrews when 'Isa Bin Mariam appeared at the Jordan river banks, the Holy Ghost descended upon him saying, "I have waited for you in all the prophets until your coming and I rest in you." So the Gospel of the Nazarenes finds in Christ, the Greatest Prophets to Beni Israel who put an end to all prophets. They find in his message a right and true prophecy, and not a sacrifice message. The death of Christ is martyrdom and not redemption. To the Christians, the death of Jesus Christ is a Sacrifice and Redemption. By His arisen, He gives Christianity strength and power to grow and prevail as a true religion of all nations.

Nazarenes' Picture of the Cosmos

The Jews used to imagine the Universe to be three heavens: the heaven of meteors, the heaven of stars and the heaven of God where the Throne and the Glory of Divinity exist. Paul had traveled and was caught up in the third heaven: Paradise, where he saw the glory of God "and heard secret words that man may not repeat..." [73] The early Christianity accepted the theory of the three heavens. But the Nazarenes alone considered the universe to be composed of seven heavens, contrary to the beliefs of the Jews and the Christians. In the erroneous Nazarenes book of "The Night Journey of Isaiah", this theory is mentioned in a night journey for Isaiah, and in the Descend of Christ from heaven to earth, and the Ascend of Christ to the seventh heaven, to the Throne of God. The Universe is composed from seven heavens: the highest is the heaven of God and the Angels live there in the seventh heaven according to their priorities and their jobs. In the seventh heaven of God, we have the Throne surrounded by the closest Seven Angels. In the lowest heaven were the wind, evil spirits and devils dwell.

In the second version of Idriss (Akhnoukh), another Nazarene erroneous "Book", he gives the same theory in details:

- The first heaven includes the high waters, the reservoirs of rains and snows and the angels in charge; and the stars with the angels who direct them.
- The second heaven is the dwelling of the sinful angels who fell from the fifth heaven.
- The third heaven has the paradise where the souls of the faithful dwell waiting for the Judgment day, the "Shoal" is there where the Disbelievers wait for the doomsday.

---

[73] The second Epistle of St. Paul the Apostle to the Corinthians 12:4

- The fourth heaven is where the sun and the moon and the angels who take charge of them.
- The fifth heaven is the place of the vigilant angels.
- The sixth heaven is the residency of the greatest angels, the seven Chief angels, the seven Cherubs, the seven Seraphs and the seven Sphinxes.
- The seventh heaven is for the glory of God.

The Nazarenes of Beni Israel believed in the theory of the seven heavens and carried it with them to Hijaz in the Arabian Peninsula. Christianity rejected that theory.

Nazarenes' Creed in Angels

The Nazarenes inherited the creed of angels from the Jews, but they did equate them to God; they accepted their nature and their jobs. Angels are from fire and are mythically very tall. The Kassa'i believed that the angles of the resurrection are "96 miles tall" as the Essenes believed too and found in Qumran's writings. They believed that the angels have ranks and jobs. The advance guards and attendants are in the highest three heavens, and the angels of the creation in the lower four heavens. Their job is to glorify God, day and night. Their other job is to urge Man to do fine deeds, and the angels of peace they lead good souls to paradise.

The Nazarenes give respect to the seven angels closest to God; they gave them the following names: Ghafreel, Raneel, Oreel, - 'Ekhtheess, - Mikhaeel, Jubraeel and 'Azaeel. All names are Aramaic, except the one in the middle is Greek 'Ekhtheess means "fish", the Nazarenes, during the Roman persecution, used to draw a fish and used different letters to represent "Jesus Christ, Son of God, the Savior". The new name was inserted in the middle of the angles to become one created angel like the others; it is intended to represent Christ.

The Nazarenes believed that Lucifer and his angels refused to bow before Adam as God ordered them to do so; God got angry and kicked Lucifer and his angels out of paradise, so they fell to earth. Neither Jews nor Christians believe this story. It is a Nazarene theory taken from the Hellenistic Gnostic Essenes doctrine, as researched by Archimandrite Al-Haddad. [74]

---

[74] Archimandrite Yusuf Durrah Al-Haddad, "AlQu'an Da'wat Nusraniah,(The Qur'an - a "Nazarene" Call)", Maktabat Albulusiah, Beirut, 1986, pp. 170-176. Copied from Martiniano Roncaglia: Histoire de l'Eglise copte T I p. 297.

In short, the Jews worshipped the angels and called them, figuratively, "sons of God", and the Nazarenes followed steps of the Judaic observances and claimed for angles a very high place of honor. St. Paul warns against such false teachings, and that there is no need, then, for outworn and abrogated Judaic rites. "Let no one, then, call you to account for what you eat or drink or in regard to a festival or a new moon or a Sabbath. These are a shadow of things to come, but the substance is of Christ. Let no one cheat you who takes pleasure in self-abasement and worship of the angels, and enters vainly in what he has not seen, puffed up by his mere human mind." [75]

Nazarenes' Creed in Christ

The Nazarenes believed that Christ is being gotten miraculously from Virgin Mary, as the Scholar Jerome testifies. But the theologians from the Nazarenes of the Ebionites, Cerinthusians, and the Kassa'iah deviated in their interpretation that Christ was born from a father and a mother similar to all human beings even if he was the master of all creation. From the evangelical references, we see the deviation of the Nazarenes, of Beni Israel, the Hebrews, that Christ is the head of the closest Angels to God; he is made like the angels, and not be gotten from God, the way Christianity believe as available in the evangelical references too.

Hermes says clearly, "that when God decided to create His close angels from fire, the Seven of them, He decided to make one of them His Son." [76] So those "Hebrews-Nazarenes" who considered Christ as the "Son of God" figuratively and selectively, did not believe in birth or self-prophecy.

We noticed other references by Epiphanius by the end of the fourth century AD that Christ to them "not begotten from God, but made, and he is one of the heads of the angels, in charge of all angles and runs God's deeds." In the falsified Codex Claromonanus teachings, it is stated clearly "that Christ is nothing more than an angel" and in another section "that he was the first head of the angels." [77]

---

[75] St. Paul's epistle to the Colossians, Chapter 2 verses 16-18
[76] Hermas, "The Shepherd" (9:12:7)
[77] Ibid.

The Nazarenes' Name Attributes of Christ

1. Christ is "the Name"

In the Biblical Hebrew, "The Name" is used for glorifying the name of God. He is the One, in Hebrew's interpretation, the Name becomes the Selfsame God, and later was interpreted "the Word of God."

Christianity adopted the term and was clearly manifested in the Lord's Prayer: "Our Father, who art in heaven, Hallowed be Thy name." Or, Hallowed is your selfsame person. "I have manifested thy name to the men …"[78] "The Name" has become to present Christ Himself, "Father, glorify thy name…"[79] and again "And now do thou, Father glorify me with thyself, with the glory that I had with thee before the world existed." [80] "The name", as an expression did represent God, and to Christians, it is also an expression to represent Christ, the God.

2. Christ is "the Beginning", "the First" or "the Word"

"In the beginning was the Word, and the Word was with God, and the Word was God," [81] St. Paul sees Christ as "the image of the invisible God, the firstborn of every creature … he is before all creatures, and in him all things hold together … he, who is the beginning, the firstborn from the dead, that in all things he may have the first place."[82] Firstborn of every creature is God Himself. The Nazarenes also believed that God begins with creation then performs it all over again.

3. Christ is "the Namous" or "the Law"

"Namous" is a Greek word. It is translated to "Torah" or "The Law", it became to the Jews "The Book of Moses". The way the "Torah" was treated, the Law became a symbol by itself and not a Book. The Law became the words of God as read in the Torah. In the Nazarenes and the Hebraism, the law became "the Word of God". Phylon [83] considers the Law to be "the Word of God", the Law is the Word and the Word is the Law, relying on the words

---

[78] According to the Gospel of St. John, the Apostle, chapter 17 verse 6

[79] Ibid. chapter 12 verse 28

[80] Ibid. chapter 17 verse 5

[81] Ibid. chapter 1 verse 1

[82] St. Paul's epistle to the Colossians, chapter 1 verses 15-18

[83] Phylon, "The problems of the Universe" 4:240

of Isaiah "... For the law shall come forth from Sion, and the word of the Lord from Jerusalem." [84]

To the Nazarenes, the Law becomes a representation of Christ. In the Shepherd of Hermes "...the law of God is given to the world. This law is the Son of God that they preach in all direction of the word." [85]

We also learned "that Waraka Bin Nofal [86] has come with "the Greatest Law" or "the Law of 'Isa", as will be explained later on.

Jesus Christ – 'Isa Bin Mariam

When the Nazarenes of Beni Israel took refuge in Hijaz, after Christianity was forced as the State Religion of the Roman Empire, they were praying with their western Aramaic Assyriac tongue where the terms Moussa (Moses) and 'Isa were used in their prayers. The original of the term "Isa" was from the Hebrew "Yashou'". It was translated into Arabic as "Yassu'" where the sheen sound changes to seen. But the real translation was not directly from Hebrew (Yashou' Masheehu); it was from Aramaic/Assyriac into Arabic. The first translation was from the Greek language, then to the Assyriac, and then to Arabic.

Historically, it is known that The Gospel was written in Greek, even in Palestine and Syria. The popular Greek name for Jesus at that time was "Issus", or by "Issu" all over the Roman world that used to speak Greek. In the Aramaic, the language of the area surrounding the Arabian Peninsula, the name was pronounced "Ishu", in the Eastern Iraqi dialect, and "Isa" in the western Aramaic dialogue and especially in Assyraic. Through local dialects, the Greek "Issu" and the Aramaic "Ishu" turn out to be pronounced "Isa" in Arabic. 'Isa becomes the popular pronunciation for Jesus in Hijaz. The name "Isa Bin Mariam" is the name revealed in the Qur'an.

Why Bin Mariam? "Is not this the carpenter, the son of Mary...."? [87] In the Eastern environment, they used the term 'Isa Bin Mariam continuously. It was witnessed by the popular songs of Aphram Al-Siryani. It was chanted by travelers on the roads. Traditionally, in the East, in general, the son is named after his father, the Jews used to call Jesus son of Mary, as an insult. But the

---

[84] From the Prophecy of Isaias, Old Testament, chapter 2, verse 3.

[85] In the book "Stromates" (collection of thoughts and theology) of St. Clement of Alexandria in the "erroneous Reports of Peters' on Christ" that Christ is called the Law and the Word."

[86] Waraka Bin Nofal was the Bishop of the Nazarenes in Mecca, during the days of Prophet Muhammad. [From Sira Al-Hashimiah.]

[87] According to St. Mark, the Apostle, Chapter 6 verse 3.

27

Nazarenes used to call Jesus, son of Mary, as a blessing, because they believe that 'Isa was born miraculously from The Virgin Mariam.

The Nazarenes' Creed in "the Trinity"

The Nazarenes of Beni Israel accepted the Gospel of Matthew only. Their Gospel was known as "the Gospel of the Hebrews", a Hebrew dialect written in an Aramaic letters. In the Gospel of Matthew, the verse before last has Christ's order that came before His Ascension to Heaven "Go, therefore, and make disciples of all nations, baptizing them in the name of the Father, the Son, and the Holy Spirit." [88] A statement is considered a creed, a law and a religion to the people of the Gospel.

The Nazarenes of Beni Israel did not have to cast this evangelical Trinity except through the understanding of the "spirit"; they put it in an angelic expression and said in "the Word of God Angel" and "the Holy Spirit Angel". In the beginning, the angelic expression for the Trinity was not a deviation from creed, because they repeated terms in the Book that called for the appearance of God as "the Angel of God". The reference of the Nazarenes to the Word of God Angel and the Holy Spirit Angel reflect the spirituality in their personalities, and nothing related to their creation. But the resemblance in the usage of the terms led them to treat the Word of God and the Holy Spirit as created angels.

The Nazarenes' description of the evangelical trinity was based on angelic expressions, and on the understanding of the biblical monotheism. Gradually the doctrine of trinity in Christianity for the Word of God and the Spirit of God were dissolved into becoming two angels very close to God, sometimes both are worshipped along God, and sometimes we see their presence to worship God.

The Nazarenes were left in confusion without becoming able to have the knowledge and able to comprehend the concept of the Spirit, during the period of their survival. That was the period from the spread of Christianity until the coming of Prophet Muhammad. The Spirit was, to them, created by God's command and their knowledge of its nature was very limited.

The meaning of the Word of God, in the Nazarenes theology, has developed slowly from the Divinity concept into an Angelic one, as seen in the Shepherd of Hermes. The resemblance in the duality is confusing between having 'Isa Bin Mariam a human and as an angel at the same time. This is one of the main reasons why the Nazarenes are considered the

---

[88] The Holy Gospel of Jesus Christ according to St. Matthew Chapter 28 verse 19.

"Shiites" (paying allegiance to Moses and Jesus), in relation to Christianity, "the Sunnis or Sunnas", paying allegiance to Jesus only.

The same duality is seen when considering the angel Michael, as the Word of God Angel, and considering the angel Jebreel, as the Spirit of God Angel. In the falsified books of the Nazarenes [89] "the Word descends to earth and was blown or breathed into the Virgin Mary's womb a new light. He (the Word) appeared in the pure and strong form of the angel Jibreel. As a Head Angel, he talks to the girl saying "Oh Virgin, accept God in your pure womb". Therefore, the Word, a Spirit of God was breathed into Virgin Mary's womb was an essential part of the Nazarenes of Beni Israel's creed.

The Trinity in the Nazarenes understanding took another confusing form based on the word "Spirit", in Hebrew and in Aramaic (*Ruh or Rooh*) is feminine. They understood what was written in their Book that the Spirit called Jesus during his baptism "You are my beloved Son" to mean that the Spirit is a mother to Christ. The popular view of the Nazarenes to Trinity was God; Christ, the Son of God; and the Holy Spirit, the mother of Christ. The Ebionites theologians rejected that popular belief and revolted against the possibility of Christ could ever have alleged to take Him and His Mother as gods, without God, the Father! Such erroneous Trinity was never considered in Christianity, it was a Nazarenes falsified interpretation of the Gospel based on their understanding of the Torah. If the Selfsame Word of God did not descend on us in the New Testament of Christ, then should Jesus be considered as a continuation to the expectation of the Torah?

The Nazarenes' Creed in "Christ Crucifixion"

Christ is immortal and does not die. This is the concept of the Nazarenes of Beni Israel inherited from the Jewish theologians. This point was based on such a quote "... We have heard from the Law that the Christ abides forever..."[90] That is why the Nazarenes believed that Christ left the body of Jesus before his martyrdom. They believed that Christ changes as he wishes from shape into another, and he throws his resemblance onto Simon who was crucified in his place, while he ascended alive, unseen, to the One who sends him. Therefore the theory of "look alike" is what seemed to the Jews when they killed Jesus. In the Nazarenes' creed, Christ is the Word of God, left Jesus, Son of Mary, before his martyrdom, and Jesus himself who was crucified and that Christ was neither killed nor crucified.

---

[89] Such as "The Epistle of the Apostles" as well as in "Oracles sybillins" VIII p. 456-461

[90] The Holy Gospel of St. John, the Apostle, chapter 12 verse 34

They also believe that Jesus Christ ascended to heaven, neither killed nor crucified, but it seemed so because he threw his resemblance upon another from his disciples, either Simon or Judas, and that look alike was crucified instead of Jesus. Irenaeus talks about their beliefs, "Wherefore he (Christ) did not himself suffer death, but Simon, a certain man of Cyrene, being compelled, bore the cross in his stead. So that this latter being transfigured by him, that he might be thought to be Jesus, was crucified, through ignorance and error, while Jesus himself received the form of Simon, and standing by, laughed at them. For since he was an incorporeal power and the mind of the unborn father, he transfigured himself as he pleased, and thus ascended to him who had sent him. ..." [91]

The Nazarenes of Beni Israel never considered the Cross a historical fact or a doctrine of sacrifice and redemption, they considered it a symbolic matter; the Cross is of glory, it follows Christ in his glory as if the Cross is alive. They call it "the Cross of light", like the star that led the Magi to the place of Christ's birth. It represents the omnipotent of Christ. It is the Cosmos Cross, reflected in the universe, all over. The Nazarenes never gave a meaning to the Wooden Cross, the symbol of crucifixion of Christ and His martyrdom as it is in Christendom.

Redemption, according to the system of Basilides' thoughts, came through the work of Nous, (Nous is a Greek word for Mind). God has emanated a series of spiritual beings, the first of which is Nous. From Nous came Logos (Reason or Word), followed by three other personified powers: Phronesis (Prudence), Sophio (Wisdom), and Dynamis (Force) in succession. Basilides treated Nous as Christ who has descended from the highest heaven into the world in the appearance of a human being. He also looked upon Salvation as a treatment for the soul alone. [92]

The Nazarenes celebrated the memory of crucifixion of Jesus, and not Christ crucifixion. And the memory of Jesus has risen from death and not Christ. Because on the day of resurrection Christ came back to the body of Jesus, and God lifted him up towards Himself. In the Nazarenes doctrine, the lifting up (Ascend) of Jesus Christ is what they stressed more than the resurrection. To them, they considered the resurrection and the lifting up (Ascend) as one act, and they declare the Ascend only because they call the incarnation of Christ as a Descend. The concept is taken from the Greek terms "Catabase – Anabase". It has its roots, also, in the epistle of St. Paul, "Now this, 'he ascended,' what does it mean but that he also first descended

---

[91] Irenaeus, "Against Heresies" discusses the Doctrines of Saturninus and Basilides (Syrian Arab by birth) in Chapter XXIV, in the fourth paragraph.

[92] Ibid.

into the lower parts of the earth? He who descended, he it is who ascended also above all the heavens that he might fill all things."[93]

To the Nazarenes of Beni Israel, there is nothing after death of 'Isa except His resurrection and His lifting up alive to God in heaven. Up to this day, the prayer at Easter, in the Melkite Churches as well as the rest of the Eastern Churches, start with the celebration - the act of "Al-Hajmeh". It takes place at the outside main door, at the entrance of the Church, in the early morning of Easter (the Day of Resurrection) to represent Jesus Christ Resurrection, His lifting up and His glorious entrance to heaven at the same time. This tradition is an evidence of the effects of the revelation of the evangelical antiquity.

The Nazarenes' Creed in "Christ Return and the Judgment Day" is based on the Gospel where it is mentioned that Christ will come again with glory to judge the living and the dead. It is mentioned in the Apocalypse [94] that Christ and the righteous rule the earth a thousand years after Christianity conquered the pagan Romans, referred to by the name of the "earthly Babylon". The symbolic one thousand years has no limit. The thousand years rule mentioned is called "the first resurrection". "And they came to life and reigned with Christ a thousand years. ... Blessed and holy is he who has part in the first resurrection..." But the true Day of Judgment is in the "second resurrection" where "hell and death were cast into the pool of fire. This is the second death, the pool of fire. And if anyone was not found written in the book of life, he was cast in the pool of fire." [95]

The Nazarenes of Beni Israel's creed compared the symbolic thousand years for Christ and Christianity by the coming back of Christ in the Judgment Day. They considered it a paradise garden on earth as the true and actual "first resurrection", and resemble it to Adam's Garden, when the end of humanity will return to where it started. So they mixed between the descriptions of Paradise in heaven as a paradise garden on earth. The Jews and the Ebionite Nazarenes understood the pleasure of the thousand years as a physical sensual pleasure that will take place in paradise at the Judgment Day. There, "the wolf and lamb shall feed together; the lion and the ox shall eat straw..." [96]

The heedful of the Nazarenes have been promised a garden in paradise where rivers of never stagnant water and rivers of milk whose flavor never changes, and rivers of wine so delicious for those who drink it, and rivers

---

[93] Epistle of St. Paul, the Apostle, to the Ephesians, chapter 4 verses 9-10.

[94] The Apocalypse, a revelation to St. John the Evangelist, written in Greek, and presented in a form of symbol, on the island of Patmos, about 96 AD, chapter 20 verses 4-6.

[95] Ibid. Apocalypse 20:14-15.

[96] Isaias, Old Testament, chapter 65 verse 25

of clarified honey. They will have every sort of fruit in it. In the garden, marriage is abundant with no limit to a number of Huriyat (an Aramaic word for beautiful women) who look like pearls and corals.

Irenaeus, in his work that took place between 182 and 188 AD "Against Heresies", copied the teaching of Cerinthus that "after the Judgment Day, the kingdom of Christ will become earthly, and the body will become a captive of his nymphomania, lust and delight. As an enemy to the Books of God, he says there will be a thousand years of a cheerful marriage." [97] "To them, the Day of Judgment will be a table God prepares it to them to feed them with everything they desire." [98]

---

[97] Irenaeus, "Against Heresies", chapter 3 verses 3:4.
[98] Ibid. 5:33:2.

CHAPTER THREE

Introducing Arab Christian Religious Culture before Islam

In this chapter, I try to show the basic confusions that take place when we study religion by introducing Arab Christian religious culture before Islam, starting with introducing how some Islamic interpretation of the Arab Christian Culture are confusing and misunderstood.

An Islamic Interpretation of the Pre-Islamic Ecumenical Councils Period

Before introducing the first five Ecumenical Councils that took place before Islam, I would like to present an interpretation of an Islamic scholar in a paragraph which I read in the interpretation of Ibn Katheer [99], when he was explaining Sura Maryam, verse 34 (**Such as Isa (Jesus), son of Maryam (Mary)** *(It is) a statement of truth, about which they doubt (or dispute)* as follows: "Abd Al-Razek: Muamaar told us quoting Katadah saying *(Such as 'Isa, son of Maryam. (It is) a statement of truth, about which they dispute)* said : Banu Israel met and picked four groups to represent them. Each group got out their best scholar to discuss how suspected was the elevation of Isa. One of the scholars said: He is God descended to Earth and gave life to resurrect and gave death to putting death, then ascended to heaven, that group was the Jacobites.

The other three scholars told the Jacobites that they were telling lies. Then two of them told the third 'what did you say' he said 'he is the son of God' and those were the Nestorius; and they also said lies. Then one of the two said to the third: 'what did you say' he said he is one of three: God is

---

[99] Ibn Katheer, *"Tafseer Ibn Katheer"* Volume 4, pages 456-457

God, He is God and his Mother is God and those are the Israelites, kings of the Nazarenes, God's curses upon them. The fourth said: you are telling lies Isa is a servant of God, his Messenger, his Spirit and his Word and those are the Muslims. Each of those scholars have followers and fought each other, and that was what Katada said by repeated verse 37 (***Then the sects differed, so woe unto the disbelievers from the Meeting of a great Day***), and so they differed about him and became different sects.

Ibn Abi Hatem narrated what Ibn Abbas, Arwat Bin Al-Zabeer told about some of the learned people of that period that the history professors who belonged to the people of the Book and others that Constantine brought them to a meeting place (Ecumenical Council) out of their three famous congregations. Two thousand one hundred and seventy bishops were in the meeting; they disagreed about Isa bin Maryam, peace be upon him. Serious discrepancies among them took place, and every band said differently, a hundred of them said something and another seventy said something different and fifty others differed, and one hundred and sixty said something dissimilar. Three hundred of them agreed upon one issue, only eight of them bond together on one saying that the King who was a philosopher brought them close to him, supported them and dismissed those who opposed them. They confided in him their great loyalty, or rather the eminent betrayal. They prepared for him the books of laws, legalized things, devised novelties, and corrupted the religion of Christ and changed it. So Constantine built for them huge churches in his entire kingdom in Al-Sham country, Al-Jazeera and Al-Roum (Greece). The number of churches that he built during his era was about twelve thousand churches, and his mother Hilaneh built a Temple in the place that the Jews pretended to be the place where Christ was crucified, they lied as God elevated him to heaven.

Such interpretation of the Qur'an, by a great Muslim scholar, Ibn Katheer, gives a gloomy picture to the Muslim readers about Christianity. Such vague and limited misinformation do not represent the 622 years of religious evolution within the Christian religion and faith that differs from the Nazarenes religion and faith.

This chapter deals with the achievements of the first Five Ecumenical Councils that took place during that period before Islam.

I will start with what I believe that the indicator to religion is "faith". Faith creates a vertical relationship with the omnipotent God.

Religion is Based on Faith

Faith is a "religious" term to overcome terror and fear. Jesus Christ, put it plainly as such "Have faith in God. Amen I say to you, whoever says to this mountain, 'Arise, and hurl thyself into the sea,' and does not waver in his heart, but believes whatever he says be done, it shall be done for him. Therefore I say to you, all things whatever you ask for in prayer, believe that you shall receive, and they shall come to you." [100] The way faith is presented in this perspective means absolute emancipation from any kind of natural law. It gives man the highest freedom to intervene in the ontological constitution of the universe, the ultimate reality beyond everything that seems to be real. Therefore faith is an internal belief, a feeling that no one can convey to others through convincing arguments, especially to other fanatics who belong to a different faith. In fact, there is no win or loss in arguing or discussing religious affairs that deal with faith and beliefs.

In order to be appreciated in initiating a religious discussion, such religious dialogues should be based on respect to all human believes and should concentrate on common ideas that create rapprochement and positive reception for others' faithful beliefs whenever they come together to define a common truth. Religions of Islam, Christianity, Judaism, Confucianism, Buddhism and Hinduism together form parts of people's cultural heritage and their lives. There ought to be the opportunity for people to learn and understand these religions in an atmosphere of respectfulness and openness. Understanding the concept of religion as a service to the human race, make people feel how trivial are the causes to fight each other.

Once I read a saying "For those who have faith in God, no proof is necessary. For those without faith, no proof is sufficient to convince them." So he addresses his writing to those who have faith in their religions and eager to acquire more enlightening knowledge.

No values exist without truth. Truth leads mankind to look for values that appreciate virtues in human behaviors. Virtues are the ultimate goals for the wisdom in searching for the truth. Religion's objective is to preach about that inner feeling of love that leads to the belief in a heavenly truth.

We find no need for argument in preaching. Preaching does not accept immediate results. Successful preaching depends on human behaviors and how people concentrate on finding out points of agreements. Finding common denominators bring accord to the understanding of each other's belief in the truth through faith. Faith is intangible and spiritual. It does not mix with materialistic substances, but it complements the human nature.

Religion is "Deen" in Arabic, and Syed Maudoodi states, "With Allah, Deen is only that a creed which makes man recognizes Allah" [101]

---

[100] The Holy Gospel of Jesus Christ according to St. Mark 12:22-24.

[101] Syed Abul A'la Maudoodi, "Fundamentals of Islam," p 8, published by Markazi Maktaba Islami, p 81

Christianity is best understood through examples. Love and humility are the basic characteristics of virtue in Christianity. Jesus Christ, the Savior based his message on examples, which demand imitation. "A new commandment I give you that you love one another: that as I have loved you, you also love one another." [102] While humility is indeed a Christian virtue, it is also a religious act as a means of salvation practiced after the Savior's example of the washing of the feet. God Jesus say: "If, therefore, I the Lord and Master have washed your feet, you also ought to wash the feet of one another. For I have given you an example, as I have done to you, so you also should do." [103]

For digging deeper in the religious roots of Islam, a brief discussion of the Ecumenical Councils of the Orthodox Catholic Eastern Church about the Trinity and the Divinity of the Son of God which the Nazarenes and the Ebionites did not believe in is needed for clarification.

The Ecumenical Councils final conclusions allowed for the way heresy was declared. They played a major role in keeping the Nazarenes inhabitants of the Arabian Peninsula devotedly confused to understand the spirit of Christianity. Nazarenes accept Jesus as a prophet while adhering very closely to the Law of Moses. They supported their new devoted leader Prophet Muhammad who led their doctrine among Arab tribes to shift from stressing religion alone to be involved in social and economic foundations needed to build a State of institutions and laws that expanded to become an Islamic Empire.

The Orthodox and Catholic Christians went along with the declarations of the Ecumenical Councils. A quick review of the Ecumenical Councils before the birth of Islam will explain the development of the early Christian dogma.

The Ecumenical Councils of the Orthodox Catholic Church before the Birth of Islam

It is impossible to understand the verses of the Noble Qur'an without understanding the growth and development of early Christianity and the teaching of the Nazarenes and the Ebionites before Islam. Confusions relate to the Nazarenes Arabs' vague understanding of the structured Orthodox Catholic Church teachings. To differentiate between Nazarenes and Christianity is very essential to understand the concept of Islam, Prophet Muhammad was introduced to the teaching of the Nazarenes only without

---

[102] The Holy Gospel of Jesus Christ according to St. John chapter 13, verse 34.
[103] Ibid. 13: verses 14-15.

knowing the in-depth growth and evolvement in understanding the Christian faith as we try to introduce in this chapter.

The Ecumenical Councils set the foundations to understanding the Christianity Dogma that was not clearly understood through the restricted Nazarenes' teachings based on primitive traditional knowledge and understanding of their beliefs. Through the spread of the heretic teaching of Nestorius and his followers in the desert of Arabia, most of the Nazarenes were more confused in understanding the true Christian dogma.

I reject the wicked approach of the most recent contemporary Zionist Jewish writers and university professors such as Dr. Geza Vermes [104] who degrades Jesus to a thief and considers Christianity as a failed Jewish movement. Arab Christians totally reject mutilating history and even devoted Muslims reject Dr. Vermes insulting Jesus (Isa Bin Maryam) who is the most respected Islamic prophet.

We took the path of the faith that Jesus is the Lord and searched the Catholic Encyclopedia [105] to give a bird's eye view about the history of the Church before the birth of Islam based the early and major ecumenical councils. The Council decrees are considered final judgment on questions of faith and morals, invested with the authority and majesty of the whole teaching body of the Church. To this end some means are absolutely necessary; others are only desirable as adding perfection to the result.

The First Ecumenical Council

Constantine the Great convened the First Ecumenical Council from May 20 to August 25, 325 AD at the Royal Palace in Nicaea, Asia Minor, to formulate the First Part of the Christian Creed by defining the divinity of the Son of God. More than 300 representatives were involved in the first council coming from Asia, Pontus, Syria-Phoenicia and some legates did travel from Rome and from throughout other regions of the Roman Empire.

---

[104] Geza Vermes is a Professor Emeritus of Jewish Studies, University of Oxford; and Director, Forum for Qumran Research, Oxford Center for Hebrew & Jewish Studies. Published a number of books such as: "A historian reading of the Gospels (1981) Jesus and the world of Judaism (1984), The Religion of Jesus the Jews, (1993), The Sacrifice of Abraham in Judaism, Christianity and Islam, (1999), An Introduction to the Complete Dead Sea Scrolls(1999), The Changing Faces of Jesus, Jesus the Jew (2000).

[105] The Catholic Encyclopedia, Volume IV, Robert Appleton Company, 1908

To the Orthodoxy of Catholic Church has always believed that the council is the chief organ whereby God has chosen to guide His people, and it regards the Catholic Church as essentially a councilor Church.

"In the Church there is neither dictatorship, nor individualism, but harmony and unanimity; its members remain free but not isolated, for they are united in love, in faith, and in sacramental communion. In a council, this idea of harmony is and free unanimity can be seen worked out in practice. In a true council no single member arbitrarily imposes his will upon the rest, but each consults with the others, and in this way they all freely achieve a 'common mind'. A council is a living embodiment of the essential nature of the Church." [106]

Timeline of early Christian events

By introducing a Timeline of events preceding the First Ecumenical Council of Nicaea, we give a short review to the major highlights in the foundation of Christianity:

30 - 33 AD

- The ministry of Christ
- Death on the Cross
- Christ's Resurrection after three days on the Cross
- The Ascension, forty days after the Resurrection
- Pentecost, fifty days after the Resurrection

33 - 34 AD

- The First Convention: The Apostles meets to discuss who should take the place of Judas. Mathias was selected. [107]

34 - 56 AD

- The Second Convention: The Apostles meet to discuss believers who would sell their possessions and give the moneys to the Apostles for the ministries. [108]

---

[106] Timothy (Kallistos) Ware, The Orthodox Church, Penguin, 1993, p. 15.
[107] Acts chapter
[108] Acts 4:31-37

- The Third Convention: The Apostles meet to discuss which deacons should be selected to serve at the table.[109]
- The Fourth Convention: The Apostles meet after Peter had baptized the heathen Cornelius and his family. [110]
- The Fifth Convention: This is considered to be the first general Council of the Church. Acts 15 explains that the Apostles met to discuss the matter as to what extent gentile converts should be subject to the Law of Moses (i.e., circumcision.) The apostles and the elders of the Church met and decided after much prayer and debate that these are the necessary things for gentiles: "that [they] abstain from what has been sacrificed to idols, and from the blood of what is strangled and from unchastely." [111]
- The sixth convention met "when all of the elders were present." [112] In that convention the 85 Canons of the Apostles were set to focus upon the maintenance of the worshiping community. Specifically, they provide detail as to the way clergy and laity is to conduct themselves and what books of the faith they ought to read.

The First Ecumenical Council Achievements

Solving the Arian Controversy

Arius, a priest at the church of Baucalis, came into open conflict with his bishop, Alexander of Alexandria, concerning the divinity of Christ. Arius reasoned and taught that if Jesus was born, then there was time when He did not exist. If He became God, then there was time when He was not. Therefore, Arius reasoned that Jesus must be understood as inferior to the Father.

The effect of making Christ less than God renders impossible our human deification (to become like God). Only if Christ is both God and man can humanity be united with God. For none but God Himself can open to humans the way of union. The Council therefore declared Arius' teaching a heresy, unacceptable to the Church and decreed that Christ is God. He is of the same essense "homousios" with God the Father.

---

[109] Acts 6:2
[110] Acts 11:2-3
[111] Acts 15:29
[112] Acts 21:18

Making the Trinitarian Doctrine of the Church

The Nicene Creed

The primary task of this council was to make the Trinitarian doctrine of the Church very precise to avoid future debate. The document produced was the Nicene Creed. The key word in this Nicene symbol is the term "consubstantial," used to indicate the relationship between the Father and the Son.

The Council dealt with the visible organization of the Church. It singled out for mention the three great centers of Christianity: Rome, Alexandria, and Antioch. The position of Jerusalem, while remaining subject to the Metropolitan of Caesarea, was given the next place of honor after these three. (Constantinople was declared the New Rome five years later).

A Date for Pascha (Easter) - The Council decided that three principles should guide the Church in determining when Pascha is to be celebrated:

a. All churches must celebrate the feast on the same Sunday.
b. It must take into consideration the full moon that follows the vernal equinox.
c. The Eastern Churches who followed the Jews in calculating the date of Pascha had to abandon their practices.

They also ratified the first parts of the seven articles of the Creed. The text of the Christian's profession of faith reads as follows:

We believe in one God. The Father Almighty. Maker of heaven and earth, and of all things visible and invisible. And in one Lord Jesus Christ, the Son of God, the only begotten, begotten of the Father before all ages. Light of Light; true God of true God; begotten not made, of one essence [CONSUBSTANTIAL, Gr. Homoousion] with the Father, by whom all things were made. Who for us men and for our salvation came down from heaven, and was incarnate of the Holy Spirit and the Virgin Mary, and became man. And He was crucified for us under Pontius Pilate, and suffered, and was buried. And the third day He rose again according to the Scriptures; and ascended into heaven, and sits at the right hand of the Father; and he shall come again with glory to judge the living and the dead; whose Kingdom shall have no end.

The Nazarenes rejected what resolved in the Nicene Creed especially the concept of Jesus as true God of true God and He was crucified. The same Nazarene's belief is reflected in the Noble Qur'an's chapters in over 25 different verses using the same words.

The Second Ecumenical Council

The Second Ecumenical Council was held in Constantinople in the year 381 AD to formulate the Second Part of the Creed, defining the divinity of the Holy Spirit.

In the year 380 AD the emperors Gratian and Theodosius I decided to convoke this council. The council opened in May of the following year and closed on July 9 of the same year (381 AD). Approximately 150 representatives from the Eastern Church were in attendance. The West did not send even one representative, yet later agreed to the things that this council decreed.

From the year 382 AD onwards, in the letter of the synod that met at Constantinople, the council was given the title of "ecumenical." The council of Constantinople was however criticized and censured by Gregory of Nazianzus. And, in subsequent years it was hardly ever mentioned.

In the end it achieved its special status when the council of Chalcedon, at its second session and in its definition of the faith, linked the form of the creed read out at Constantinople with the Nicene form, for being a completely reliable witness of the authentic faith.

The fathers of Chalcedon acknowledged the authority of the canons - at least as far as the Eastern Church was concerned - at their sixteenth session.

Pope Gregory, the bishop of Rome accepted the council's dogmatic authority in the western church venerated the four councils (Nicaea, Constantinople, Ephesus and Chalcedon).

The Second Ecumenical Council Achievements

This Council took up the work of the first Council, expanded and adapted the Nicaean creed. They developed the teachings concerning the Holy Spirit and condemned the blasphemy of Macedius who declared that the Son created the Holy Spirit.

This Council struck down the works of Apollinarius, the Eunomians, the Marcellians, the Photians, and every other heresy that had arisen under the rules of the emperors' Constanius, of Julian, and of Valens.

Solving the Macedonian Controversy

Macedonius, somewhat like Arius, were misinterpreting the Church's teaching on the Holy Spirit. He taught that the Holy Spirit was not a person ("hypostasis"), but simply a power ("dynamic") of God. Therefore, the Spirit was inferior to the Father and the Son. The Council condemned Macedonius' teaching and defined the doctrine of the Holy Trinity. The Council decreed that there was one God in three persons ("hypostasis"): Father, Son and Holy Spirit.

The Creed – The Profession of Faith

The holy fathers of the Council added five articles to the Creed. They read as follows:

1. And (We believe) in the Holy Spirit, the Lord, the Giver of Life, who proceeds from the Father:
2. who with the Father and the Son together is worshiped and glorified:
3. who spoke by the prophets. In one Holy, Catholic, and Apostolic Church.
4. I acknowledge one baptism for the remission of sins.
5. I look for the resurrection of the dead, and the life of the world to come. Amen.

The holy fathers in this Council concluded that:

*   The profession of faith of the holy fathers who gathered in Nicaea in Bithynia is not to be abrogated, but it is to remain in force.
*   Diocesan bishops are not to intrude in churches beyond their own boundaries nor are they to confuse the churches: but in accordance with the canons:
    1. The bishop of Alexandria is to administer affairs in Egypt only.
    2. The bishops of the East are to manage the East alone (whilst safeguarding the privileges granted to the church of the Antiochenes in the Nicene canons).
    3. The bishops of the Asian diocese are to manage only Asian affairs.
    4. Those in Pontus should manage only the affairs of Pontus.
    5. Those in Thrace should manage only Thracian affairs. Unless invited bishops are not to go outside their diocese to perform an ordination or any other ecclesiastical business.

Because it is new Rome, the bishop of Constantinople is to enjoy the privileges of honor after the bishop of Rome. Etc.

The Third Ecumenical Council

The Third Ecumenical Council of the Church was held in Ephesus, Asia Minor. It opened on June 7, 431 AD under Emperor Theodosius II (grandson of Theodosius the Great) at the request of Nestorius, whose teachings had been condemned by Celestine, Patriarch of Rome. [113] Two hundred bishops were present. Cyril of Alexandria was the presiding bishop. When the first session was held, many Bishops, especially those who were affiliated with Nestorius, had not yet arrived. This allowed St. Cyril and the council time to condemn Nestorius for blasphemy before his supporters could defend him. Once the representatives of Nestorius arrived, they refused to join the Council, and in turn, formed their own council that condemned and excommunicated Cyril and Memnon, the bishop of Ephesus.

Shortly thereafter, representatives from Rome, the first see of the Church arrived. They sided with St. Cyril of Alexandria and condemned Nestorius.

This council was full of controversy and condemnation. They affirmed that:

1. Jesus Christ possesses two natures, divine and human, at the time of His incarnation.
2. The Church confesses Jesus Christ as both True God and True Man.
3. The Church confesses the Virgin Mary as "Theotokos", (the bearer of God).

The Third Ecumenical Council Achievements

Solving the "Nestorians'" concept - A Christological Controversy

Nestorius, bishop of Constantinople, believed and taught that the Virgin Mary gave birth to a man, Jesus Christ, not God, the "Logos" ("The Word," Son of God). Thus, he reasoned that the Logos only dwelled in Christ, as in a Temple (Christ, therefore, was only Theophoros: The "Bearer of God"). Consequently, the Virgin Mary should be called "Christotokos," "Mother of Christ" and not "Theotokos," "Mother of God."

Ferguson says, "For Nestorius himself, salvation required that both the human and divine natures of Christ be complete, to guarantee the integrity

---

[113] It is interesting to note that Celestine's judgment was not sufficient to condemn Nestorius' teachings. Another judgment was still required, that of a Great and Holy Council as their judgment was decisive and final.

of carnation and to protect the divine Logos from the blasphemous assertion that God could suffer pain and weakness." [114]

Nestorian over emphasized the human nature of Christ at the expense of His divine nature. He emphasized the two separate natures of Christ. But Our Lord Jesus Christ is one person, not two separate "people": the Man, Jesus and the Son of God, Logos.

The Council therefore decreed that the Lord Jesus Christ, the Son of God (Logos), is complete God and complete man, with a rational soul and body. The Virgin Mary is "Theotokos" because she gave birth not to man but to God who became man. The union of the two natures of Christ took place in such a fashion that one did not disturb the other.

The Creed:

The text of the "Creed" decreed at the First and Second Ecumenical Councils were deemed complete.

The Council forbade any changes (additions or deletions). This Council decreed new eight Canons to deal with provincial bishops who were not present at the Holy Synod and have joined or attempted to join the apostasy of the deposed Nestorius. They will be deposed from the priesthood and degraded from their rank.

The Fourth Ecumenical Council

The Fourth Ecumenical Council was convoked by the Emperor Marcius and was held in Chalcedon, a city of Bithynia in Asia Minor from October 8th to November 1st, 451 AD. Six hundred thirty bishops were present to define Christ as Perfect God and Perfect God and Perfect Man in One Person.

They asserted the Orthodox doctrine against the heresy of Eutyches and the Monophysites, and addressed issues of ecclesiastical discipline and jurisdiction.

Melkites are those Christians who adhered to the Chalcedonian faith since 451AD. Melkites faith was supported and defended by the Byzantine Bacillus in Constantinople.

---

[114] Everett Ferguson et al., eds., "Nestorius" in the Encyclopedia of Early Christianity, New York: Garland, 1970, p. 648

The Fourth Ecumenical Council Achievements

Solving the Monophysite Controversy

The Third Ecumenical Council, held at Ephesus, did not put an end to the debate over the Person of Christ, failing to reconcile those sympathetic to Nestorius with the Church. Not long afterwards, however, in the 430's, reconciliation was attained by means of a union, i.e., a unification that, for all intents and purposes, brought an end to the division within the Church.

Since Nestorius so fully divided the Divine and the human in Christ that he taught a double personality or a twofold being in Christ, it became incumbent on his opponents to emphasize the unity in Christ and to exhibit the God-man, not as two beings but as one. Some of these opponents in their efforts to maintain a physical unity in Christ held that the two natures in Christ, the Divine and the human, were so intimately united that they became physically one, inasmuch as the human nature was completely absorbed by the Divine. The result was one Christ not only with one personality but also with one nature.

John of Antioch [previously a follower of Nestorius], in the name of all the bishops of the region of Antioch, sent to Saint Cyril a confession of faith, the essence of which is included in the following excerpt:

We [wrote the Antiochian bishops] confess, therefore, our Lord Jesus Christ, the only-begotten Son of God, perfect God, and perfect man of a reasonable soul and flesh consisting. Begotten before the ages of the Father according to His divinity, and in the last days, for us and for our salvation, [was born] of the Virgin Mary according to His humanity; that He is consubstantial with the Father according to divinity and consubstantial with us according to humanity. For in Him there is a perfect unity of two natures. For these reasons do we also confess one Christ, one Son, and one Lord? According to this understanding of such an unconfused union, we confess the all-holy Virgin to be the Theotokos; Because God the Word was incarnate and became man, and in His very conception He united Himself to the [bodily] temple received from her. We know the theologians make some things of the evangelical and the apostolic teaching about the Lord common as pertaining to the one Person, and other things. They divide as to the two natures, and attribute the worthy ones to God on account of the Divinity of Christ, and the lowly ones to His humanity.

At the end of the epistle there is a condemnation of Nestorius and his doctrine, with a declaration to the effect that Maximian is received into communion. Cyril of Alexandria accepted this confession of John and the bishops of like mind with him as a gift from heaven, acknowledging it as wholly Orthodox. Peace began to spread throughout the ecclesiastical world, and disputes began to die down.

Those who held Saint Cyril in high respect however were the forerunners of the soon to be revealed Monophysite heresy. They considered the communion between Saint Cyril and John of Antioch to be a betrayal of Orthodoxy and perceived heresy in the teaching of Saint Cyril on the two natures in Christ. Despite their great number, they behaved with restraint while Saint Cyril was alive, for he enjoyed tremendous respect with the Church. But with his death matters changed.

Eutyches

In Alexandria, enemies of the union began openly and forcefully to act against it in the name of Orthodoxy, yet in actual fact in the name of their own heretical doctrine, which has become known in the history of the Church under the name Monophysitism ["mono," one and "physis," "nature"].

Monophysitism: is referred to in the "Encyclopedia of Early Christianity" by "Monophysitism" and defined it as "a movement that emphasized the divine nature of Christ in the Christological dispute in the fifth century AD." [115]

The principal representative of the Monophysite heresy was Eutyches, the abbot of one of the monasteries in Constantinople who at the time of the Third Ecumenical Council showed himself to be a zealous partisan of Saint Cyril of Alexandria in his struggle against the heresy of Nestorius.

Eutyches only respected Saint Cyril as the champion of Orthodoxy against Nestorius. He considered his activity during and after the union a betrayal of Orthodoxy. Eutyches did not recognize the treatises authored by Cyril in preparation for the Union and in defense of it as the idea of two natures in the Person of the Lord Jesus Christ was developed and forcefully maintained.

Eutyches instead proclaimed that: "After the incarnation of God the Word I worship one nature-the nature of God Who took on flesh and became man"; "I confess that our Lord consists of two natures before [their] union, and after [their] union I confess one nature." He boldly proclaimed, "He Who was born of the Virgin Mary is perfect God and perfect man, but does not have flesh which is consubstantial with ours."

The Church sought to investigate Eutyches' case. The Council of Constantinople of 448 AD strove mainly to ascertain whether Eutyches was in agreement with the epistle of Saint Cyril (referred to above) and with

---

[115] Everett Ferguson et al., eds., "Monophysitism" in the Encyclopedia of Early Christianity, New York: Garland, 1970, p. 620.

the words of the confession of John of Antioch. At the council in 448 AD, Eutyches made the following statement: "I confess that our Lord consisted of two natures before [their] unification, and I confess one nature after [their] unification." There no longer remained any doubt that Eutyches was a heretic.

To prevent the heresy of Eutyches from resulting in grievous consequences for the Church, the fathers of the council proposed that he anathematize all that was contrary to the dogmas read out at the council. But Eutyches rejected this proposal in a bitter tone of voice. Then the fathers of the council, rising up, proclaimed: "Let Eutyches be anathema!" Later, after a conference, a statement was made regarding Eutyches, signed by Archbishop Flavian, 31 bishops and 23 Archimandrites. The Council of Constantinople in 448 AD did not, however, bring an end to the disputes. The Church of Alexandria or Egypt or the Church of Jerusalem did not recognize it. And from the days of the First Ecumenical Council they had gone hand in hand with the Church of Alexandria in resolving disputed questions of dogma, or even the Church of Rome, which was poorly acquainted with the details of disputes taking place in the East.

Relying on the Court's sympathetic relations with him, he determined to wage war on the council and his own archbishop: Eutyches submitted a petition to Emperor Theodosius, and Eutyches did manage to convince the Emperor that a new, Church-wide council should be called to investigate current contrary dogmatic views.

In history this council has not come to be known as the Fourth Ecumenical Council, but rather the "Robbers' Council," for the activity it directed was not for the triumph of Orthodoxy, but for heretical beliefs proposed by Eutyches.

Under such unfavorable conditions for the defenders of Orthodox Truth, the council convened in Ephesus on August 8th, 449 AD; its sessions were held in the Church of the All-holy Virgin Mary, which had been the site of the sessions of the Third Ecumenical Council. The number of fathers participating in the council fluctuated between 122 and 130.

Eutyches was summoned to the council, to set forth before the council "justifications beneficial for him." Thus was the Monophysite heresy proclaimed instead of the Truth at the unlawful council, and Orthodoxy was trampled underfoot. Eutyches, as the principal champion of the Monophysite heresy, was thereafter declared to be Orthodox and was restored to the dignity of Archimandrite and the rank of a priest.

Emperor Theodosius, the protector of the Monophysite, soon died; General Marcian took his place in August of 450 AD, by the election of the army and the senate. Deeply committed to Orthodoxy, Marcian subsequently married Theodosius' sister Pulcheria, who was also renowned for her zeal for Orthodoxy. For the Orthodox, the affairs of the Church thus took a turn for the better.

The activity of the Fourth Ecumenical Council at Chalcedon consisted of:

- Judgment over the "Robbers' Council" of 449 AD and Dioscorus of Alexandria, its head; and
- An investigation into the true teaching concerning the two natures in the Person of the God-man, Jesus the Christ.

The definition of Faith was given its final form and read out at the council on 22 October 451 AD. The Orthodox Church commemorates the Fourth Ecumenical Council on the 16th of July.

The Fifth Ecumenical Council

The Emperor Justinian the Great convoked the Fifth Ecumenical Council in the year 553 AD in the capital city of the Byzantine Empire, Constantinople to reconfirm the Doctrines of the Trinity and Christ.

This synod was opened on May 5th in the Secretarium of the Cathedral Church of Agia Sophia. Among those present were the Patriarchs, Eutychius of Constantinople, who presided, Apollinarius of Alexandria, Domains of Antioch, three bishops as representatives of the Patriarch Eustochius of Jerusalem, and 145 other metropolitans and bishops, of whom many came also in the place of absent colleagues (164 in total). This Council concluded its work on June 2nd 553 AD after eight sessions. The Fifth Ecumenical Council was held seventeen years before the birth of Prophet Muhammad in 570 AD.

The Fifth Ecumenical Council Achievements

Solving the Nestorian Controversy

The Council was called in hope of putting an end to the Nestorian and the Monophysite controversies.

Nestorius, bishop of Constantinople, proposed that the Virgin Mary gave birth to a man, Jesus Christ, not God, the "Logos" ("The Word," Son of God). He reasoned that the Logos only dwelled in Christ, as in a Temple (Christ, therefore, was only Theophoros: The "Bearer of God"). Consequently, the Virgin Mary should be called "Christotokos," "Mother of Christ" and not "Theotokos," "Mother of God." The Third Council dealt with the history of the events surrounding this controversy.

The Monophysite Controversy

Eutyches, the Archimandrite, in his efforts to maintain a physical unity in Christ held that the two natures in Christ, the Divine and the human, were so intimately united that they became physically one, inasmuch as the human nature was completely absorbed by the Divine. The result was one Christ not only with one personality but also with one nature. See the Fourth Council for the history of the events surrounding this controversy.

This Second Council of Constantinople confirmed the Church's teaching regarding the two natures of Christ (human and divine), and condemned certain writings with Nestorian leanings.

The Emperor Justinian himself also confessed his Orthodox faith in the form of the famous Church hymn "Only begotten Son and Word of God" which is sung after the Second Antiphon during the Divine Liturgy.

In the year 527 AD, Justinian, an ecclesiastically devout and learned man, was consecrated as Emperor of Byzantium. He ruled the Empire for nearly thirty years maintaining the ideal of reconciling heretics to the Church. Unfortunately, it was through his efforts that both the church and the state continued to experience great divisions.

Influenced by his empress Theodora, Justinian was secretly devoted to the Monophysite teaching, he was condemned by an edict the Antiochian teachers' most detestable to the Monophysite: Theodore of Mopsuestia (the teacher of Nestorius), Theodoret of Cyros, and Ibas of Edessa.

On Easter Eve, April 11, 548 AD Vigilius, likewise issued his Judicatum (judgment). He generally subscribed to the Emperor's wishes but he added a proviso that nothing should put in question the decisions of the previous four Ecumenical Councils. This was what was at issue. Since Chalcedon had not condemned the letter or Ibas, to do so now might seem to undermine the fourth ecumenical council. This was the aim of those who had promulgated the imperial decree (the Monophysite), that is, the credibility of the Council of Chalcedon.

Opposition to the Judicatum soon arose. Vigilius was accused of treachery. As a result Vigilius excommunicated a number of those, who criticized him, including deacons from Rome as well as some people from Africa. From Gaul, Illyria, and Dalmatia there came still stronger opposition to Vigilius. As a result Vigilius withdrew his Judicatum in 550 AD.

Justinian, without concurrence from the Roman Pontiff, summoned the synod at Constantinople to address these matters. Pope Vigilius, refused to take part in the council, because Justinian had summoned bishops in equal numbers from each of the five patriarchal sees. For this reason, Eutychius,

Patriarch of Constantinople, presided. The council opened on May 5th in the Church of Agia Sophia with 164 bishops in attendance.

On 14 May 553 AD, Pope Vigilius issued his "Constitution," which was signed by 16 bishops (nine from Italy, two from Africa, two from Illyria and three from Asia Minor). This rejected sixty propositions of Theodore of Mopsuestia, but spared his personal memory and refused to condemn either Theodoret or Ibas since, on the testimony of the council of Chalcedon, all suspicion of heresy against them had been removed. This council issued no canons, as it did not debate ecclesiastical or disciplinary matters. Most important, the Council of Chalcedon was not discredited as the Monophysite had hoped.

The refusal of the condemnation by the council created the formulas of the "Three Chapters":

a. The person and writings of Theodore of Mopsuestia;
b. The anti-Cyrillian writings of Theodoret of Cyros;
c. The writings of Ibas of Edessa to Maris

The Three Chapters were controversial because of the three, long since dead, personalities involved. Theodoret of Cyros and Ibas of Edessa were one-time companions of Nestorius who had been deposed from their Episcopal thrones for their heretical beliefs. Upon their acceptance of the teachings of St. Cyril of Alexandria (d. 444 AD) and of the Council of Ephesus, however, Chalcedon restored them to their Episcopal sees.

Theodore of Mopsuestia was a priest from Antioch and the head of the Syrian school who had tried to maintain the truth of the two natures of Christ against Apollinarianism. To Theodore the term "incarnation of God" seemed dangerous for it suggested that God the Word changed into a human being. This is why he preferred to recognize only the indwelling or "enoikeesis" of the Word in man. Thus he divided the one Christ into two, the man Jesus and the God who dwelt in him. In this respect Theodore was the father of the heresy that was attached to Nestorius. The Council of Ephesus, however, did not condemn Theodore, probably because he was already dead when the Council took place.

After carefully considering the matter for six months, Vigilius, evaluated the persecutions of Justinian against his clergy and having sent a letter to Eutychius of Constantinople, approved the council, thus changing his mind. Furthermore he anathematized Theodore and condemned his writings and those of Theodoret and Ibas.

On 23 February 554 AD, in a second "Constitution," he tried to reconcile the recent condemnation with what had been decreed at the council of Chalcedon.

This council was not universally recognized for some time by western bishops, even after the vacillating Pope Vigilius gave in his assent to it. The event caused a temporary schism between upper Italy and the Romans see. As to its importance, it stands far below the four previous councils. It did further confirm the first four general councils, especially that of Chalcedon whose authority was contested by some heretics.

What has been reviewed shows the complexities of concepts within the Christian ideologies and the different sects, congregations or religions such as the Nazarenes, Hebrew-Christians, Messianic Judaism that were developed and floating before the coming of Islam.

CHAPTER FOUR

Christianity in the Arabian Peninsula

All Semitic people have their beginnings in the Arabian Peninsula. The Arabian Peninsula, including Syria (Ash-Shaam), is a cradle of the most influential of human cultures. The great Semitic cultures and civilizations of the early period belong to emigrants who left the Arabian Peninsula for Mesopotamia, Palestine, and Africa.

The Red Sea in the west and the Persian/Arabian Gulf in the east separate the Arabian Peninsula from its parent continent, Africa, and from Asia. Although it is surrounded on three sides by water, there are no good harbors, save for Aden, and both the Red Sea and Persian/Arabian Gulf.

The Arabian Peninsula can be divided into two distinct climactic and geographical zones. In the south is an area along the coast of the Arabian Sea that gets regular rain and has an astonishing variety of plant life. Its wealth, tropical plants, cities, frankincense and myrrh knew it.

From a very early period, sedentary populations living in cities and relying on agriculture heavily populated the south of Arabia. Many of these civilizations were very wealthy and powerful, and Semitic peoples in Africa largely owe their origin to these privileged southerners.

Northern Arabia includes all of Arabia north of the southern coast, is one of the most uninviting places. To the east is a vast desert—one of the largest continuous areas of sand in the world—bordered by arid steppes in the west. The western portion of northern Arabia consists of mountains and steppes. Across this vast land, there are no rivers to connect peoples together. While the people in the south have historically lived close together and in constant contact, the people in the north live far apart and in relative isolation.

The most forbidding part of northern Arabia is the expanse of sand desert on the eastern side. There is little or no precipitation and so no support for agriculture—the only substantial flora in eastern Arabia is the date palm, a plant magnificently adapted to an arid climate. This area throughout almost all of human history has been inhabited by nomadic, pastorals Arabs called Bedouins who lived in small, tightly knit tribal groups. The western coast is slightly less forbidding and the Arabs that settled there, and lived in sedentary and larger tribal groups.

These two regions, the south and the north, were homes to two entirely separate Semitic peoples: the Sabaeans in the south and the Arabs in the north.

The Pre-Islamic Arab Christian kingdoms:

At least five different Arab monarchies flourished in the Arabian Peninsula before Islam. In short, they are:

1. The Sabaean kingdom of south Arabia that displayed an elaborate civilization in the vicinity of today's Yemen. According to the historian Diodorus from Sicily in the first century B.C., the kingdom of Sheba in south Arabia surpassed "not only the neighboring Arabs but all other men in wealth and in their extravagancies besides." [116] It is interesting to note what Muhammad Shukri al-Alusi wrote about Sabaeans[117] that: "The Sabeans have five prayers similar to the five prayers of the Muslims. Others say they have seven prayers, five of which are comparable to the prayers of the Muslims with regard to time [that is, morning, noon, afternoon, evening and night; the sixth is at midnight and the seventh is at forenoon]. It is their practice to pray over the dead without kneeling down or even bending the knee. They also fast for one lunar month of thirty days; they start their fast at the last watch of the night and continue till the setting of the sun. Some of their sects fast during the month of Ramadan, face Ka'ba when they pray, venerate Mecca, and believe in making the pilgrimage to it. They consider dead bodies, blood and the flesh of pigs as unlawful. They also forbid marriage for the same reasons as do Muslims."

2. The remarkable Natataean kingdom with its renowned capital of Petra established itself as the primary Arab power in the north of Arabia.

3. The Palmeryne kingdom flourished in north Arabia was famous with its caravan city of Palmyra to the northeast of Damascus and with its Arab beautiful queen Zenobia (Queen of the East). During

---

[116] Diodorus 3.47.5-8

[117] Muhammad Shukri al-Alusi, *"Bulugh al-'Irab fi Ahwal al-Arab"*, Vol 1, p 121-122

that period, an Arabian leader named Philip, from the city of Shahba, south of Damascus, rose to power to become emperor in Rome. "Philip the Arab" ruled the Roman world from 244 A.D. to 249.[118]

4. The Ghassanids kingdom, descended of a south Arabian tribe, was centered in Houran, a neighborhood of Damascus and adopted the monophysitism Christianity as the religion of the state.
5. The Lakhmid kingdom centered in Hira, southwest of the Euphrates and adopted the Nestorianism Christianity.

The Immigration of the Nazarenes to Hijaz

The Nazarenes had fallen between two fires, that of the Jews on one hand, and the fires of the Christians on the other. They had no other choice, but to immigrate to Hijaz where the desert and the country's political neutrality acted as a security buffer from the intervention of both the Persians and the Romans. The Nazarenes moved to Hijaz and settled there, mainly in Mecca, because the Jews had already penetrated into Taif and Yathreb (Medina).

No tangible reference to the Nazarenes can be traced in Christianity. No one can deny the historic events and facts that Christianity, mainly the Nazarenes, was well established in the Arabian Peninsula before the birth of the Prophet Muhammad in 570 AD. Christianity was prevailing in the northern and southern parts of the Arabian Peninsula; they had bishops in every location, and under each bishop a minimum of twenty priests and deacons.

The Roman historian Sozuminius [119] recorded that "each town was represented by a bishop, even bishops of the tents (Saracen, Arab nomadic peoples), who participated with representatives from every country in the General Church Councils and signed the minutes of the sessions they attended. In the first General Council of the Church at Nicaea, 325 AD, six Arab bishops attended the Council; while in the fourth General Council of the Church at Chalcedon, in 451 AD, seventeen Arab bishops managed to attend the sessions out of twenty." To have such number of Arab Bishops reflects the strength of those Arab Christian communities (parishes) to afford to have consolidated authority of independent bishops.

Christianity spread extensively in the Arabian Peninsula, in-spite of the persecution of the Roman Empire, and before Christianity became the

---

[118] Irfan Shahid, "Rome and the Arabs: A Prolegomenon to the Study of Byzantium and the Arabs," Washington D.C.: Dumbarton Oaks, 1984, pp. 65-93.
[119] Father Al-Haddad quoted the information from the "Revue Biblique" magazine, #476, 1930.

Empire's Religion. For example, St. Hironimus [120] through his missionary work converted all the Bedouin Tribes of Gaza to Christianity. The historian Sozuminius, also, relates that Mawia Albadawia fought against the Emperor Walnus (364-378). She had a condition in her peace treaty to give a pious hermit called "Moses" to become a bishop on her Arab Bedouins; he accepted in-spite of the fact that he himself was persecuting the Christians. Again, Kirilus Al-Bissani relates in his writing about the life of St. Aftimus the Great, who lived, in his monastery East of Jerusalem that Asdabet, an Arabian Tribe Sheikh, had a disabled boy who was cured by a miracle, through the prayers of St. Aftimus.

Asdabet and his tribe became Christians, and Asdabet himself, became a bishop on the nomadic peoples of the tents, as he signed his name on the minutes of the third General Council of the Churches at Ephesus, in 431 AD. It was also known that the Patriarch of Jerusalem St. Ilya was an Arab Bedouin. [121] In the fifth century AD, Nonnos, the Bishop of Baalbeck guided 30,000 Bedouins into Christianity.

When the Theodorian Constitution forced Christianity as the State Religion, the Jews felt that they had no choice to stay; they immigrated to Persia, the enemies of the Romans, to become their spies on the Romans. Archimandrite Al-Haddad stresses, "This is what the Jews do best through history. ... And that ... the Jews live as parasites; they penetrate the body of every ruling government of any 'Great Nation', whether in the eastern or western countries." [122]

Contemporary history acts witness to what was taking place in ancient and elapsed history. History tells us that the "Jews" penetrated deeply in Yemen, and tried to make the people Jewish, by seizing the power from the Christian Authority of Ethiopia to be ruled under the crown of the Persian Shah. Again, history recorded the struggle that took place in the fifth century AD, between the Christianity in Ethiopia and Judaism to control Yemen, and to control the communication routes between the East and the West. These events are well known in History.

---

[120] St. Hironimus, a Roman scholar, lived and engaged in worship in Bethlehem, mentions about Bedouin conversion in writing about the devout Hilarion (291-371 AD), in "Vita Hiharionis XXV".

[121] Fliche and Martin in "Histoire de l'Eglise" IV, 517 no. 2

[122] Archimandrite Al-Haddad, "Al-Qur'an wa Al-Kitab... p. 32.

The "Hunafa'" Christians in Syria and Hijaz

Al-Ghassasinah, Arab Christians, as most Arab tribes in Hijaz and in Syria was Christians. Al-Ya'kubi [123] says, "... The Arab Tribe of Kadha'a came to Syria, and Tannukh Ben Malek was their first king to rule Syria; he became a Christian, and was appointed a king by the Roman Emperor". Al-Mass'udi states, "... The tribe of Wardat Saleeh Al-Shaam, came to Syria after Kadha'a, and conquered Tannoukh; she became Christian, and was crowned to rule the Arabs in Syria by the Roman Emperor. The third Arab Tribe, Ghassan, came to Syria, became Christians, and ruled Syria until the coming of Islam to Syria." [124]

Christians of Syria used to call the Nazarenes of Beni Israel "Hunafa', plural of Hanif", an Aramaic term denotes the deflection of that group from the true Christian religion of the Syrians. Mohammed Kurd Ali says, "... Numerous Arab Tribes came to (Al-Shaam) or Syria and shared the control over Syria with the Roman Emperors, the most famous among them was Ghassan in the South, Tannoukh in the North, and Taghleb in the East. All these Arab tribes were Christians." [125] But the Nazarenes used their new portrayal as Hunafa' to become their new traits or characteristics. They made their new name in Hijaz very popular, and created a new relationship between their sect and Abraham the grandfather of "Israel" and "Ismayel". They referred to themselves as the sect of Abraham. The Hunafa' of the Arab Nazarenes of Beni Israel were lost between their nationality and their religion, they were independent from both Judaism and Christianity; they formed an in-between religion and a nation. The Hunafa' Nazarenes called themselves living in peace with God or "Muslims", before the spread of Islam as a consequence of the coming of the Prophet Muhammad.

Dr. Jawad Ali wrote, "The students of monotheism used to come to Syria where monotheism prevailed. The Hunafa' or Hanifs or (Nazarenes) were spread all over Syria, to the highest mountains of Hijaz and the highest mountains of Iraq, where most of the inhabitants were Christians, at that time. There were priests and monks to answer their questions about monotheism and discuss the concepts with them."[126] We read the same thing in Mohammed Darwazat's research and analysis, he writes, "...Not only in Syria Christianity was prevailing, the influence of Christianity was

---

[123] Al-Ya'kubi, "History Book of Al-Ya'kubi", p. 234

[124] Al-Mass'udi, "Muruj Al-Zahab", 3, p.216

[125] Mohammed Kurd Ali, "Khuttat Al-Shaam", 1: p.105.

[126] Dr. Jawad Ali, a member of the Iraqi Scientific Council, "History of the Arabs before Islam", 5: 2: p. 399.

spread up to Hijaz and to the northern parts of the Arabian Peninsula where Christianity prevailed. ..." [127]

The Christian Arab State of Ghassan, Al-Ghassasinah, was extended from Damascus "doors" and its desert, to Najd in the middle of the northern part of the Arabian Peninsula. After the destruction of the Dam of Ma'reb by the end of the third century AD, the most drastic, catastrophic economic event in the ancient Arab History, forced the tribes of Al Jeffnat to relocate in the land of Houran and Al-Balka'. The Al-Jeffnat adopted the Aramaic language, similar to the people of Syria. But, they kept their original Arabic tongue alive among them, so they became bilingual similar to the rest of the Arab tribes who lived in the Fertile Crescent as reported by Philip Hitti. [128]

The Ghassasinah acted as a strong castle in the face of the attacks of the nomadic Bedouins of the desert to the "civilized" towns under the Romans' control. The Roman Historian Ruferus mentions that a monk by the name of "Moses" was ordained to serve the tribes of Ghassan in the year 347 AD. [129]

In the sixth century AD, four Bishopric districts were present among the tribes of the Ghassasinah and the neighboring tribes. It is an established fact that no Bishopric district can be afforded, if Christianity is not well established and strong in that locality. And those Arab Bishops (Monks) were nomadic and were known as the bishops of the Tents (Saracens). Those tribal Monks were different than the Syrian Bishops of Houran and Al-Balka'. The Eparch Bishop of Busra, alone, was in charge of over twenty other bishopric districts. From these areas, where the Christian Arabs of Beni Ghassan lived, Christianity and Nazarenes were spread among the rest of the Arab tribes of the north, penetrating the tribes of Kalb, Kadhaa, Zubbian and others.

When the Syrian Aramaic dwellers in the State of Ghassan accepted the Monophysitism, the one nature doctrine; the Ghassasinah followed their steps. By giving a quick background to the Christian theology of that period, we start by reviewing the dispute that took place between the monk Nestorius, who became patriarch of Constantinople in 428 AD, and Cyril, Patriarch of Alexandria (412-444), about the two natures (divinity and humanity) in Christ. Nestorius overemphasized the humanity of Christ and so took exception of the traditional description of Mary as Theotokos (mother of God), declaring her proper title to be 'mother of Christ', since she was the mother of the human nature alone, and referred to Jesus as 'Issa Bin Mariam'. There was a ferocious argument between Cyril and Nestorius, in which Rome joined on the side of Alexandria against the pretentious claims of Constantinople. The third General Council of the Church was convened

---

[127] Mohammed Darwazat, "Sira Al-Rassoul – The Life of the Prophet", 2: p. 143.

[128] Philip Hitti, "History of the Arab", 1: p. 102.

[129] Ruferus, "Ruferus History Book", 2: p. 6.

at Ephesus, in 431 AD, called by the two Roman Emperors, Theodosius II of the East, and Valentinian III of the West. The Council condemned Nestorius and his Nestorianism, and Nestorius was exiled to the 'Egyptian' desert in 435 AD. [130]

A further fifth century AD dispute took place between the patriarch of Alexandria (supported by Rome) and the patriarch of Constantinople centered round the teaching of the Archimandrite Eutyches of Constantinople, who held that after the incarnation there was only one nature in Christ, the doctrine of Monophysitism. The fourth General Council of the Church at Chalcedon condemned Monophysitism, in 451 AD. Emperor Marcian called for this council, and attended the final session, personally. All Christians, Catholic and Orthodox adopted the Chalcedonian Definition of the doctrine of the Trinity. Trinity was asserted by the Letter of Pope Leo I that "Jesus Christ is one person, the Divine Word, in whom the two natures, the divine and the human, permanently united before and after the incarnation, though not confused and unmixed." [131]

This statement of belief, together with the other doctrinal definitions of the first four General Councils of the Church, have ever since, been accepted by Eastern and Western Orthodox, Catholic Christians, and even by Protestants. But the followers of Nestorius seceded and formed a schismatic church (unrecognized by Catholics and Orthodox alike) after the Council of Ephesus in 431 AD. While the upholders of one nature in Christ after the incarnation seceded from the main body of Christians after 451 AD, those followers had rejected the faith of the Empire, and to be saved from persecution, they found refuge among the Ghassani tribes. [132]

The Ghassani, AlHarith Althani Ben Jabalah, who was in Constantinople in 563 AD, helped the monk Jacob Al-Baradai' to be ordained as the Bishop of the Arab Syrian Church, under the protection of the king of the Ghassan State. Al-Baradai' was so energetic and made most of the Syrians and the Arabs to belong to his Church, and so the Monophysite became known by the 'Jacobite' Church. "Jacob Al-Baradai' died in 578 AD, but he left the Jacobite Church to grow, and is still has a Patriarch in Antioch and churches in Syria, Lebanon, Iraq, Jordan, Palestine, Cyprus, Egypt, Armenia and Ethiopia." [133]

---

[130] [Nestorius teachings were perpetuated in the Christian School at Edesa, which was transferred to Nisibis in 489 AD and received the support of the Persian king.]

[131] Parrinder, Geoffrey, ed. "World Religions: From Ancient History to the Present", the Hamlyn Publishing Group Ltd., 1983, p.432.

[132] Ibid.

[133] Ibid.

Philip Hitti states, "…As the Nestorius followers in Al-Hirra had influence on the Arabs living close to the borders of Persia, so the Monophysites who lived in the land of Ghassan had an influence on the Arabs of Hijaz." [134] Hitti quotes what John of Ephesus said, "The Arab tribes of Syria were fanatic in their belief in Monophysitism. … And in the 'Collections of Wright Sculptures no. 468', it appears that the leaders of the Ghassan and their tribes, specially the brothers of al-Munther Ben al-Harrith were Melkite." [135]

The Nazarene "Christians" in Al-Hirra among the Lakham Tribe

History tells us that after the destruction of the Dam of Ma'reb, the tribes of Al'zd and Tannukh migrated to the north of the Arabian Peninsula, to the land of the Fertile Crescent. As the Ghassan dwelled in the northwest, Al Lakham settled in the northeast. Al Lakham ruled Al-Hirra at the time Al Sasaan took over the rule in Persia, in 227 AD. The Byzantine Emperor appointed the Emir of Ghassan to rule the land of Syria on the Empire borders, while the 'Akassira in Persia appointed the Emir of Al Lakham on the Persian borders to rule the area and to prevent the nomadic attacks. The inhabitants of Al-Hirra, Syrians and Arabs, were Christians known as Nazarenes. When the Nestorius sect appeared in Iraq and in Persia, the Christians in Al-Hirra followed Nestorius teachings, they were known by "Al'Ubbad" or "Worshippers" or "the worshippers of 'Issa (Jesus)". The ruler of Al-Hirra did not declare their Christian faith officially, observant of the feelings of the King of kings Kissra, the enemy of the Byzantine Christian Emperor.

In the first half of the fifth century AD, both Arab and Greek reports used to tell us that the Nomad Arab Bedouins and the people of Al-Hirra used to come, in groups, to the north of Syria to visit St. Simeaan Al-Amoudi, of Arab origin. St. Simeaan was a hermit, renouncing worlds' pleasures by sitting on the top of his "Column", praying and making miracles. His influence was great, it forced Emir Al-Hirra, Al-Nu'maan I, known by "Al-'Awar" (one-eyed), who was a "mushrek", a sharer or an associator in his beliefs, to permit his people to make their pilgrimage to Al-'Amoudi. But Al-'Awar saw a vision of the saint Al-'amoudi threatening him; he became a Christian and made his people Christians and allowed them to visit Al-'Amuni.

---

[134] Ibid.

[135] Philip Hitti, "History of the Arabs" 1: p.150.

The Roman historian Sozuminus[136] mentions, "Christianity penetrated the royal family of Al-Hirra during the rule of Queen Maa' Al-Samaa' and Hind Al-Ghassaniah. Hind was the daughter of Al-Harrith Al-Ghassani, married to Al-Munther III Al-Lakhami, son of Maa' Al-Samaa', she brought with her, her Christian belief, and she established a monastery for the nuns, under the eyes of the King Kissra Anu Sherwaan. The nuns' numbers grow to over four hundred. This showed that Christianity became well established to have an abbey with such a number of nuns' worshippers. Dr. Assad Rustum quoted what Al-Yakut copied from the entrance of the monastery, the words read as follows:[137] "Hind, the daughter of Al-Harrith Ben Umru Ben Hajar, the Queen daughter of kings, and the mother of the King Umru Ben Al-Munther, servant of Christ, and the mother of His servant and the daughter of His servants; in the realm of the king of kings Khessru Anu Sherwaan, in the days of St. Afram, the Monk. And God, for whom this Abbey was built, bless her and bless her son, and accept her and her people in His righteousness, and let God be with her and her son forever and ever."

When the war broke between the Roman and the Persian, Al-Munther fought well, defeated the Roman in Syria and proceeded with his attacks on the borders of Antioch. During those attacks for special favoritism from Kissra, the son of Maa' Al-Samaa' was forced to kill the four hundred plus nuns in the monastery, and sacrifice them to the goddess Al-'izza.[138] This innocent blood that was shed had its revenge, when Al-Harrith Ben Jebalah (Al-Ghassani), supported by the Byzantine, conquered Al-Munther (Al-Lakhami) and killed him in the battle known as "Yom Halimeh" in 554 AD. Many Arab Christians were killed whenever the war used to break between the Romans and the Persians.

Christianity was spread heavily along the Arabian Gulf coast, and five Churches were established as bishopric districts: in Al-Hirra, Sakat, Qatar, Al-Huffuf and Al-Bahrain. There, the two sects that of the Monophysitism and of Mestoriusism were the leading religions in the area, up to the days of the Prophet Muhammad. There were two religious centers in each location, one Church for the followers of Nestorius and the other for the Jacobite. The Nazarenes who lived to the south of the Euphrates, acted as teachers to the "associators" of gods to teach them reading and writing and religion, as reported by Hitti. At that time, Christianity spread from Emirate of Al-Hirra to the north to Taghleb and 'Iyat tribes, to the south to Beni Shaiban and Beni Hanifeh and Beni Rabieh and some of the descendants of Bakr

---

[136] Sozuminus, "A History Book", 6: p. 38.

[137] Assad Rustum, "History of the Great City of God Antioch".

[138] This event is reported by Zacharie le Rheteur in "Histoire Ecclesiastique VIII" and in Michel le Syrien II, p.178

Ben Wa'el. To the northern part of Najd, Christianity came with Beni Taa'i and Tha'labah. To the southern part of Najd Christianity was introduced by Beni Tamim and Kadha'a.

Mohammed Hussein Haikal states, "There were three stories that showed how the Nazarenes entered Najran. One says, it came from Syria from patriarch of Antioch; some says from the Jacobite of Al-Hirra who belongs to the Monophysitism and also it was said that a certain Najrani became Christian while in Al-Hirra and brought the religion with him to his tribe and his people."[139]

Therefore, the Nestorius followers in Al-Hirra had carried the thoughts and beliefs of the people in the north, from Aramaic, Hellenistic and Persians to the heart of the Arabian Peninsula including their Christian faith.

When Al-Munther Ben Al-Harrith conquered King Kabous of Al-Hirra, in 570 AD, at Ain Abagh battle, he called for a Council and excommunicated the "Christian" sect that called for the trinity of the three: God, Mary, and Jesus. Later on, the noble Qur'an prohibits the same form of trinity: "Don't say: three".

The Nazarene "Christians" in the southern part of the Arabian Peninsula and in Yemen and Najran

Yemen is one of the oldest Spot where ancient world civilization grew. The happy Arabia – Yemen - was named from "Al-Yumen" for the fertility of its land. Pre-historic Yemen was well known for its striving life, even before the historic biblical tribe of "Noah" flourished there into statehood for nearly 950 years (the age of biblical Noah). This tribe had branched to Sam, Ham and Yafeth after 500 years. The main branch of the tribe, to escape the flood, moved from Al-Tabba in Salma Mountain, north of Najd to the southeast of the city of Ha'el in Hijaz. [140]

Yemen was the educational, economic and political center to connect the Old East with the Old West. The written history of Yemen starts with the Ma'eeniah State (1200–650 BC). Then came the Saba'eeah State (650-150 BC), and the Himyariah State (150 BC-525 AD). The Himyariah was broken by the destruction of the Dam of Ma'reb by the end of the third century AD to start the second phase from (300–525 AD). With the catastrophic destruction of the Dam, most of the local tribes migrated to Hijaz and Syria as we have mentioned before.

---

[139] Mohammed Hussein Haikal, "The Life of Muhammad" p. 30

[140] Read the details of this interesting interpretation of the biblical story of Noah in Dr. Kamal Salibi's book "Khafaya Al-Tawrat wa 'Asrar Sha'ab Israel" pp. 47-71

Yemen was attacked by the Ethiopian army, after which King Abraha Al-Ashram, an Ethiopian agent ruled Yemen in 525 AD. After 570 AD, the year of the elephant ('Aam Al-Feel), when Saif Ben Yazen asked for the help of Kissra who came and occupied Yemen until replaced by the coming of Islam.

The people of Yemen were atheistic; their religion was astronomic. Their worship concentrated on the "Moon" (god Wad), the Noble Qur'an kept the name for us. They considered the "Sun" his wife, and their son/daughter "'Athtar" or "Venus". 'Athtar became 'Atshar in Babylon and 'Ashtarout in Phoenicia. The worship of the Arabs in the south was that of the stars. It represented a family of three: Moon, the Father; Venus, the Son; and the Mother, the Sun. This type of worship led a sect of the Nazarene in Hijaz, to falsify the meaning of Trinity, to include God, Mary and Jesus, whom Christians reject and so the Qur'an rejects.

Yemen had contacts with the followers of Yahweh, the Israelites, who were known by "the people of the Book". They were the first to believe in monotheism in the southern part of the Arabia Peninsula, in the Asir district, where the kingdom of Israel and that of Judea were established and Solomon built the Temple. [141]

Emperor Costandius sent the first Christian missionary to reach Yemen in 356 AD, led by Thaophylis Andes who followed the Arius teachings. From the beginning, Christians had asserted the belief in the divinity of Jesus Christ. It was a matter of time before the question of the relation of God the Father, and Jesus Christ, the Son, would arise. It took place in the fourth century, when the great Arianism controversy split the Church into two. It stemmed from the preaching of the Alexandrian presbyter, Arius, that the Son was created being that did not eternally exist and, therefore, was a sort of demi-god, subordinate to the Father (the God of the Old Testament). Arius argued that Jesus was less than God and that his true role was to serve as a model of virtue to humanity.

Athansius called Arius interpretation as heresy and an assault on Jesus Himself. Arius misused Scripture to obscure the central mystery of the Christian faith; he believed that the only way to save mankind from mortality, sin and death; God, out of his infinite love for us, descended into the human flesh and suffered that we may be given eternal life. The Emperor Constantine summoned the first General Council of the Church at Nicaea, in 325 AD, to settle this dispute and so reunify the Church. It condemned the teaching of Arius and produced a creed, which declared that the Son is of one substance with and Eternal with the Father.

---

[141] To familiarize oneself with the detailed research and his astonishing analysis on the subject, we suggest the reading of Dr. Kamal Salibi's book "The Bible Came From Arabia".

Theodosius I convened the second General Council of the Church at Constantinople, in 381 AD, which endorsed his definition of Catholicism in 380 AD, condemned Arianism and also Appollinarianism which over-stressed the divinity of Christ, in opposition to Arianism, and reaffirmed the Nicene Creed. The triumph of the Nicene Creed meant that Christ is God, and that the "Christological" controversy was over. [142] But the teaching of Arius penetrated the Arabian Peninsula, through Yemen, as it went along the Nazarene teachings. Thaophylis was successful in spreading Nazarenes (Christianity) among the "Taba'eah" tribe, and building famous churches in 'Aden on the coastal area, in Zafar, in Hadramout, and in Hermez at the entrance of the Arabian Gulf.

The State of Al-Himyariah in Yemen was weakened, after the route of communication shifted from Yemen to Egypt. Dr. Mustafa Al-Rafi'I [143] states, "...When Egypt fell in the hands of the Romans, Batlimus II reopened the channel between the Nile and the Red Sea. The Romans, with the help of Ethiopia, managed to reach the Indian Ocean by passing Yemen, Petra and Tadmur. The age of decline took over Yemen and at that time the Arabs of Yemen split between Jews and Nazarenes."

In that third phase of the State of Himyariah, the competition between the Jews and Christians was at its utmost. "...During that period, one of the Taba'eah tribe leader, Aba Karab, As'ad Kamel became a Jew, and forcefully imposed Judaism on his people. He and another Jewish king Yusuf thoo Nawas (the owners of the Trench) attacked the Christians for national (Ethiopian) and religious (Christian) struggle, between 510 AD and 523 AD. The most famous massacres of Zafar and Najran occurred in October 523 AD. The Christians for not accepting Judaism was killed; in Najran alone (437 priests), and in Yemen four thousand priests and over twenty thousand Christian martyrs." [144]

The massacres of Zafar and Najran were kept alive in the memory of the Arabs and are eloquently remembered in the Qur'an ("1 By the sky holding constellations 2 and the promised day, 3 and a witness plus his evidence, 4 the owners of the Trench slained! 5 The fire was full of fuel, 6 as they were crouching over it, 7 and themselves were witnesses of what they were doing to believers. 8 They persecuted them merely because they believed in God, the Powerful, the Praiseworthy, 9 Who holds control over Heaven and Earth. God is a Witness for everything.)" [145]

---

[142] Parrinder, Geoffrey, ed. "World Religions ... p.431.

[143] Mustafa Al-Rafi'i, "Al-Islam Intilak la Jumoud" p. 149.

[144] Ibn Hisham, "Al-Sira", 1: 37.

[145] Sura Al-Buruj, 85: 1-9

Doos Thoo Tha'laban escaped the massacre and asked for the help from the Roman Emperor Justinius who called upon the King of Ethiopia to support Doos. An army of seventy thousands of the Ethiopian Christians led by Ariyatt attacked and conquered Yemen before the end of 523 AD. King Abraha assassinated the Ethiopian leader and ruled Yemen in 525 AD.

To show gratitude to the King of Ethiopia, King Abraha built a magnificent Cathedral in Sanaa', he called "Al-Qleess" (a Greek term in origin). The Ethiopian decided to convert all the people of Hijaz into Christianity, and compete closely with the "atheist" Mecca. Ben Hisham recorded the message King Abraha sent to his King of Ethiopia. It reads: "I have built for you, Oh King, a Church, no one ever built one similar to it to any king before you, and I'll never stop until I make it the Ka'ba for the pilgrimage of all the Arabs." [146]

King Abraha Al-Ashram kept his promise to fulfill his goal from 525 AD, until the year of the Elephant ('Aam Al-Feel) in 570 AD. He persecuted the Jews and the atheists and spread the teaching of monotheism of Nazarenes' Christianity in all direction. The people of Mecca and those who worship its Idols and traders of her pilgrimage were annoyed from that Christian Emir. Ben Hisham relates "Al-Kanani, in protest, left Mecca to Al-Qleess and settled inside it, King Abraha got furious and swore to invade the House in Mecca and demolish it." [147] He raised an army and rode his elephant and arrived to Mecca and was about to demolish Al-Ka'ba. But smallpox effectively spread among his army and King Abraha decided to return and died affected by the smallpox. Ben Hisham mentions, "That year (570 AD) was the first time smallpox appeared in the land of the Arabs." [148]

The memory of the attack and the spread of smallpox survived, and the House of Mecca was magnified with praise, so they used the year 570 AD to date events and write history with it. With that year, the Arabs dated the birth of Prophet Muhammad. The noble Qur'an preserved the "legendary myth" about what happen then in Sura Al-Feel (The Elephant) on how the Lord dealt with the owners of the Elephant? And sent birds in flocks (Tayr Ababeel) against them, which threw stamped clay pellets (Hijarah men Sajjil) at them? [149]

King Abraha's two sons Yaksoom and Massrouq ruled Yemen after the death of their father. The plague wrecked Yemen and Saif Ben Thee Yazen

---

[146] Ben Hisham, "Al-Sira", 1: 44.

[147] Ibid. 1:47.

[148] Ibid. 1:57

[149] Sura Al-Feel 106: 1-5. [Ben Hisham (1:56) considers the words Sajjil and Ababeel as Persian words. The Qur'an copied the public opinion of the people of Mecca that smallpox is done by strange birds.]

Al-Himyari asked the help of Kissra, who attacked and kicked out Ethiopia from Yemen. He crowned Wihrez and his descendants after him to rule Yemen until the arrival of Islam to take over. The only remaining to obey Islam, under the sword of Ali and Khalid, were the Christians of Yemen. They were the first to cause the war of apostasy, and were defeated the second time. After which the Caliph Omar expelled those who refused to accept Islam, as their new religion, to Iraq in 635 AD.

The Christians fighters in Najran grew in number to over forty thousands. Abi Jaafar Al-Nahhas reported that "... their increased number made the Caliph feel afraid of their might and the possibility of creating deflection, so he decided to expel them to Syria." [150] The Nazarenes in Yemen stayed until 840 AD and their Bishop in Sanaa' was called Mar Butrus.

Christianity, as expressed by the Nazarenes, spread the monotheistic doctrines in Yemen, the Arabian Peninsula before the coming of the Prophet Muhammad with the message of Islam. Ben Hisham mentions Abdullah Ben Al-Tamer who called for the religion of God and the Law of Islam before Muhammad. The people of Najran followed the religion of Abdullah Ben Al-Tamer according to 'Issa Ben Mariam teachings in the Gospel and His Discretion. [151]

It is important to remember the three major events that took place in the sixth century AD, before the coming of the Prophet. These events show the in-depth spreading of Christianity in the Arab lands from the North to the South and in Al-Hijaz.

1. The first event was the massacres of 523 AD in Zafar and Najran where thousands of clergymen were slained.

2. The second event was the massacres of Al-Hirra, Yom Halimeh, in 554 AD; over four hundred nuns were sacrificed. A peace army of Arab Priests, Clergymen and Nuns were anchoring on the border of Hijaz ready to invade peacefully with the spread of monotheistic Christianity of Ben Al-Tamer, if events had given him the opportunity to do so.

3. The third event has a political tone, when King Abraha attacked Mecca in the year of the Elephant, 570 AD, to demolish Al-Ka'ba and get rid of the atheistic monopoly over the Arabs of Hijaz. But that objective was destined to be accomplished by someone else.

---

[150] Abi Jaafar Al-Nahhas, "Al-Nasikh wal Mansukh", p.162.
[151] Ben Hisham, "Al-Sira", 1: 36.

Islam took over the Nazarenes' religion and invaded Al-Hijaz completely and spread its collected teachings of monotheism all over the Arabian Peninsula.

The Nazarene "Christians" in Al-Hijaz

Al-Hijaz confines the middle area of the Arabian Peninsula from Yemen and from the North with the surrounding deserts. But Al-Hijaz was never confined from the outside world or the Arab World, because it was the route of communication. The people of Al-Hijaz, specially the tribe of Quraysh, led the transit trade business, and were in continuous contact with the Christian Arabs world and the Christians' world. Al-Hijaz was surrounded by Christians, and the monks of Najran used to visit Suq 'Ukkazz and preach Christianity. Jews were spread all over Al-Hijaz. Mr. Darwazat states, "The Bible was handled by the learners, from the Jews who had large Jewish communities and had settled in Al-Hijaz, as it is well known." [152] A large number of the Arabs in Hijaz became Nazarenes in Aylat, Dumat Al-Jundul, Wadi Al-Kura, Tymaa', Ma'an, Yathreb, Mecca and Al-Taif. No apparent locations were noticed for the Nazarenes except in Aylat, Dumat and Tymma', because the associators were abundant among the inhabitants of Mecca in Hijaz. They took advantages during the season of pilgrimage for a profit and to make a living.

When Prophet Muhammad wanted to prevent the associators from participating in the pilgrimage, the Muslims in Mecca got afraid from becoming poor and hungry. Such event resulted in the following, "You who believe, associators are nothing but filthy, so they should not approach the Hallowed Mosque after this year that they still have. If you should fear destitution, God will enrich you out of His bounty if He so wishes. God is Aware, Wise".[153] The nature of the Bedouin nomadic life did not give the Bedouins time to care for their religious affairs.

Prophet Muhammad died in desolation from the desert Arab Bedouins rejection of God's monotheism: "Desert Arabs are quite stubborn when it comes to disbelief and hypocrisy, and the least inclined to acknowledge the limits that God has revealed to His messenger." [154]

Having observed the Desert Arabs natural propensity, the Bedouins Nazarenes adapted to the Desert life, and accepted nomadic monks to lead them, travels with them, and was called the "monks of the tents". We have

---

[152] Mohammed Darwazat, "Sira Al-Rassoul", 2: 41.
[153] Sura Al-Tawbat (Repentance,9) verse 28
[154] Ibid. Verse 97.

seen their signatures in the General Council of the Church by "X Monk of the Nomads" or "X Monk of the Allied Eastern Tribes", or "X Monk of Desert Arabs". Since the fourth century AD, the historian Sozuminus wrote about "the monks were among the Arab Tribes living in tents." How about Bedouins Nazarenes and their monks by the end of the six-century! Such events could not happened in Al-Hijaz, but "Tarikh Al-Ya'koubi", Al- Ya'koubi in his History book, left us with an authentic certification that "from those who became Nazarenes among the Arabs of Al-Hijaz was a group from Quraysh; and from Yemen, Taa'i, Bahraa', Saleeh, Tannukh and Ghassan." [155].

The most important fact to remember is that a group from Quraysh became Nazarene "Christians", the tribe that ruled Mecca and its Ka'ba, and controlled its trades and its religions.

The Nazarenes "Christians" penetrated the following cities in Al-Hijaz.

The Nazarenes in Najd:

In short, the tribes of Kindat and Ma'ad were in direct contact with the Roman Emperors. After the death of the family of 'Imrau' Al-Kaiss, the famous pre-Islamic poet, this wandering King found refuge in Emperor Yastinianus who crowned 'Imrau' Al-Kaiss to become the Emir of Najd and the tribes of Kindat and Ma'ad. That was a political move to block the route of the Persians who had the ambition to invade Najd and to protect the Christian Ethiopian privileges in Yemen.

After the event of the year of the Elephant took place, 'Imrau' Al-Kaiss story went to say that the Emperor moved him to Palestine to become an Emir on the Arabs living on the borders of his territories. This shows us that the Christian Emperor reached Najd and was in control of its leaders.

The Nazarenes in Aylat (Al-'Akabah):

Yakout states "Aylat [156] is at the end of the Hijaz land" northward. The inhabitants of that part of the Arabian Peninsula were Arab Nazarenes. Al-Mas'udi mentions that "Youhana Ben Ru'yat was the monk in Aylat came to the Prophet Muhammad in the year 9 Hijriah, (631 AD), when the Prophet

---

[155] Sozuminus, "A History Book", 1:98

[156] [Up to date we have four 'Akabas: the 'Akaba of Saudi Arabia, 'Akaba of Jordan, 'Aylat of Palestine and 'Akaba of Egypt in juxtaposition.]

was in Tabouk, and made peace with him and every inhabitant pays one Dinar". [157] Ibn Saad confirms this testimony, but he considers the arriver to meet with the Prophet a King and not a Monk; but by mentioning the Cross carried on his chest, it indicates that the arrival is indeed a Monk. He says "Youhana, King of Aylat came accompanied with people from Jarba' and Athrah and having a Cross from gold; the Prophet made peace with them and agreed on pay a known tribute." [158] By knowing the name of the negotiator and the Cross of Gold carried on his chest, these are signs of a Monk, and the peace treaty with the tribute confirms that the setup of the land of Hijaz starting from the North adopted the religion of the Nazarenes.

The Nazarenes in Dumat Al-Jundul:

In describing the invasion of Tabouk, Ibn Hisham said, "that the Prophet called Khalid Ben Al-Walid and sent him to see 'Ukeeder of Dumat. 'Ukeeder Ben 'Abdullah, King of Kindah who was a Nazarene... When he left to meet with Khaled, they were intercepted by the horsemen of the Prophet and took him; they killed his brother who had an outer garment decorated with gold pieces. Khalid plundered the King from them and took him to meet the Prophet who spared his life and made peace with him and agreed on a payment of a definite tribute. He was left alone to return to his village." [159]

Al-Mas'udi and Ibn Saad both mentioned 'Ukeeder in their books as the King of Dumat Al-Jundul who was a Nazarene, and was taking orders from Hirakel, the Roman Emperor. His peace treaty with the Prophet and the arrangement for paying the tribute was mentioned, too. [160]

So, the second major city in the north of Hijaz was Christian and ruled by a Christian. Dr. Jawad Ali states, "With the emergence of Islam, there were no locations ruled by Christians in the Arabian Peninsula except in Dumat Al-Jundul, Aylat and Al-Yamamat."[161] This statement could be true if it is applied to Hijaz area only, and not to the Arabian Peninsula.

---

[157] Al-Mas'udi, "Al-Tanbih wa Al-Ishraf"

[158] Ibn Saad, "Wafadaat Al-Arab". [A copy of the message that the Prophet sent to Youhana Ben Ru'yat, to the people of 'Alyat and to those who accompanied him from Syria and Yemen is documented in "Sira Ibn Hisham" (4:169.)]

[159] Ibn Hashim, 4:169.

[160] Yakout, 2:626

[161] Jawad Ali, "The Arabs before Islam".

The Nazarenes in Mu'an:

Mu'an is described by Yakout, it is located at the end of the Syrian Desert opposite to Hijaz from the Balka' direction. Its inhabitants were Nazarenes under the control of the Romans similar to the Ghassassinah, or similar to the family of 'Imra' Al-Kaiss in Najd. Mu'an was ruled by Farwat Ben Abi 'Amer, the Chief of the Nazarene Beni Jazzam.

It is mentioned that Farwat, in Mu'tat invasion, fought the Muslim army under the leadership of Zaid Ben Harithah, Ja'far Ben Abi Taleb and Abdullah Ben Rawwahat. They also mention that the Roman army under Thaodorus, known by the Deputy, consisted of 100,000 soldiers, and another 100,000 fighters from the Arab Nazarenes. Muslim Army ran away after the killing of their leaders. Those who remained in the city scoffed at them, and called them "Ya Furrar!" (Oh Deserters, running away) [162]

An area that can levy troops of 100,000 soldiers, in a very short period, shows that it has hundreds of thousands of the Arab Nazarene-Christians to accommodate a large numbers of volunteers. So, north of Hijaz and up to Najd, the absolute majority of the people were from the believers in monotheism of the Book, mainly Arab Christians. The rulers of Aylat, Dumat Al-Jundul and Al-Yamamat were Nazarene-Christians too.

The Nazarenes in Teema':

Teema' is located between Syria and Wadi Al-Kura (the valley of villages). The stronghold city of Teema' was for the Jews and the Nazarenes. There, the Christian tribe of Taa'I lived and it was a bishopric district. The citizens of Teema' paid tributes after the invasion and the fall of Khaybar. It was also the town of (the poet) Al-Samaw'al, the owner of the only spotted pinto. The religious identity of Al-Samaw'al was unknown. From his name Samuel appeared to be Jewish. But he was expected to be a Christian due to his origin; he belonged to the Ghassan tribe. He made reference to the names of the Disciples of Jesus in his poems, and mainly for 'Imru Al-Kaiss who trusted him with his sister and his armors. [163]

The Nazarenes in Tabouk:

Tabouk is a fortified location between Wadi Al-Kura and Syria, inhabited by the Christian tribe of Kadha'ah. Their neighbors were Beni Kalb from

---

[162] Al-Ya'koubi and the Mu'jam (Dictionary) of Yakout.

[163] Father Shikho, "Divan Al-Samaw'al", Beirut, 1920

the Christian tribe of Taghleb, as stated by Ibn Khaldoun copying Ibn Saad, "For Kadha'ah was an Emir Kalb Ibn Dubrah Ben Taghleb, who was also in charge of Al-Sukoon of Kindah. Kalb had Dumat Al-Jundul and Tabouk too. They were all Nazarenes." [164] When Prophet Muhammad and his Muslim Army invaded Tabouk, he could not conquer; it was well fortified and received support from the surrounding Arab Christians. He besieged the city for twenty days and then unsuccessfully withdrew. That event proved the strength of the Arab Christians in Tabouk, Mu'tat and Mu'an in southern Arabia and delayed their brothers the Arabs of the north to conquer them without death defiance.

The Nazarenes in Wadi Al-Kura:

The name Wadi Al-Kura represents a concentration of villages within the same location in a valley (Wadi). It is situated between Syria (Al-Shaam) and the Medina. Jew dwelled there first, then the Nazarene tribes of Kadha'a and Saleh. That area was restricted no Jews were allowed to live in, or any Arab who is not Christian. That meant only Arab Christians lived there [165].

The Nazarenes in Yathreb (the City of the Prophet):

Yathreb was colonized by the Jews from the tribes of Beni Kuraytha, Beni Al-Nadhir and Beni Al-Kaynuka' and surrounded by twenty other Jewish tribes. Yathreb of Hijaz was famous by its seventy strongholds as referenced in "Al-Khazraj" of the Islamic Department of Information. These strongholds were mentioned in the Noble Qur'an "...they thought that their strongholds would keep God away from them..." [166]. The tribes of Al-Awss and Al-Khazraj from Yemen joined the Jewish tribes of Yathreb. They came to Yathreb on a basis of an established covenant among them. Each time the Jews try to defect and oppress them, the non-Jewish Arab tribes used to ask the help and support from the Tubba' or the Ghassasinah tribes. It materialized many times, and the Nazarenes Arabs got stronger in Yathreb during the era of Muhammad.

Nazarenes penetrated Yathreb, slowly at intervals, until it grew strongly among the Arabs to compete with Judaism. Al-Shahrastani mentions "the two opposing teams, before Muhammad, are from the people of the Book

---

[164] Ibn Khaldoun, Mukadamat, 2:249

[165] According to Al-Asfahani, 'Al-Aghani' 7:171

[166] The Noble Qur'an, Sura Al-Hashr 59-The Gathering-Banishment, from verse 2

and the illiterate of the Book (Al-Ummiyoun). The Jews and Nazarenes were in Al-Medina and the illiterate were in Mecca." [167]

Hassan Bin Thabit, in his Diwan that included the "Elegy of Prophet Muhammad", mentions that the Jews of Yathreb got happy when the "atheist" (Prophet Mohammad) vanished in his grave. [168] Such a statement indicates the Jews were still strong enough in Yathreb after the death of Prophet Muhammad. It also reflects the presence of Christians there.

The records in the Nestorius Church tell us that they had a Bishopric district in Yathreb, and the three churches built carried the names of Ibrahim Al-Khalil, Mussa Al-Kalim and Ayoub Al-Sadik. From the writing of Dr. Heal, we read that the Arabs in Yathreb were closer to monotheism belief from the people of Mecca because they were neighbors to the people of the Book and the influence of its emphasis on monotheism. We are convinced that the Monotheism belief in the Book had prevailed in most of the Hijaz's land.

The Nazarenes in Mecca and the Environment of the Prophet:

Mecca was the stronghold for the associators. It had the Old House of worship and all the advantages of pilgrimage that was prevailing as the main profitable income to the leaders of Mecca and their descendants until the coming of Islam.

The old Arab idolatry became in Mecca as it was over Hijaz, an association of someone with God, Who has no associators. That type of associations was in form, but not a religious creed, deep in the heart of the people, because the written monotheism teachings of the Book prevailed. No doubt that Jews and Nazarenes were well established in Mecca before Islam. From

---

[167] Al-Shahrastani, "Al-Milal wa Al-Nihal" (p. 162). [The discrepancy is over the meaning of (Ummi). Is he the illiterate who does not read or write? Or (Ummi), contrary to Kitabi - who belongs to a Book - and has no Book to guide him!]

[168] From -Diwan Sayyidina Hassan ibni Thabit radya Allahu 'anh- (Tunis: Matba'at al-Dawlat al-Tunisiyya, 1281/1864) p. 25 "Prophet Muhammad gave Hassaan his slave Sirin, the sister of Muhammad's wife Maria al-Qibtiyya. The sisters were EgyptianCopticChristians sent as gifts to Muhammad by Muqawqis, a ruler of Egypt, in around 628. Sirin bore Hassaan a son, 'Abd al-Rahman ibn Hassaan." From Tarikh Tabari, p. 131

reading a number of history books, we observe that Mecca was inhabited with Nazarenes and Jews. [169]

The presence of the Nazarenes in Mecca is very old. Ibn Al-Atheer and Ibn Khaldoun mentioned that the sixth king of Jurhum tribe in Mecca was called Abed Al-Massih Ben Bakiah Ben Jurhum. While Al-Asfahani asserts that "the House of Mecca, under King Abd Al-Massih Ben Bakiah Ben Jurham had no roof at that time. The Nazarenes in Mecca were indeed in charge of the Old House, during the realm of Jurhum, and a Bishop was in control of Al-Ka'ba." [170]

Mr. Mohammed 'Izzat Darwazat said that "the Nazarenes as we have concluded had a presence as a foreign Nazarene Community in Mecca, and a possibility of having foreign Nazarene Community in Yathreb; and a preponderance of Arabs Nazarenes settlers, too, in the Prophet environment and his Age." Mr. Darwazat continues "if the spreading of the Nazarenes was narrow, we believe that the Nazarenes, similar to Judaism, was a source for knowledge and religious thoughts for the Arabs of Hijaz." [171]

We see same references recorded in much of the Qur'anic verses. All of these references indicate that the Arab of Hijaz and specially Arab of Mecca had a tremendous knowledge in the Nazarene doctrines and sect and their opinion of Christ's Birth, His message and His crucifixion. It was natural that such talks created a feedback in their knowledge, minds and dogma. Even the associators of Mecca used to say that the Prophet himself learned and was affected by them. [172]

We should not forget the thousands and thousands of the Christian Arabs, with whom the people of Hijaz used to meet in their travels, and deal with them as brothers, and talk together in a common Arabic tongue. Let us not forget that during the pilgrimage to Mecca they were seen in their

---

[169] The book of Mohammed 'Azzat Darwazat's "Sira Al-Rassoul" (the Life of the Prophet), (1:308) has reported that Al-Ya'coubi (1:298) mentioned Beni Assad Ben Abed Al-'Azzi among those who became Nazarenes from the tribe of Quraysh. Al-Azraqi in "Akhbar Mecca" (p.50) shows us the location of "a Nazarenes' graveyard at the rear end of the quarry on the road to 'Anbassa Bethee Tawa Well. The quarry is a mountain at the lower part of Mecca to the right of the person who is leaving Mecca toward Madina. Al-Feiruzabadi in "Taj Al-'Arouss" (the Crown of the Bride) mentions a location in Mecca known by "Mawkeph Al-Nusrani" (the station of the Nazarene).

[170] Al-Asfahani, "Al-Aghani"13: 109.

[171] Mohammed 'Izzat' Darwazat 'Asr Al-Nabi (Sad) wa Bi'atahu Kabl Al-Bi'that – "The Age of the Prophet and his Environment Before the Revelation", p. 452.

[172] As stated in the Noble Qur'an verses of (Sura Nahel – Bees 103) and (Sura Al-Furkan – The Standard or Criterion 4).

markets, some of them used to lecture and preach like Al-Kouss (the Monk) Ben Sa'eda. [173]

Darwazat says, "The tribal traditions and blood relationship are deeply rooted among Arab Nazarenes (Christians) fathers and grandfathers, and together they created strong bonds that were apparent through ages. The Arabs who were not Nazarenes, mainly in Hijaz, used to intermarry with the Arab Nazarenes, building even stronger bonds and more power. Out of this interaction, the Arabs of Hijaz had more opportunities for knowledge, reading and studying and be effective." [174]

Darwazat also states: "We have arrived to conclusions that among those who met the Prophet (Sad) were Arabs. And even those who were not Arabs used to speak and understand Arabic, as we are told by the Qur'anic verses from one side, and from the witnessed historic events. They all reported that thousands and thousands of Arabs who were Nazarenes, nomad Bedouins and urbanized town Dwellers. Arab Christians had their own States and had influence in the land of Al-Shaam (Syria) and Iraq. They have their Christian monks and bishops and priests and churches and enormous monasteries." [175]

Darwazat writes, "In pursuance to what being said, it is true to state that much of the Bible of the Old Testament and the Gospel were translated into Arabic before Islam. It might have lost among so many written Arabic antiquities and relics during the war, invasions and conspiracies. ... These are the facts that remain straight including the presence of tens of thousands of Nazarenes and thousands of Christian Arab monks and priests, and hundreds of churches and Arab monasteries." [176]

The Archimandrite Rev. Al-Haddad adds to what Darwazat's stated that "we need to take into consideration what the great Arab scholars Al-Bukhari and Mussalem had written in both of their 'Saheehs'. They wrote that Waraka Ben Nofal, the Bishop of Mecca, was translating the Book and the Gospel of Mathew's Hebrew in Aramaic to Arabic in the presence of Muhammad." [177] This important fact deserves in depth study and a detailed discussion. My intention is to do that shortly.

I start by reporting how Father Al-Haddad was surprised to find out how ignorant Abed Al-Fattah Tabbarah was of historic events. Tabbarah contradicts what we read in the Hadith and in the Qur'an itself, when he says: "On the other side, it was proved historically that there was no Arabic

---

[173] Mohammed 'Izzat' Darwazat, ... P. 452

[174] Ibid.

[175] Ibid.

[176] Ibid. p. 468

[177] Archimandrite Rev. Al-Haddad, "Al-Qur'an Da'wat Nusrsaniah" AlMaktabat Albulusiah, Beirut, 1986, p. 105.

translation to the Gospel and the Bible exist at the time of the Prophet (Sad)"[178]. Rev. Al-Haddad asks whether Tabbarah feels ashamed from the testimony of the Qur'an when the Prophet challenges the Jews: "SAY: Bring the Torah and recite it if you have been truthful."[179]

Is it possible to the Qur'an to challenge the Jews to bring their Torah and read it in Hebrew before an Arab Audience? There is no doubt that it was translations into Arabic and was read in Arabic before offering the challenge, or else what is the use of having a strong and decisive confrontation! If no Arabic copies translated from Aramaic or Hebrew were found due to the invasions, conquests and conspiracies that Mr. Darwazat mentioned; it does not mean that it never existed during the period of Muhammad.

How do we explain Tabbarah's reference to a few "hundreds of Christians"? Is it possible that the few hundred of the Nazarenes could be able to control the work and the trade of Mecca, and have preachers! Those Nazarenes in Mecca were led by two bishops or monks: they were Waraka Ben Nofal and 'Addas of Ninawa, his assistant.

Most Arab historians wrote about the life of the prophet and his environment, events that testify the presence of the Christians who laid siege to Hijaz from the "Four Corners". They were supported by the Christian State of Al-Kindah in Najd, backed by the presence of the Ethiopians, as paid soldiers. Such events, with time, led to social and religious revolutions in Mecca and Hijaz through the immigration of the Nazarenes of Beni Israel and the continuous infiltration of the Christians. The time came for the appearance of Muhammad himself to become the Imam of the Nazarenes in Mecca, succeeding his relative the Bishop of Mecca, Waraka Ben Nofal. Muhammad was the first Muslim to force the Nazarenes' teaching on the Arabs, under the Qur'anic Call.

Usually, they say the people follow the religion of their kings. If that is true, then why the historians of the Middle East fail to recognize that Mecca was under the mundane ruler: King Abed Al-Massih, as previously mentioned, and a religious leader the Monk of Mecca!

A Note from Ibn Khaldoun on the rulers of Mecca and Al-Hijaz before Quraysh:

Ibn Khaldoun, the father of the Arab sociological and architectural studies, writes the following political indications about the prevalence of

---

[178] Afif Abed Al-Fattah Tabbarah, "Ruh Al-Deen Al-Islami" (The Spirit of Islam), fourth edition, p. 431.

[179] Holy Qur'an, Sura Al-Imran, 3: verse 93.

Christianity over Mecca and Al-Ka'ba, during the realm of the Tribe of Quraysh. Ibn Khaldoun says: "The reign of Al-Ghawth Ben Murra on the House was appointed by the Kings of Kindah. The Ruler of Hijaz for the Tababi'a was Hajar A'kel Al-Marrar." [180]

The Tatabi'as were from Himyar, between the first Ethiopian invasion of Yemen and the second one in 523 AD, they were Christians, resembling their Leaders in Ethiopia. "The Al-Harith Al-Ra'eech, the grandfather King of Al-Tatabi'a, was called "Taba'an" or (Emperor in the language of that time)"[181]. "He was a believer as reported by Al-Suheili" [182]. Other Taba'and were Tabban Asa'ad and Hassaan Tabba', the later was the first to dress Al-Ka'ba and made its door with a key [183]. Hassaan Tabba' married to the daughter of Amru Ben Hajar A'kel Al-Marrar, from the kings of Kindah, in the Eastern part of Yemen, and she gave birth to Al-Harith Ben Amru. "Tabba' Ben Hassaan ruled after him and he who sent his nephew Al-Harith Bin Amru Al-Kindi to the land of Beni Ma'ad Ben 'Adnan in Al-Hijaz as their king." [184]

"Al-Tabbabi'a were in-laws with Beni Kindah, who let them rule Beni Ma'ad of 'Adnan in Hijaz. The first to rule was Hajar A'kel Al-Marrar, Ibn Amru Ben Ma'wiah, the older, then Tabba' Ben Karab who dressed Al-Ka'ba, then followed by his son Amru Ben Hajarand then his son Al-Harith Al-Makksour, he who refused to disbelieve and go along Kabaz, King of Persia. He was killed at Beni Klab, and his riches were stolen. He already had conferred his sons to rule Beni Ma'ad, but most of them were killed. Hajar Bin Harith ruled Beni Asad cruelly, so they killed him. His son Imra'u Al-Kays, dedicated his time to secure revenge, he went to Caesar for help." [185]

Imra'u Al-Kays is the poet who composed the famous first suspended poem in the Arabic literature; he shows in the poem his monotheistic inclination of his Christian belief. It was said that Caesar gave him Palestine to rule, and where he died.

We have seen that kings of Hijaz were Nazarenes assigned by the Christian kings of Kindah. Five years before the Revelation upon Muhammad, the Ka'ba was renewed and pictures of angels, prophets, Christ and His Mother, decorated its internal walls. These real historic demonstrations, that the Islamic resources are witnessed in the Qur'an, indicate the prevalence of the evangelical doctrines in Mecca and Hijaz before Islam.

---

[180] Ibn Khaldoun, "The History", published by Dar Al-Kitab Al-Lubnani, Vol. 2, p. 580.

[181] *Ibid.* p.89

[182] Ibid. p.95

[183] Ibid. p.100

[184] Ibid. p.109

[185] Ibid. p. 576

The Arabs of Mecca accepted Judaism and Christianity as religions for the believers in the Book; and their religious beliefs were reflected on the walls of Al-Ka'ba as religious drawings. Al-Azraqi narrates that when Prophet Muhammad entered Al-Ka'ba sent Al-Fadel Ben Al-Abbas Ben Abed Al-Mutaleb to bring water from Zamzam, and requested to put water on a cloth to wipe out all the pictures on the walls except for the ones he covered under his hands. The picture of Issa Bin Mariam and His Mother were covered under the Prophet's hands and were preserved. The same story was narrated by Al-Azraqi as well as Ibn Al-Arabi, and by Al-Harawi, and Al-Beyhaqi. An event or story shows how much the Prophet Muhammad had respected deeply Isa Ben Mariam and His Mother. Not only by keeping the pictures of Jesus and Mary on the walls of Al-Ka'ba, but in their praise that the Noble Qur'an verses included glorifying Jesus and Mary. One example is "And she who guarded her chastity, so we breathed some of our spirit into her, and set both her and her son up as a sign for [everyone in] the Universe. [186]

Furthermore, I quote Muhammad Shukri al-Alusi [187] who describes: "*The Arabs during the pre-Islamic period used to practice certain things that were included in the Islamic Sharia. They, for example, did not marry both a mother and her daughter. They considered marrying two sisters simultaneously to be a most heinous crime. They also censured anyone who married his stepmother, and called him dhaizan. They made the major [hajj] and the minor [umra] pilgrimage to the Ka'ba, performed the circumambulation around the Ka'ba [tawaf], ran seven times between Mounts Safa and Marwa [sa'y], threw rocks and washed themselves after intercourse. They also gargled, sniffed water up into their noses, clipped their fingernails, plucked their hair from their armpits, shaved their pubic hair and performed the rite of circumcision. Likewise, they cut off the right hand of a thief.*"

A Note from Ibn Khaldoun on How the Environment of Mecca transferred from Jurhum to Quraysh:

Ibn Khaldoun tells us that "the civilization and advancement in Maddar for Al-Kananah, then to Quraysh; Beni Lu'ay Bin Ghalib Bin Fahar Bin Malek Bin Al-Nadhar led the advancement of Quraysh." [188] Their Leader was Kussi' Bin Klab Bin Murra Bin Ka'ab Bin Lu'ay. Kussi' had four sons: Abed Al-Dar, Abed Munaf, Abed Al-'Azzi and Abed Kussi'. A story to relate the transition of the responsibility of Al-Ka'ba from Jurhum to Quraysh

---

[186] Noble Qur'an, Sura Al-Anbiya', verse 91.

[187] Muhammad Shukri al-Alusi, "*Bulugh al-'Irab fi Ahwal Al-'Arab*", vol.2 p. 122

[188] Ibn Khaldoun, "The History", published by Dar Al-Kitab Al-Lubnani, Vol. 2, p. 690.

went like this: "The grandfather of Kussi' was al-Ghawth Bin Murra, and his mother was from Jurhum; she was sterile. She made a vow to God if she gave birth, she will dedicate the child to the service of Al-Ka'ba. She gave birth to Al-Ghawth, his uncles from Jurhum gave way between him and his competitors, and so the dedication for Al-Ka'ba was left for him and for his son. They were called: Sufah" [189]

The second story, according to Ibn Khaldoun, shows the real political reason, Al-Suheili said that the transmitted news he received tell that kings of Kindah appointed Al-Ghawth Bin Murra, a ruler over Mecca. And he is the one who gave inheritance to his grandson Kussi', who took exclusive possession, (against the will of his cousins). "Kussi' felt he had the right to take charge of Al-Ka'ba and rule Mecca and the tribe of Khaza'a and Beni Bakr because he belonged to Quraysh; at that time, Quraysh was the largest and the most influential." When the people of Mecca sought the wisdom of the oldest among the Kananah, he "ruled for Kussi' to lead them. Kussi' took over the House and settled in Mecca, and brought the tribe of Quraysh and subdivided them into four branches. Quraysh ended up into two major groups: Quraysh Al-Bitah (the main stream), and Quraysh Al-Dhawaher (the supporters from the others). From Quraysh Al-Bitah was born Kussi' Bin Klab and the rest of Beni Ka'ab Bin Lu'ay." [190]

It became clear that the penetration of the Nazarenes doctrine among the people of Quraysh started with the transfer of the rule to Quraysh from Jurhum, by the grace of the kings of Kindah, who appointed the Tabbabi'a of Himyar to rule Hijaz. "Those who became Nazarenes from the Arab tribes, people from Quraysh." [191] Now, it makes sense that the surname of Sufah was applied to them. Benu Abed Al-Dar disputed with Beni Abed Manaf in collecting the benefits from the Pilgrimages, resulted in an honorable agreement to divide the prominence and the benefits. The collection of benefits from giving water and dresses to the Pilgrims was assigned to Beni Abed Manaf, and from screening and housing the Pilgrims to Beni Abed Al-Dar. Both teams were happy, and the people were restrained. Such events took place at the time of Abed Al-Muttaleb, the great grandfather of the Arab Prophet Muhammad, who was in charge of the House of Al-Ka'ba.

---

[189] Ibid.

[190] Ibid.

[191] Al-Ya'koubi, "History Book", Vol. 1, p. 298.

The "House" of the Prophet was from the Nazarenes:

Benu Abed Manaf arranged for Hisham, the son of Abed Al-Muttaleb the First, to rule Mecca, according to Ibn Khaldoun, his brother Abed Al-Shaam, (the grandfather of Beni Umayyad), was involved in trade on the route to Damascus. Hisham did a great job in taking care of welcoming and feeding the Pilgrims. It is said that he fed them with "the Thareed (porridge) of Quraysh". Ibn Khaldoun tried to explain how the Thareed of porridge is cooked from water and flour because that food was not local to the people of Mecca. This indicates that the social life in Mecca had been changed with the immigration of the Nazarenes of Beni Israel, and the Arab Nazarenes were affected with them and their traditions and eating the porridge is one example. After Hisham, his son Al-Muttaleb took over Mecca.[192]

When Hisham was in Yathreb, he got married from Beni 'Addi, from a woman who was married to Uhayhah Bin Al-Hallaj, leader of Al-'Awss at his time; and gave birth for Umru Bin Uhayhah. (In another story, it is stated that the woman was Salma the daughter of Umru Bin Labeed Al-Khazraji.) That women had the right of the marriage knot accepted Hisham Abed Al-Muttaleb in marriage and gave birth to boy called Shibah. Shibah was left with his mother until he grew up to a young adult. Hisham passed away in a trip he made to Gaza of Palestine (used to be referred to as part of the Land of Al-Shaam, "Syria"). Al-Muttaleb succeeded his father Hisham.

Muttaleb left to Yathreb looking for his brother Shibah. He took care of his brother and let him ride Muttaleb's camel into Mecca. Quraysh said that the young man was a servant that Al-Muttaleb bought, and his name was changed from Shibah to Abed Al-Muttaleb, that was the name of his grandfather too. In a trip to Yemen, Al-Muttaleb died. So Abed Al-Muttaleb Bin Hisham took charge of Beni Hashim; he was Abed Al-Muttaleb, the Second, Grandfather of the Prophet Muhammad. Abed Al-Muttaleb did a great job in welcoming, feeding and housing the Pilgrims; he had direct contact with the Kings of Yemen of Himyar, and welcomed their delegations, and did the same with the Ethiopians; such contacts hinted towards his real religious affiliation. [193]

When Abed Al-Muttaleb, the Second, the grandfather of Muhammad, decided to dig the well of Zamzam, Quraysh objected. He took an oath upon himself that "one of his sons will be sacrificed for God at Al-Ka'ba," if he would have ten boys, and when they grew, he must fulfill the dream. He had ten sons, and he struck randomly at the ten sons to pick the victim, and it fell on Abed Al-Allah, the father of Muhammad. But Abed Al-Muttaleb

---

[192] Ibn Khaldoun, "The History ..." Vol. 2 from pages 690 and on
[193] Ibid.

ransomed his son with one hundred camels and slew them in surrender to God that was one of the charisms that the people had it for him." [194]

Then Abed Al-Muttaleb II, the grandfather of Muhammad, arranged for his son Muhammad to marry Amenah Bint (daughter of) Wahab, from Beni Zahrah in Yathreb. Abed Al-Allah slept with her and she got pregnant with Muhammad. When Abed Al-Allah returned from a trip to Syria (Al-Shaam), he passed by Yathreb to meet his wife. In Yathreb, Abed Al-Allah got sick and died while Amenah was pregnant with Muhammad.

Abed Al-Muttaleb II, the grandfather of Muhammad "lived for one hundred and forty years, some said one hundred and ten, while others said less than that." He was the one who dug the well of Zamzam and surrounded it with a basin – reservoir - for people to drink from. He also painted the ornament of Al-Ka'ba with gold, and put an iron gate at its entrance. Ibn Khaldoun ends up his narration by saying: "then Abed Al-Muttaleb spent his time taking care of his role as the leader of Quraysh, and the universe listens to the domination of the Arabs, and the world gives rise to a decisive prophecy." [195]

Ibn Khaldoun narration testifies that the leadership of Mecca and Al-Ka'ba was in the hands of the grandfather of Muhammad of Quraysh before Islam. The same grandfather is the one who took Muhammad under his protection after the death of his father Abed Al-Allah. This historic event differs from the "myth" that it is repeated by ignorant people that Muhammad was an orphan, a poor and worked as a shepherd for a living. The relationship and the in-laws between Abed Al-Muttaleb and then his son Abed Al-Allah in Yathreb is a living proof of the success of the immigration of the Nazarenes to Yathreb, and the help Muhammad received during his struggle for leadership in Mecca.

Muhammad in Mecca before the Revelation:

From reading the different Sira (Life) of the Prophet, we conclude that Muhammad was "Yatahannaf" (the Nazarene way in fasting and praying like a Hanafi) similar to his Grandfather Abed Al-Muttaleb, with Waraka Bin Nofal, the Bishop of Mecca. The first to go to Al-Harra' to pray and fast, was Abed-Al-Muttaleb, he used to feed the poor during the month of fasting "Ramadan". (Ramadan was the month for the Nazarenes to fast through)

---

[194] Ibid.

[195] Ibid.

and then followed by those who were praying such as Waraka Bin Nofal and Abi Umayyah Bin Al-Maghirrah [196].

The connection of the name of Waraka Bin Nofal with "Al-Tahannuf" is a major point to prove that he was from the Nazarenes. Let me summarize the major testimony for the Nazarenes influence in Mecca, starting with Abed Al-Muttaleb II, the grandfather of Muhammad, who was a Hanafi (a Nazarene) from Quraysh in close association with the Bishop of Mecca, Waraka Bin Nofal. The conclusion that the grandfather of Muhammad was the first to become a Nazarene is sound and correct. It was the tradition of the Nazarene to spend one month of the year in prayer at Harra'.

Another important fact to remember, before the Qur'an, that the month of Ramadan was a month for fasting for the Nazarenes in the Jahiliyah. Abed Al-Muttaleb and his grandson, [197] Muhammad, practiced such a tradition, proved that the Nazarenes were influential in Mecca.

Again, history witnesses that the Hanafiah Movement started in Mecca and Hijaz before the coming of Islam, a movement that was somehow mysterious to a good number of historians and researchers to relate it to the Hanifah Nazarenes. It was the first movement that the Nazarenes of Beni Israel brought it in with their immigration. The second movement is seen in the Muslim Nazarenes before the Qur'an: "... He has named you Muslims both previously and right now ... [in this Qur'an]" [198], (And the third movement was in the Qur'anic Call: "...I have been ordered to be one of the Muslims..."[199] That is, the Nazarenes, the people of the Islam Al-Hanif.

We would like to come to an end of the talk about Mecca, by quoting our Arab scholar Mr. Mohammed 'Izzat Darwazat. He states, "...The environment of Al-Hijaz, specially Mecca and Al-Medina, was a commercial environment, in direct contact with the neighboring countries that enjoyed much of their cultures and civilization. In the Hijaz environment, there were learned Jewish and Nazarene communities. Communities that believed in the written Book, and brought with them the knowledge into Hijaz from the neighboring civilized countries. Those communities had religious and non-religious books under their disposal, and they were reading and writing them. It is irrational for the Arabs who lived in that environment to remain stupid and ignorant, not to adopt the most necessary tools for their economic

---

[196] Ibid

[197] The Sira Al-Halabiah, vol. I, p. 259, and the Sira Al-Macciah, written on the margin of Al-Halabiah, published by the Istekamah press in Cairo, 1962, (pp. 177-178) based on what Ibn Al-Atheer wrote in his History book.

[198] Noble Qur'an, Sura Al-Hajj- Pilgrimage 22, verse 78.

[199] Noble Qur'an, Sura Al-Naml –The Ants 27, verse 91.

survival, their businesses and trades and one of the greatest resources for development and for building a civilization." [200]

The Qur'an testifies about the presence of the Nazarenes in Mecca and Al-Medina

Some facts deserve our attention: the Qur'an never knows the name "Christians", and never references it, especially this is the only name "Christians" use wherever they are. The Qur'an mentions only the name "Al-Nassara" (the Nazarenes), the name that describes a special sect of believers in Jesus and the Law of Moses among a group of Beni Israel.

The Holy Qur'an can be looked at as a continuous dialogue with the people of the Book from Jews and Nazarenes. The positions of testimony by the Nazarenes and their support to the Qur'anic call, and their affiliations to that mission, does not mean in the Qur'an, except the Nazarenes of Beni Israel – due to the Qur'an's position, similar to their position, from the trinity and the divinity of Christ. The Arab Prophet direction is to follow the believers state of affairs "Those are the ones to whom We have given the Book, along with Discretion and Prophet hood ... Such are the ones whom God has guided, so copy their guidance..."[201]. The people of "the Book, with Discretion, the Bible and the Gospel" are the Nazarenes and not the Jews.

Who are the Nazarenes in the Noble Qur'an?

They are the ones noted in "Do they not have a sign since the scholars Children of Israel knew about it?" [202] In view of the fact that the Jews with the associators are "the first infidel in Him" and they are the "evil among creation", then those scholars Children of Israel are the Nazarenes of Beni Israel. Their testimony to the Qur'anic call was enough an excuse to the Prophet Muhammad in) "Those who disbelieve say: "You are no emissary." SAY: "God suffices as a Witness between me and you (all), as well as anyone who has knowledge about the Book."[203] Again, in "God testifies there is no deity except Himself and so do the angels and persons possessing knowledge... Religion with God means [Islam] or commitment to [live in]

---

[200] Mohammad 'Izat Darwazat, "Al-Qur'an Al-Majeed" (The Glorious Qur'an), p. 308.

[201] Noble Qur'an, Sura Al-Ena'am, 6: verses 89-90.

[202] Ibid. Sura Al-Shuaara' (the Poets), 26: verse 197

[203] Ibid. Sura Al-Raad, 13: verse 43

peace." [204] Those persons possessing knowledge are not Jews, and they are not Christians, as testified by the Qur'anic indications; they are the Nazarenes of Beni Israel.

This is a clear declaration that "Out of Moses' folk [there grew] a nation who guided by means of the Truth and dealt justly by means of it."[205] This nation of believers of Moses' folks is the sect of Beni Israel who believed in Christ. The Qur'an came in support of its monotheistic call in Mecca, in Hijaz and in all the Arabian Peninsula. "A faction from the Children of Israel believed [in Christ], while another faction disbelieved [the Jews]. We assisted the ones who believed against their enemy, till they held the upper hand.[206] The Holy Qur'an asserts the presence of the Nazarenes of Beni Israel in Mecca. The Nazarenes being there in Mecca and Hijaz, constituted an established reality, clearly and sharply, stated in the versions of the Holy Qur'an.

The Sira Al-Nabawiyat testifies the immigration of the Nazarenes to Hijaz.

(The story of Salman Al-Farisi)

The story of Salman Al-Farisi is told in the Hashimiah, the Halabiah and the Mecciah prophecy Siras. Muslim commentators believed that the story is being narrated to proof that the Nazarenes' monks were predicting the coming of Muhammad, the Arab Prophet. This objective is very doubtful because the Nazarene monks were not prophets. But the true scholars take the truth behind the story as a proof for the withdrawal of the Nazarenes of Beni Israel from Al-Shaam (Syria), Iraq, and Anadol to Al-Hijaz.

Ibn Hashim has written the oldest biography for the Prophet, where the story of Salman Al-Farisi (Salman the Persian) was a Magus (Majussi), from a noble family. [207] He passed by a Nazarene Church and acquainted himself with their Nazarene teachings, and learned from the Persian monks that their religion was originated in Syria [208]. Salman agreed with the monks to take off to Syria. He says: "When I arrived there, I asked: Who is the best informed about this religion? They said the monk who is in the Church. I approached

---

[204] Ibid. Al-Imran, 3: verses 18-19

[205] Ibid. Al-'Araf (the Heights), 7: verse 159

[206] Ibid. Al-Saff (Battle Array), verse 14

[207] Mustapha Al-Sakka, *"Al-Sira Al-Nabawiah (the Life History of the Prophecy)* of Ibn Hisham, Cairo, 1936.

[208] Ibid. 1:228.

the monk and told him: I have an interest in this religion, and I would like to be with you and serve you in your Church, so that I can learn from you, and pray with you. He said: Come in and I entered with him." [209]

That monk, who is referred to in the Nazarene language, as a priest, was bad and passed away, and was succeeded by another monk who was virtuous. "I lived with him for a long time. Then before he was about to meet with his creator, I told him: Oh (Fulan) I loved you very much more than anything I loved before, and you are ready to accept God's will, whom do you recommend me to? And whatever you order? He said, "Oh son, I swear by God, I do not know, today, anyone who follows our conditions." (My) people passed away; they were reduced and left what they were expected to do, except a man in Al-Moussel, he is (Mr. X Fulan), he was on the same state of affairs of mine, follow him." [210]

The Sira testifies that the Nazarenes in Syria disappeared and the others or the Christians. "They were reduced and left more than what they had." No one remains with the same belief that the Nazarene monk believed in. So he sent his pupil Salman to the Nazarene monk in Al-Moussel. But all historic references testify that the people of Syria in totality, in the seventh century AD, were Christians. They were divided into four major groups: The Orthodox, the Melkites, the Jacobite and the followers of Nestorius. The Orthodox and Melkite Christians prevailed in Damascus. Even with the Islamic invasion to Syria, Christianity was still prevailing. How come the Sira considers that the monk was the last of those who followed "our state of affairs?" The testimony of the Sira shows that the monk was a Nazarene and not a Christian, because the Christian monks stay up-to-date on the head of their parishes in Damascus, as well as it shows that by the death of the monk from Damascus, the Nazarenes in Syria were nearly vanished.

Salman arrived to Al-Moussel. He found the Nazarene monk to whom he was sent. "I lived with him, and found him to be one of the best to follow his friend's state of affairs; but it did not take long before he died. And when he was on the bed ready to pass away, I told him: Oh (Fulan), Mr. X recommended you to me, and ordered me to follow you, and now you answer the will of God as you are going through: To whom do you recommend me? And whatever do you order me? He said: Oh son, I swear by God I do not know anyone who follows our state of affairs and what we believe in, except a man in Nassibeen, he is (Mr. X Fulan), follow him." [211]

We know that Al-Moussel and all of Iraq believed in Christianity. The group that prevailed there, were the Christians who followed the teaching

---

[209] Ibid. 1:229.

[210] Ibid. 1:230.

[211] Ibid. 1:231.

of Nestorius. They were (and still are) there before and after the invasion of Islam. "The presence of no one to follow our beliefs" indicates that monk was a 'Nazarene'; and that the Nazarenes withdrew from Iraq too, and disappeared.

Nassabeen is a city, in the Syrian Island, extends between the Euphrates and the Khabour. Salman also says: "when the monk passed away, I went to the one in Nassabeen. I told him my story, and what my friend ordered me. He said: "stay with me; and I did. I found him following the same track of his friend, and so I lived with of the best of men." By God, it did not take long before he drew his last breath, at that moment, I told him that (Fulan) recommended me to (Fulan), and then (Fulan) asked me to come to you: whom you recommend me to? And with whatever you order me to do? He said: Oh son, By God, I do not know anyone still living and keeping up with our state of affairs to send you to, except a man in 'Amouriah in the land of the Romans. If you want to go to him, you can do so because he is one of us." [212]

Likewise, The Syrian Island was on the Christian faith before the coming of Salman and his monk, and after. Confining Christianity "on our state of affairs" indicates that the monk was of the Nazarenes, Salman witnesses its withdrawal.

Salman continues with his story: "I went after the one in 'Amouriah, and told him my story. He said "stay with me, and I stayed with the best man of all people; he believes in the guidance and course of his friends." ... Then, his time came. And before he expired, I asked him to recommend me to someone, and whatever he orders? He said, "Oh son, by God, no one remains, today, to follow our state of affairs among men to order you to go and seek. But, it is the time now to go under the protection of a Prophet. He is coming with the religion of Abraham, peace be on him, emerging from the land of the Arabs, and immigrating to the independent land between Harratayn (two areas —expected to be Persia and the Roman Empire) where palm trees are plentiful. He carries well-known signs: he eats the donation (Al-Hidiah), but he does not eat the charity (Al-Sadakah); between his shoulders the Prophethood Seal. If you can go there, follow him and do not hesitate."[213]

This is a true certification that the Nazarenes had withdrawn to Hijaz, (land of the Arabs). Al-Shaam, Syria, Moussel, Syrian Island, Iraq and Anadol followed the course of Christianity, considering the spread of its four major known groups, before Salman and after Salman. The last Nazarene monk telling Salman: "By God no one remains, today, to follow our state of affairs among men" indicates that the Nazarenes had reduced from the lands where

---

[212] Ibid. 1:231.

[213] *Ibid.* 1:231-232.

Christianity prevailed. The last Nazarene monk directed Salman Al-Farisi to go to Hijaz where "the time to have a prophet coming with the religion of Abraham". This direction testifies that the Nazarenes are gathered in Hijaz to be led by an Arab Prophet, or else why should the Nazarene monk ordered Salman to go to him?

Al-Sira Al-Halabiah states "Salman Al-Farissi is a scholar, honest, ascetic and austere pontiff of 'Isa Nazarenes religion." [214] After Salman tracing the withdrawal of the Nazarenes from the land of Al-Shaam to Hijaz, he himself arrived to Medina to become the Nazarenes' Bishop there. He met with the Prophet, and joined his Call. It is related that Salman, in Al-Medina, suggested the erection of the ditch surrounding Al-Medina from the south, to protect the city from the invasion of the associators of Mecca.

The Sira Al-Nabawiyat testifies the Story of the Monk Gregarious Buheira.

Another story confirms the presence of the Nazarenes in Hijaz is the story of the Al-Raheb (Monk) Gregarious Buheira, of Bousra, Houran, in Syria. Monk Buheira was known as 'Isa's Custodian of His religion or (the Pope of the Nazarenes) to whom Bishop Waraka Bin Nofal reported The story of the Monk Buheira and the relationship of Muhammad with that monk are related in the Sira too. Houran was similar to all other cities of Al-Shaam, Syria, believed in Christianity. Bousra was the Bishopric center of Houran. In retrospection, the following facts should be taken in consideration:

Muhammad traveled while he was 9 years young. He, then, traveled several times as a merchant in the summer trips to the lands of Al-Shaam. He used to meet with the Nazarene Monk only, and not any other Christian clergymen.

Muhammad married Warakat Bin Nofal's niece Khadija fifteen years before his inspiration with the revelation. He kept in continuous relationship with the monk Warakat Bin Nofal, the monk of the Nazarenes in Mecca. Muhammad's meetings with Al-Raheb (Monk) Buheira revealed that the Monk was a Nazarene, living along the control road of the caravans. This is also an indication for Muhammad's inclination toward the Nazarenes under the influence of Waraka Bin Nofal in Mecca, as I am going about to show.

When Muhammad took up the Call, and went through spiritual struggle, his wife Lady Khadija sought comfort in Waraka Bin Nofal in Mecca, and did the same with monk Buheira in Bousra to tell about what happened to Muhammad in Ghar Harra'. She never met any other Christian scholar. This

---

[214] Al-Sira Al-Halabiah, 1: 215.

is another proof to indicate that the leadership of the Nazarenes had settled in Mecca, and Monk Buheira was the only Nazarene monk to live outside the borders of Hijaz.

The story of Buheira is "a true story as related in the Sira of the Prophethood, and abstracted from the talk of Abi Moussa Al-Asha'ri by Al-Tarmathi (4:296). He said: (this talk is agreeable), I said: and its resource is true and correct, as reported by Al-Jazari." [215]

The Monk Waraka Bin Nofal is the "Head of the Nazarenes" in Mecca.

By the acceptance of Abed Al-Muttaleb II, the grandfather of the Prophet Muhammad, the Hanafi Movement, we are sure that the Nazarenes had invaded the house. The House "of the leadership in Quraysh", quoting Ibn Khaldoun; and that the house in which Muhammad was born in, was a Nazarene house, a leading house both in politics and in religion.

By going over the story of Waraka Bin Nofal, the story of his niece or some historians referred to her as cousin Khadija, we need to remember that Khadija Bint Khuwayled Bin Asad is the cousin or niece of Waraka Bin Nofal Bin Asad. She was the "Lady of the ladies of Quraysh", and "a leading merchant with honor and wealth", and "A Qurayshi related, most famous among the women of Quraysh and their richest in wealth", "Her trade is equivalent to all of Quraysh trade". Borrowing the terms used in Al-Sira for Ibn Hisham as well as in Sira Al-Halabiah and Sira Al-Macciah. Also, Abed Al-Razzak Nofal states "...then Muhammad left to trade with Khadija's merchandise whose value was equal to the values of all Quraysh's trading power combined." [216]

The Lady Khadija, the cousin or the niece of the monk Waraka Bin Nofal used to consult her uncle or her cousin for her marriage from Muhammad. He agreed and encouraged her by saying: "He will be the Prophet of this Umma (Nation)." (As narrated in the Sira Al-Hashimiah)

Was Waraka Bin Nofal a prophet to predict the prophecy of Muhammad? A prophecy happened 15 years before it took place? Was Waraka's prediction a sign to prepare Muhammad for the task of the Call? We know that Khadija is related to Waraka Bin Nofal, the Bishop of Mecca, before her accepting the marriage from Muhammad. That marriage was blessed by her uncle, and after the consultation with the Nazarenes religious leaders only, Al-Raheb Buheira,

---

[215] Muhammad Al-Ghazali, *"Fiqeh Al-Sira"* as stated in the margin of page 68.
[216] Abed Al-Razzak Nofal, *"Muhammad - Messenger and Prophet"* p. 97.

Waraka and 'Addas, Khadija showed that she belonged to the Nazarenes religion of her uncle, the Bishop of Mecca.

With Waraka, Abed Al-Muttaleb, the grandfather of Muhammad, and the Lady Khadija, the civil, and the religious, and the commercial leadership in Mecca was in the hand of the Nazarenes. Muhammad, close to Khadija and under the direction of Waraka, was preparing himself to inherit the total leadership of Mecca.

Our conclusion is based on the consideration of all the testimonies, as presented in the Islamic resources, from the immigration of the Nazarenes of Beni Israel to Mecca and Hijaz to their success as true and complete.

We also would like to affirm the words of Al-Ya'koubi that "...those who become Nazarenes among the Arabs a tribe from Quraysh." [217] This testimony indicates that the Nazarenes invaded and converted the tribe of Quraysh, the leading tribe in Mecca and Hijaz.

The Sira Al-Hashimiah states the full name of Waraka Bin Nofal Bin Asad Bin Abed Al-'Azza "he was a Nazarenes, followed the Books and taught whoever needed to be taught from the people." [218] He was a Nazarene Scholar, and was a monk as confirms the Hadith of the Prophet "I have seen the monk in Heaven".

The Sira Al-Halabiah states "that he followed the religion of Moses, and then he followed the religion of 'Isa, peace be with their souls. In another word, Waraka was a Jew, and then he became a Nazarene." [219]

Archimandrite Yusuf Durrah Al-Haddad explains, "No Jewish Scholar will shift to become a Nazarene Scholar, and lead the Nazarenes as such. A misunderstanding of the Nazarene of Beni Israel took place, and led to a misleading interpretation of Waraka's Nazarene based on Moses' Law. And the Sira also states that Waraka was a monk. A monk, in their language, and according the Law of Moses is set to signify "head of the Nazarenes", is not possible. It is not by the Law of Moses that a Nazarene becomes a monk, 'head of the Nazarenes', but according to the Gospel. This similarity in expression indicates that Waraka was a Nazarene monk in Mecca. The Monk in the Aramaic and Syriac languages of the Nazarenes is equivalent to a Bishop in the Roman and Greek languages; so Waraka was the head of the Nazarenes, he was their Bishop in Mecca." [220]

The contemporary Arab Scholar Archimandrite Al-Haddad, of the Greek Catholic Melkite Church in Damascus, made it clear that history

---

[217] The "History of Al-Ya'coubi" 1:298.

[218] Sira Al-Hashimiah, 1:202.

[219] Sira Al-Halabiah, 1:263.

[220] Archimandrite Al-Haddad "The Qur'an - a "Nazarene's Call", Beirut, 1986, pp. 97-8

did not preserve for us much of the truth about the real conditions of "Al-Jahiliyah Al-Arabiah". Most of these conditions went away with the attacks, revolutions, invasions, occupations and conquers that took place as a result of the spread of Islam. The only knowledge we have for the prevalence of the evangelical call in Mecca and Hijaz is by researching the history books, the "Jahiliyah" poems and the Holy Qur'an. The gloomy picture that the Islamic resources try to present to the era before Islam that of associators was ruling in Mecca and Hijaz, the worship of idols only is biased and incorrect. [221]

Father Al-Haddad copies the testimony of Dr. Jawad Ali that "the monotheism of the people of Mecca was very close to the monotheism in Islam... and that the Jahiliyah poems neglects the mentioning of idols." [222]

Father Al-Haddad commends that monotheism was spread indeed through the teaching of the Book and the Gospel, through Judaism and Christianity. Mainly through the Nazarenes who transferred them from pageantry to monotheism; as it appears in the Qur'an who calls "monotheism" an association with God, this is done because they used to take the angels as their guardians (protectors or mediators), or "in order to bring them nearer to God... But those who take for protectors other than Allah (say): "We only serve them in order that they may bring us nearer to Allah." Truly Allah will judge between them in that wherein they differ. But Allah guides not such as are false and ungrateful". [223]

The monotheistic inclination appears in the poems too. There is a Hadith that says, "The most truthful word said by a poet was that of Labeed from (the Jahiliyah period) "Everything is null and void except God". Where can we find better witnesses than Al-Hadith about Labeed and the Qur'an as proofs that the people of Mecca were not all idol worshippers? They were Nazarenes.

Furthermore, Father Al-Haddad insists that the Qur'anic environment was related to the Book. The Qur'an refers to the people of the Book and to their presence in Mecca. The Qur'an distinguishes them from the other Arabs because they believe in God, in a monotheistic Book. The Qur'an has a verse that says that it is "... not invented by anyone except God; but exists as a confirmation from the Lord of the Universe for what He already has and is an analysis of the Book which contains no doubt." [224]

Envision this historic fact, a Nazarene Bishop and his followers in Mecca, including the political leader Abed Al-Muttaleb, the grandfather of Muhammad. Is such prediction not enough to confirm that the immigration

---

[221] Ibid

[222] Jawad Ali, "Arabs before Islam" 5:415.

[223] Noble Qur'an, Sura Al-Zumar (Throngs), 39: verse 3.

[224] Ibid. Sura Yunis, 10: verse 37.

of the Nazarenes to Mecca, led to their success in converting many the people from Quraysh to the Nazarene faith!

Another essential fact to consider Mathew's Gospel that Waraka was translating into Arabic. "At the start of the revelation, Khadija took Muhammad to Waraka Bin Nofal.

Waraka Bin Nofal was a Nazarene bishop of Mecca prior to Islam as recorded in Halabieh, Maccea and Hashimieh Siras. As a Bishop of Mecca, he was reporting to his Patriarch or (Pope of the Nazarene sect, located in Busra Ash-Shaam) Raheb Gregarious Buheira. Waraka was writing the Hebrew Book written in Aramaic, he was writing from the Gospel as much as he can write." [225] Accordingly, Waraka was copying the Gospel that was written in a Hebrew lettering in Aramaic, and translating it into Arabic. It is known facts that none of the Gospels were recorded in Hebrew expect the one according to Matthew intended to his people, the Jews, and was adopted by the Nazarenes only; while Christians have adopted the four Holy Gospels of Mark, Luke, John and Mathew that were written in the Greek language.

As we know from the testimonies of clergymen and scholars, mainly the authentication by the Scholar Jerome who translated that Gospel into Greek and Latin. The Gospel according to Matthew that was the only Hebrew Gospel written in the Aramaic-Assyrian language, but with the Hebrew lettering that was sacred to them. That was the only Gospel, the Nazarenes admitted to accept. The original writings of the Gospels were in Greek.

Consequently, we see the collaboration of the Muslim and the Christian testimonies on this decisive conclusion: that Waraka Bin Nofal, 'head of the Nazarenes' in Mecca was writing and translating the Nazarene Gospel for his followers. The Nazarenes with their Bishop and their Gospel were, in effect, present in Mecca. And Muhammad, for a period of fifteen years, between his marriage from Khadija and the start of the Call, was close to Waraka watching him writing the Gospel and translating it into Arabic.

We learn the truth from the discourse of 'Aeesha, when she ended up her declaration by saying "and it did not take long before Waraka passed away, and the revelation cooled off." Is it so? The inspiration cooled down by the death of Waraka.

Since Muhammad's marriage until his inspiration, and its cooling down, was connected with a Nazarene Monk, Waraka Bin Nofal taken from Sira (Life of Muhammad), according to the narration of 'Aeesha. The fading away of the revelation was an indication that the hand of Waraka was involved. Knowing the story of Waraka Bin Nofal, and the unfolding of the revelation, both events witness the presence of the Nazarenes in Mecca led by 'a head

---

[225] ['Aeesha reported that, in both Saheeh Al-Bukhari (1:18-19) and Saheeh Mussalem (1:97-98)].

of Nazarenes'. And from the language of the Nazarenes' Gospel and its particles, and the way Waraka has been described in the Sira. We confirm that those who were there, at that time, were the Nazarenes of Beni Israel and those Arabs followed their steps and became Nazarenes.

To disclose the mystery in the use of the name "Nazarenes" in the Qur'an, the Qur'an never mentions the name of "the Christians". Therefore, the Qur'anic Call was based on the support of the "Nazarenes" of Beni Israel only.

To proof the Muslim resources, the reader should review: the Qur'an, the Sira and the Hadith that testify the immigration of the Nazarenes to Hijaz, and their settlement in Mecca. Such resources show how convert a group of the Arabs from the tribe of Quraysh became Nazarenes; they made Muhammad himself a Nazarene when he got married to Khadija - the cousin or niece of Waraka Ben Nofal, 'the head of the Nazarenes' in Mecca, a Nazarene. How could it be that the Bishop of Mecca and, his cousin or niece, the richest Lady among the merchants of Quraysh, accepted to go through a marriage if Muhammad was not one of them?

The final decisive word is for the Holy Qur'an to affirm the truth of the Nazarenes, a faction of the children of Israel, who believe in 'Isa Bin Mariam. It is spelled out in, "You who believe, act as God's supporters just as" 'Isa Bin Mariam told the disciples: "Who will be my supporters [along the way] towards God?" The disciples said: "We are God's supporters." A faction from Beni (the Children of) Israel believed, while another faction disbelieved. We assisted the ones who believed against their enemy, till they held the upper hand." [226]

---

[226] Noble Qur'an, Sura Al-Suff (Battle Array), 61: verse 14.

CHAPTER FIVE

The Religious and Social Traditions of the Nazarenes/Islam

The Nazarenes were monotheists, they believed in the Books and in Prophets in praying, in fasting, in almsgiving, in pilgrimage to the House of God. They believed in Jesus as a Prophet and kept their commitment to Moses' Law and compared to Christianity. By explaining the traditions of the Hebrew-Christians as it is adopted in the Muslim religion in the followings:

A- The prayers:

As the Jews, the Nazarenes started their day in praying the Morning Prayer, and they end the day in praying the Evening Prayer. The Essenes and their priests in Qumran had added the "Middle prayer" at noon. They "performed the prayers at dawn, when the sun is in the middle of the day, and when the sun sets at its usual location." [227] When the Essenes became Nazarenes, they brought the middle of the day prayer with them. Including the Day prayers, the followers of Christ used to wake up at night to pray and chant the verses of the Book.

The Nazarenes followed the same steps as reported in the early years of the third century AD. [228] The Nazarenes used to pray "the Lord's Prayer", three times a day, facing Jerusalem, contrary to the Christians who pray facing the East. The Nazarenes used their national language, the Aramaic-Syriac, and not the Greek language as the Christians. [229] The pious Jews used to pray three times a day, while Christian priests used to pray seven times.

---

[227] "Manual of Discipline" (15:1).

[228] Hippolytus, "Apostolic Traditions" p.35

[229] Ireneaus, "Against Heresies"

B- The Eucharist:

When the Temple in Jerusalem was destroyed in 70 AD, the Jews stopped from giving blood offering. The Essenes sect were saying that their preference was to give the offering of thankfulness instead of the blood offering, and when they became part of the Nazarenes, they accept their offering that was made of bread and water. While Christians believe that through Jesus Christ, God changes the offering of livestock, to the offering of Bread and Wine.

The followers of Christ used to present the offering in an evening celebration they called "the Supper of Love", in imitation of their Master; they called it the Eucharist, from the Greek word "eucharestia" (thankfulness), or the "Lord's Supper." [230] Christians stopped the supper celebration for the abuse that accompanied it and Paul rejected completely. [231] But that custom remained effective among the Nazarenes and was referred to as "the table of the Lord".

With their deflection, they gave it a generic term "the Table" only. After the offering, the supper of the Nazarenes was limited to milk, honey, and fruit; as recorded in a number of Nazarenes' references, such as in Solomon "Song of songs" [232]

The Nazarenes sees in 'Issa Bin Mariam, a true offering of the Table, that they ask God to descend it from heaven upon them, and that such offering is repeated in the cerebration of the Nazarenes each Sunday.

The Story of the Table in Islam:

In the year 759 Hijriah the knowledgeable Al-Imam Al-Hafez 'Imad-el-Deen Abi Al-Fidah Isma'eel Ben Katheer Al-Kurayshi al-Dimashki', explains the story of the Table (Sura 5) as related in the Qur'an in his interpretation of the "Noble Qur'an".[233] He wrote the followings: "This is the story of the table that the chapter took its name, the Table. The table [banquet] is given from Allah to His Servant and His Messenger Isa (Jesus) in response to his call to send it down. Sending it down is clearly expressed in the revealed graceful

---

[230] St. Paul's First Epistle to the Corinthians, 11:20.

[231] Ibid. 11:17-22.

[232] [Thy lips, O [my] spouse, drop [as] the honeycomb: honey and milk [are] under thy tongue; and the smell of thy garments [is] like the smell of Lebanon (4:11)]. Also mentioned in the epistle of Barnabas 6:8:17

[233] Al-Imam Al-Hafez 'Imad-el-Deen Abi Al-Fidah Isma'eel Ben Katheer Al-Kurayshi al-Dimashk, "Tafseer Al-Qur'an Al-'Azeem" Volume Two, pages 679-686,Dar Al-Andalus, Beirut, 1966.

verses, an evident plea. Some knowledgeable authorities mentioned that this story is not mentioned in the Gospel, and al-Nassarah (Nazarenes) does not know about, only the Muslims know about it …. Copying Ibn Abbas talking about (Jesus) Isa, that Isa spoke to the Israelis saying: Can you fast for Allah thirty days, and then you ask him for what you want and he gives it to you; the worker gets a fee for his work. They did that and said: Oh teacher of charity, you told us that the worker gets a fee from whom he works and you ordered us to fast for thirty days, and we did. We never worked for any one thirty days without giving us food to eat all what we can. Is it possible for Allah to send down on us a banquet from heaven? And so the verses 112-115 of surat al-Ma'idah (The Table) were revealed."

Ben Katheer continues with his explanation and said: "The angels came flying carrying the banquet from heaven having seven fishes and seven loaves of bread and settled it in front of them, all the peoples ate. …. Ammar Ben Yaser quoted the Prophet saying: The banquet came down from heaven with bread and meat on it, and were ordered not to betray and not to hide and not to save food for the next day, and said: People, who betrayed, concealed and saved, Allah transformed them into apes and pigs."…

Again, Ben Katheer quotes Suleiman Al-Khair and hereby, I summarize what he says that when the disciples of Isa, son of Mary, asked him about the table (banquet), he disliked the question very much and said: Be contented with what Allah gave you on earth and do not ask Allah to send the banquet from heaven; because if it came down it would be a revealed sign from Allah. Remember how Thamud was destroyed when the people asked their prophet for a sign they were afflicted with it and ruined by. But they insisted that he should come with it; and that is why the Qur'anic verse says (*We only wish to eat of it and satisfy our hearts*); and when Isa (Jesus) saw that they insisted that he should pray to Allah to send it down. Jesus stood up and took off his coat, and dressed with a black toupee, and a jubbah from hair, and a cloak from hair, and performed the ritual ablution and entered his oratory and prayed; after completing his prayers, he stood up facing kiblah, put his heel bone to stick together, and extended the fingers and put his right hand over his left above his breast, closed his eyes and bow his head with piety, and start weeping until his tears dropped on his cheeks and poured from the edges of his beard to reach the ground under him that got wet from his devoutness; and then called (*O Allah our Lord, send a table from heaven to us*); and Allah sent upon them a red dining table between two clouds, one from above and one from below, they were watching it falling down from heaven while Jesus was weeping from the conditions that Allah attached with, including thread to torment the one who disbelieve after sending it *Allah will punish him with penalty such as I have not inflicted on anyone among all the peoples*, Isa was calling upon Allah saying : Oh Allah make the banquet a blessing for them and do not make it a torture, My Lord how many miracles did you send me when I asked you for, My Lord let me be thankful, My Lord I pray for you not to send it as a punishment while you are furious, but My Lord makes it safe and healthy, and not an ordeal and a drawback. Jesus kept invoking Allah until the banquet settled before him; the disciples and friends around him smelling the aroma which they never smell such a fragrance before. Jesus and the disciples prostrating themselves for Allah, thanking Allah for giving them what they did not expect, showing them a great sign, a lesson and a wonder. The Jews came to watch and saw an amazing event grievance and sadness upon them, and left angrily. Jesus and the disciples sat around the banquet but it was covered with a veil. Jesus said: "who is willing to uncover the veil over the banquet and thank Allah for his gift? The disciples said: O spirit of Allah and his Word, you are the one who deserve to uncover the table. Jesus, peace be upon him, then, performed the ritual ablution, entered his oratory and prayed prostration; wept for a long time and called Allah to permit him to uncover the banquet for him and for the crowd. Jesus said: In the name of Allah, the best provider, and he uncovered the banquet that had a roasted huge fish, with no piles and no spikes inside, fat flowing from it, fixed with it all kinds of vegetables, next to leeks, vinegar at the head and salt at the tail, five loaves of bread; one loaf had olives on it, and dates on another, and on another five pomegranates; Sham'oun, head of the disciples, said to Jesus: Oh Spirit of Allah and His Word, Is this food from this world, or is it the food from paradise? Jesus said: Isn't now time for you to think highly of what you see from signs and refrain from carving problems? I am afraid that you will be penalized from having this sign sent down. Sham'oun said: Oh no and by the God of Israel I never intended to question you, Oh the son of the virgin; Jesus, peace be upon him, said: There is nothing like what you see in the food of the world and not from the food of heaven, but it is a thing Allah created from nothing by his almighty power when he says: Be and it happens in a flash, so eat from what you asked for in the name of Allah and praise Allah to supply you with more; he who is magnificent, empowered and grateful. They said: Oh Spirit of Allah and his Word, we really like to see such a sign of such greatness; Jesus said: glory to Allah, didn't you satisfied with what you have seen to ask for another sign? Then Jesus, peace be upon him, approached toward the fish and said: Oh fish return, in the name of Allah, to your original form, and Allah brought it, by his power, alive, thrashing like the lion, twirling and glittering eyes, piles and spikes came back, the people became afraid and moved away, and when Jesus saw what they have done and said why do you wonder after having seen the sign, you hate it? I am afraid about you will get punished, and then asked the fish to go back as sent roasted. They said: Oh Jesus, you the Spirit of Allah eat first, and then we eat. Jesus said: Allah forbid, those who requested it should start eating. When the disciples and friends found out that Jesus refused to start eating, they got afraid that the sign was a wrath and eating from it a fault. When Jesus found out their rejection, he called upon the poor and lay people to eat from Allah's gift, and thank Allah for sending it to enjoy eating it and a punish to the others, telling them to start eating in the name of Allah and say praise be to Allah when you finish. They did that and one thousand and three hundred persons, men and women, ate their satisfaction and burped; Jesus and the disciples looked at the fish and found that its shape is the same as it was sent, nothing missing, and ascended to heaven while watching, those poor who ate from it got rich, and stayed rich and healthy until passing away. The disciples and their friends repented for not eating from it…"

In short, I wonder why the Gospel did not mention the story that Muslims know about. (Al-Nassarah) or Nazarenes vanished when they became the essential part of Islam, but in Christianity, we find in the Gospel of Mathew, chapter 14, passages 15-21, the following story: *"Now when it was evening, his disciples came to him, saying, "This is a desert place and the hour is already late; send the crowds away, so they may go into the villages and buy themselves food." But Jesus said to them, "they do not need to go away; you yourselves give them some food," They answered him; "We have here only five loaves and two fishes." He said to them, "Bring them here to me. And when he had ordered the crowd to recline on the grass, he took the five loaves and the two fishes, and looking up to heaven, blessed and broke the loaves and gave then to his disciples, and the disciples gave them to the crowds. And all ate and were satisfied; and they gathered up what was left over, twelve baskets full of fragments. Now the number of those who had eaten was five thousand men, without counting women and children."*

I related the story as it is mentioned in the Noble Qur'an just to show the confusion and misinterpreted information in story-telling influenced by reflecting stories in that period of time adopted from the teachings of earlier religions such as the Nazarenes', Hebrew-Christians' or Messianic Judaism'.

C- The Nazarenes Social Life:

The religious codes had interfered nearly in every aspect of Jews, Nazarenes or Hebrew-Christians social life. They have adhered to the Torah and the Mathew's Gospel that was intended to the Hebrews to learn the story of Jesus based on the Torah, Talmud and Hebrew traditions and understandings in that era, for example:

1. Prevention of Adoption

The Jews did not know adoption; it is not treated in the Torah, so did the Nazarenes and carried such a passive concept with them to Mecca and Hijaz, while adoption was spread among the Arab Bedouins. Christianity accepted adoption among people based upon the Divine adoption of God for the Christian Believers. We read in the Gospel of St. Paul, "But the fullness of time came, God sent his Son, born of a woman, born under the Law, that he might redeem those who were under the Law, that we might receive the adoption of sons. And because you are sons, God has sent the Spirit of his Son into our hearts, crying "Abba, Father."[234]

2. Prevention of Alcoholic Beverage

Beverage was permitted in Hebraism and later on in Judaism, and in Christianity as long as not getting drunk. But the Nazarenes of Beni Israel, under the influence of the Essenes Nazarenes, called for the prevention of beverage; even they refused its use in the communion and changed the bread and wine to bread and water. Irenaeus found out "that the Ebionite Nazarenes prohibits the mix of the celestial wine with water they want to use the earthly water only, instead." [235]

3. Prevention of Eating Filthy Pork

Contrary to Christians, the Nazarenes of Beni Israel were affected by the codes of the Torah, the Hebrew Bible preventing followers from eating blood that was shed, from what is strangled and from pork. Pork was treated as filthy meat, from filthy pigs. Christianity was liberated from the Law of Moses; but the Nazarenes were observant of the Law, "we ourselves have written our decision that they abstain from idol offerings and from blood and from what is strangled and from immorality." [236] They made their decision and made it part of the letter they sent to the Gentiles in Antioch and Syria and Cilicia. "For the Holy Spirit and we have decided to lay no further burden upon you but this indispensable one, that you abstain from things sacrificed to idols and from blood and from what is strangled and for immorality..."[237].

---

[234] The epistle of St. Paul the Apostle to the Galatians, (4:4-6)
[235] Irenaeus, "Against Heresies", (5:1:3).
[236] Acts 21:25
[237] Acts 21:25

While Paul was teaching Christians that "every creature of God is good, and nothing is to be rejected that is accepted with thanksgiving. For it is sanctified by the word of God and prayer"[238]. It is the teaching of Jesus Christ when he called the crowd to him and said to them, "Hear me, all of you, and understand. There is nothing outside a man that, entering into him, can defile him; but the things that come out of the man; these are what defile a man. If anyone has ears to hear, let him hear." [239] Yes, Jesus made it clear that "...Do you not realize that nothing from outside, by entering a man can defile him? For it does not enter his heart but his belly, and passes out into the drain." Thus Jesus declared all foods clean. "The things that come out of a man are what defile a man. For from within, out of the heart of men, come evil thoughts, adulteries immortality, murders, thefts, covetousness, wickedness, shamelessness, deceits, jealousy, blasphemy, pride, foolishness. All these things come from within, and defile a man." [240]

4. Washing & Bathing for Cleaning

Washing before prayer is an old biblical tradition. "The Lord said to Moses, 'For ablutions you shall make a bronze laver with a bronze base. Place it between the Meeting Tent and the Alter, and put water in it. Aaron and his sons shall use it to wash their hands and feet. When they are about to enter the Meeting Tent, they must wash with water, lest they die.

Likewise when they approach the Alter in their ministry, to offer an oblation to the Lord, they must wash their hands and feet, lest they die. This shall be a perpetual ordinance for him and his descendants throughout their generations." [241]

Washing and bathing were part of the Nazarenes of Beni Israel dogma, mainly the Ebionites. Taking a full bath after contacting with any women is needed for purification, and is a must for the Nazarenes, but it is not an obligation in Christianity.

5. Prevention of Friary

Marriage was a biblical ceremony. The Gospel called for it after modification that included the prevention of polygamy and allowed for no

---

[238] The First Epistle of St. Paul the Apostle to Timothy, 4: 4-5.

[239] The Gospel According to St. Mark 7: 14-16.

[240] Ibid. 7:18-23.

[241] The Old Testament, Exodus, chapter 30 verses 17-21.

divorce. The Gospel calls for chastity and abstinence to those who intend to serve "the Kingdom of God". This is Friary – a monastic order.

The Essenes of the Jews enforced abstinence among their followers in the Qumran monasteries. When they became Nazarenes, they introduced the concept of abstinence led to have two drifts: a moderate one, it permits marriage but encourage abstinence; and the second extremist, it enjoins abstinence on every one. St. Paul opposed the second. "Now the Spirit expressly says in after times some will depart from the faith, giving heed to deceitful spirits and doctrines of devils, speaking lies hypocritically, and having their conscience branded. They will forbid marriage, and will enjoin abstinence from foods, which God has created to be partaken of with thanksgiving by the faithful and by those who know the truth." [242]

It is stated that the Nazarenes defined the law of marriage, and that the real prophet declared it legal, with a recommendation of abstinence. [243] As the number of Nazarenes grew less and less, they forced marriage upon all followers, and discouraged abstinence. Even their Bishop got married as reported by Epiphanius "At that time, the Nazarenes declared abstinence sacred, similar to the sects that resembled them. But earlier, during the apostolic era in Jerusalem, they respected chastity and abstinence, the Kasa'ee was known for commanding marriage as a must, and forbidding celibacy." [244]

The Nazarenes, before their migration to Mecca and Hijaz, had a logo "No Friary in the Nazarenes"! At that time, the Christian world was full of clergy, priests, friars and monks. It is also known that Judaism rejects Friary, except among Essenes who looked upon celibacy as natural and dictated by law. The Nazarenes were not Jews and were not Christians, they were "in-between"

6. *The Nazarenes and Circumcision*

Circumcision among the Jews and the Jewry was a distinguishing mark; the Jews used to divide the world into two groups: the circumcised and the uncircumcised. When Christianity started its fast spread among the "gentiles" inhabitants of Syria and the Hellenic world. They were not circumcised.

Some of the Pharisees who followed the teaching of Jesus of Nazareth wanted to make circumcision imperative on all Christians. A dogma rejected by both Paul and Barnabas, as discussed earlier, they wanted to liberate Christendom from circumcision and from the Mosaic Biblical Laws.

---

[242] The First Epistle of St. Paul the Apostle to Timothy, 4:1-3.

[243] The "Third Homilies of Clement", p. 26.

[244] Epiphanius, "Panarion – (known as Refutations of All Heresies)", 30:2:6.

Christians of all nations kept their tradition and did not accept circumcision as part of their practice and their beliefs.

The Nazarenes of Beni Israel kept to the tradition of circumcision and baptism. Circumcision is also a Semite tradition wide spread in Syria and among the Arabs. The Nazarenes did not find any difficulty in promoting this tradition in Mecca and Hijaz.

7. The Nazarenes and Fasting

The Nazarenes followed the way the Jews of Beni Israel applied in fasting. They fast all day, were starting "at daybreak when the white thread can be distinguish from the blue one; until the white streak of dawn can be distinguished from the black thread of night till night." [245] Both the Jews and the Nazarenes of Beni Israel followed such a Talmudic law.

Fasting to the people of the Gospel starts forty days before Easter, including the Passion Week. The Nazarenes fast for one full lunar month knowing that the lunar fasting is mobile.

8. The Nazarenes Ban on Women

In the Nazarenes society, women were forbidden to leave home, according to the inherited mentality of the people of the Torah. Society belonged to men, no place to women accordingly. In the Talmud "the male Jew has to pray three times a day thanking God not having him born a pagan, a slave or a woman."

In the Jewish and the Nazarenes of Beni Israel societies, social life was for men, and women were to live in veil and in their homes. Virgins were not allowed to leave home, and married should veil her face before stepping out their doors to the street.

Twice a year, young girls were allowed to go to the orchards, on the 15th of August and the Day of Atonement after prayer. In these two occasions, girls were allowed to meet boys to know each other and plan for their future homes. "If a woman uncovered her hair, and showed her face in public should be divorced without forcing the husband for the deferred payment of the dowry. The following five cases were the tickets for husbands to divorce their wives without commitment:

- Walking in the street without veil,
- Running in the street,

---

[245] The Mishnah: Berakhoth 1:2.

- Talking to stranger in the street,
- Cursing her children in the presence of the husband,
- Crying to allow the neighbors hear her cries." [246]

In such a close society, no wonder why the Disciples of Jesus were surprised to see Jesus speaking to a Samaritan woman near Jacob's well. "At this point his disciples came; and they wondered that he was speaking with a woman. ..." [247] Jesus Christ revolted against such a close society and ministered some women. "...And with him were the Twelve, and certain women who had been cured of evil and infirmities: Mary, who is called the Magdalene... and Joanna, the wife of Chuza..., and Susanna and many others who used to provide for them out of their means ..."[248] This evangelical revolution on the closed society made the Talmudic laws weakened among the Nazarenes of Beni Israel, but it did not overcome them.

In the Talmud, the birth of "a baby girl" was catastrophic to the father, he tried not the see people to tell them the omen of such bad news. The Nazarenes rejected to consider the birth of a baby girl as a bad omen.

9. The Nazarenes Women' Veil

Arab Bedouin women never veiled their faces in the Jahiliah, before Islam. The Nazarenes of Beni Israel veiled their women affected by the Jewish custom; the veil did not penetrate the Hellenistic women. The veil became a distinguishing factor between the Christian women and the veiled Nazarene women.

This Nazarenes of Beni Israel carried the veil custom with them to Mecca and the Hijaz, and was accepted in Islam.

10. The Nazarenes' Marriage

The daughter of Beni Israel can marry at age twelve and half. In exceptional cases, she can marry at age seven. Prophet Muhammad did that when he married 'Aeesha daughter of Abi Bakr.

The Nazarene girl cannot marry without a guardian and a dowry. Dowry is a Hebrew biblical term (Moher). "Increase the marriage price and gifts as you will. I will give you whatever you demand of me; only give me the girl as

---

[246] Talmoud, "The Chapter on Engagement", 6:7.

[247] The Gospel of St. John 4:27.

[248] The Gospel of St. Luke, 8: 1-3.

wife." [249] And "when a man seduces a virgin who is not betrothed, and lies with her, he shall pay her marriage price and marry her. If her father refuses to give her to him, he must still pay him the customary marriage price for virgins." [250] In the Talmud, 'Moher' is equivalent to engagement.

The Talmudic law divides the dowry into two payments: an advanced payment and a deferred one, in an attempt to minimize divorce. The Nazarenes followed that law.

Polygamy is allowed in the Torah, and the Talmud allows up to four to layman and up to eighteen to prophets. The Nazarenes went along the Talmud and allowed for four wives, while Christians, in general, marry only one, with complete restriction on divorce. In the Talmud, the king is allowed to marry up to eighteen women. The Prophet married more than the limit allowed in the Qur'an, applying the Talmudic law upon him.

The right of having the marriage knot, in the Hebrew Bible and in the Talmud lies with man. The Nazarenes of Beni Israel followed the same law. Man can divorce at his pleasure. But the prophets discouraged it because God hates divorce.

"..Despise not the wife of thy youth...thou shalt hate her put her away." [251]

Nazarene wives have the right to own what they receive from their fathers or guardians, but they have no right to deal with what they own as they wish according to the Torah.

The Talmud enumerates seven conditions where the wife has rights over her husband. These rights are for: feeding her, dressing her, giving her a place to live in, giving her medication, sleeping with her and redeeming her if she was fallen captive in an invasion. Such commitment was applied to the Nazarenes too.

---

[249] The Old Testament, Genesis, 34:12.

[250] Ibid. Exodus, 22:15-16.

[251] Ibid. Malachias, 2:16-17.

CHAPTER SIX

The Birth of Islam

The Arabian Environment:

Islamic resources, through history, tried to present a gloomy picture for the pre-Islamic period in Arabia, called a period of "Jahiliyah" (ignorance) and considered it a period of "associators" and idol worshipers that rules in Mecca and Hijaz before the rising of Muhammad in the seventh century AD.

To a large extent, the worship of idols was exaggerated, biased and incorrect, and that could not mean Arabs before Islam were ignorant. [252]

Outstanding poets existed among Arabs during the period; many of them belonged to the Christian tradition. Analysis of their poetry yields evidence of tremendous wisdom literature and sophisticated metering as well as mature art and literary styles. [253]

Christian influences had been increasingly felt, although the Christian idea had never caught hold of the tribal Arab imagination. But the stage was set and the time had come for the rise of a great religious and national leader. [254] But a form of an early Christianity was prevailing before Islam, the monotheism of the Nazarenes and Ebionites were well known as presented by Muhammad's mentor the Nazarenes Bishop Waraka Bin Nofal and by Muhammad's wife Khadijah Bint Khweiled who was related to the Bishop. Muhammad started his religious life as a Nazarenes preacher as revealed in

---

[252] Philip K. Hitti, "History of the Arabs from the Earliest Times to the Present," London MacMillan Education, 1970, pp.87-108

[253] Ibid.

[254] Philip K. Hitti, "The Arabs: A Short History," revised edition, South Bend Ind. Regnery/Gateway, 1970, p. 25

the first few chapters in <u>AL-Muddaththir (the Cloaked One, the man wearing a cloak)</u> *"O you who are clothed! Arise and warn,"*[255]

The truth is that the monotheism of the people of the region was prevailing over idol worshipers and that monotheism of that period of those Nazarenes is very close, if not the same monotheism revealed in Islam. It is also important to keep in mind that nearly all of the "Jahiliyah" (pre-Islamic) poems neglect the mentioning of idols, based on personal experience from reading those poems.

The Birth of a Prophet

Arab historians state that about 570 AD, a child was born in an Arab tribe of Quraysh to a family living in Mecca. Abdullah, the father of the child passed away before the child's birth. The child was named Muhammad, which means the "highly praised." Six years later, Muhammad's mother Amineh Bint Wahab died, and was raised by his grandfather Abd-el-Muttalib until the age of eight, and then was adopted by his uncle Abu-Talib. [256] During his youth, Muhammad became involved in the trade business and built a reputation of integrity. At the age of twenty-five, Muhammad married Khadija, the richest lady in Mecca and the niece of the Nazarenes' bishop Warakah bin Nofal of Mecca, who was fifteen years his senior. According to Garraty and Gay, "Her money provided him with the ease and independence needed to investigate and appraise the religious situation in Arabia." [257]

Muhammad is "Head of the Nazarenes":

The Arab historians spoke about the Arab Prophet who was born and grew up in a rich environment among political and religious leaders of the House of Al-Ka'ba and Mecca. Other conclusions are devious tales must be discarded concerning being poor, uneducated and orphan Muhammad before the Revelation. Our inferences and reasoning indicate clearly that Muhammad grew in a Nazarenes' environment. Since his childhood, the political leader of the House and of Mecca, who happened to be his grandfather, Abed Al-Muttaleb was a Nazarene, and took care of the orphan Muhammad. His

---

[255] Noble Qur'an, Sura Al- <u>Muddaththir (the Cloaked One)</u> 74: verse 1-2.

[256] Al-Sayyed Abd el-Aziz Salem, "Tarikh al-Dawlah al-Arabiyyah", [History of the Arab Nation], Beirut: Dar al-Nahdhah al-Arabiyyah, 1986 pp. 309-40.

[257] John A. Garraty and Peter Gay, eds., "The Columbia History of the World," New York: Harper & Row, 1972, p. 259.

marriage from Khadija "the richest lady in Mecca", who was a Nazarene, and whose uncle was the Bishop of Mecca.

Muhammad was aware of the importance of the Nazarenes in Mecca and Hijaz. It was reported that he was a part of the plan to be the next political leader of Mecca after his grandfather Abed Al-Muttaleb, and the next religious leader of the Nazarenes after his wife's uncle, Waraka Bin Nofal, who led the Nazarenes or the Hunafa' Muslims in Hijaz. Muhammad studied the Nazarenes' doctrines, and followed their traditions. He used to pray at night with them and fast during the Nazarenes' month of Ramadan at Harra' with his teacher the Bishop of Mecca. He did that for at least fifteen years before he received the sign from heaven to start the Call and impose the Nazarenes' doctrines on the Arabs. "He has instituted the religion for you as He recommended for Noah, and what We have inspired in you and recommended for Abraham, Moussa and 'Issa to maintain religion and do not stir up any divisions within it." [258] The intention was clear to make the Nazarenes, the guidance and the true religion, the religion of the Arabs.

Therefore, the Nazarenes located Muhammad, and in turn, Muhammad, the Arab Prophet, brought the Nazarenes to take over Judaism and Christianity that prevailed over Syria and the Arabian Peninsula, through his Qur'anic Call and in the name of Islam. Muhammad, from the point of view of Jews and Christians, was a Muslim Hanafi like the Nazarenes. From the point of the Nazarenes of Beni Israel and of the Arabs, Muhammad was a Muslim and one of them.

The only religion known to the Qur'an is the religion of Moses (Moussa) and Jesus ('Isa), as one religion that was carried by the Nazarenes. It is very important to remember that in history before Islam the term "Nusrani" and "Nassara", the Nazarenes never used to represent the Christians and Christianity wherever they lived through out their history.

The Nazarenes is the name confined to a sect of Beni Israel who believed in the coming of Christ, and deflected from the main streams of Christianity since the first Council of the Churches that took place in Jerusalem in 49 AD. Christians refer to them as the "Shiites" in relation to their "Sunna" Christianity, in faith and in dogma. With their presence in Mecca and Hijaz, the name "Nazarene" prevailed, as they had monopolized the "Gospel".

The best proof is the Raheb Gregarious Buheira of Basra Ash-sham who was labeled, in Al-Sira Al-Nabawiah, "the caretaker of 'Isa on His religion", and to whom Waraka Bin Nofal belonged.

The Qur'an never used the term Christianity and Christians. The only reference was to Jesus, as 'Isa Bin Mariam, and to the Nazarenes all the time. Therefore any translation from Arabic into English for the Holy Qur'an

---

[258] Noble Qur'an, Sura Ash-Shura (Consultation), 42: verse 13.

is misleading if 'Isa is considered a presentation for "Jesus Christ", or any reference to the Nazarenes as "Christians". It is out of control, erroneous and misleading. Such translation causes confusions and is purely political, without any religious value.

The Qur'an does not refer to the doctrines of Christianity, and what is being said represents the Nazarenes beliefs. It causes perplexity and adds to the conflict between the Christians and the Muslims. The current misrepresentation of the nobility and the in-depth knowledge of the Qur'an in the Nazarenes beliefs cannot be mixed up with the Christians dogma. Anyone, who neglects or ignores the presented facts, shows disrespect, deceives himself and prevents himself and his community from understanding the real message of the Holy Qur'an.

The Qur'an is a true reflection to the Nazarenes or Hunafa Muslims' religion before the coming of Islam.

Understanding these facts create a better understanding between modern Islam and Christianity. Both religions branched from the same source - the written Book of God.

Jews, Christians and Muslims believe in one God Only and one Book Only. Together, Jews, Christians and Muslims can work faithfully to block the spreading of contemporary atheistic waves, and the increased trickery of the enemy of Christianity and Islam as represented in the Zionism and the Messianic Judaism movements worldwide.

Judaism denies both Jesus Christ or 'Isa Ibn Mariam and the Prophet Muhammad. To the Jews, any person who follows the Torah and the Talmud is a true believer, and the rest are heretics and enemies to their "true" God and to their Judaism. A Jew who does not abide with the Judaic code is a non-Jewish Jew, according to the Jewish belief. The Jewish way of thinking is presented in Dennis Prager and Joseph Telushkin's book "Why the Jews?" [259] Dr. Jamil Effarah rebutted the Book "Yes. Why the Jews? [260]

Just recently, a certain influential Jewish Rabbi by the name Ovadia Yosef said about the Arabs, on the Jewish New Year celebrations, "God should strike them with a plague, them and these nasty Palestinians," he also has likened "non-Jews to donkeys and beasts of burden, saying the main reason for their very existence is to serve Jews."

On the other hand, there are modern western historians who doubt the existence of the personality of Muhammad as the Prophet as well as the writings of the Qur'an as well as the location of the City of Mecca such

---

[259] Prager, Dennis, and Telushkin, Joseph: "Why the Jews? The reason for Antisemitism". A touchstone edition, 1983, New York.

[260] Effarah, Jamil, "Yes Why the Jews? No Reason for Judenhass" Feb. 2001

mentioned before using the name Robert Spencer, Gred Puin and Patricia Crone [261].

Crone believed that by using non-Arabic sources, she could study more of the context for the rise of Islam. She argued that Islam, as represented by contemporary, non-Muslim sources, was in essence a tribal rebellion against incursions by the Byzantine and Persian empires and noted that it had deep roots in Judaism, and that Arabs and Jews were allies in these conquering communities.

Furthermore, Muslim scholars have seen no reason to doubt what is commonly believed about Mecca's location, but in recent years, some historians have raised questions about Patricia Crone's theory that received much attention and eventually strong opposition, so much so that Crone's later arguments about Mecca were obscured and eventually lost to the wider Muslim audience.

I believe that modern historical investigators have a responsibility to be truthful and able to delve further into all religions' origins including Islam based on the newly archeological discoveries.

I venture to say that people have long questioned whether Moses or Jesus existed, why not the same question should not be asked about Mohammad.

The Chronological Qur'anic Call and the Nazarenes' Doctrine

Traditionally, according to the chronological order of the revelation in the Qur'an, the first chapter starts by calling for Reading. "Read in the name

---

[261] Patricia Crone (March 28, 1945 – July 11, 2015) was a Danish-American author, scholar, orientalist, and historian, specializing in early Islamic history. She noted in *"Meccan Trade and the Rise of Islam"* (1987) that the descriptions of Mecca in Islamic literature don't seem to match the present day location of Mecca. Crone argued that the importance of the pre-Islamic Meccan trade has been grossly exaggerated. She also suggested that while Muhammad never traveled much beyond the Hijaz, internal evidence in the Qur'an, such as its description of Muhammad's polytheist opponents as "olive growers", might indicate that the events surrounding the Prophet took place near the Mediterranean region.

Dr. Crone first authored a book with Michael Cook called *"Hagarism: The Making of the Islamic World"* (1977), in which they proposed a theory that *"Islam, as represented by contemporary, Non-Muslim sources, was in essence a tribal rebellion against the Byzantine and Persian empires with deep roots in Judaism, and that Arabs and Jews were allies in these conquering communities."* Such quote is taken from an article by Sean Gannon written in **The Jerusalem Post** titled, "The gospel truth?" on December 4, 2008

of your Lord Who created. He created man from a clot. Read and your Lord is most Honorable, Who taught (to write) with the pen, Taught man what he knew not." [262]

But what to read, the answer came in the second revealed Sura (chapter) Al-Qalam (The Pen) "(Letter n - noon). By the pen and that which they write (therewith), By the grace of your Lord you are not mad. And most surely you shall have a reward never to be cut off. And most surely you conform (yourself) to sublime morality. So you shall see, and they (too) shall see." [263]

In this second chapter of the Qur'anic revelation we find the real surprise by mentioning the Muslims and reading the book with them as it appears in "Shall We then treat those Muslims as We treat the guilty? What has happened to you? How do you judge? Or have you a book wherein you read, That you have surely therein what you choose? On the day when there shall be a severe affliction ..." [264] "and they shall be called upon to make obeisance, but they shall not be able ~. And it is naught but a reminder to all the worlds." [265]

It is the first time that the word "Muslim" is used in comparison to the associators the "criminals." Then, who are those Muslims? By knowing them we predict the secret of the Qur'anic Call.

It was reported that at the beginning of the revelation, no one believed in Muhammad except his wife Khadijah. Therefore who were those Muslims that the verse refers to? No doubt they were the people of Muhammad, the people of the book, the Nazarenes, as compared to the associators, the criminals. They were neither the Jews nor the Christians in particular. They were a sect from within Beni Israel who believed in Jesus and adhered to Moses' Law; who followed their early "Christian" faith among the Arabs for whom the revealed Call came in their support against Judaism as referred to in chapter As-Saff (The Ranks) "O you who believe! Be Allah's helpers (in the cause), as Isa son of Maryam said to (his) disciples: Who are my helpers in the cause of Allah? Said the disciples: "We are helpers (in the cause) of Allah. So a party of the Beni (children of) Israel believed and another party disbelieved; then We aided those who believed against their enemy, and they became uppermost." [266] It is the Nazarenes, as we shall see in the verse 143 of the chapter (Al-Baqara - The Cow). This verse supports the emergence of the middle nation between Judaism and Christianity "Thus We have appointed you a middle nation that you may be witnesses against mankind, and that

---

[262] Sura Al-Alaq, the Clot, 96: verses 1-5

[263] Sura Al-Qalam (The Pen), 68: verses:1-5.

[264] Ibid. verses 35-38

[265] Ibid. verses 42 and 52

[266] Sura As-Saff (The Ranks - Battle Array), 61: verse 14

the messenger may be a witness against you. And We appointed the qiblah, which you formerly observed only that we might know him who followed the messenger, from him who turned on his heels. In truth it was a hard (test) save for those whom Allah guided. But it was not Allah's purpose that your faith should be in vain, for Allah is Full of Pity, Merciful toward mankind." [267]

We also observe how the revealed Call attempts to force the religion of Moses and Isa as one religion on the Arabs. As it is revealed in "The same religion has He established for you as that which He enjoined on Noah - which We have sent by inspiration to you - and that which We enjoined on Abraham, Moses, and Isa. Namely, that you should remain steadfast in religion, and make no divisions therein: to those who worship other things than Allah, hard is the (way) to which you called them. Allah chooses to Himself those whom He pleases, and guides to Himself those who turn (to Him)." [268]

These verses affirm that the Nazarenes were in Mecca. It is an affirmation made for the attempt to "Christianize" the associators-criminals. And an affirmation that urged the associators to join the Nazarenes as Muhammad has done, as revealed in Sura An-Naml (The Ants). "I am commanded only that I should serve the Lord of this city. Who has made it sacred, and His are all things, and I am commanded that I should be one of those Muslims." [269]

Clearly the second Sura (Al-Qalam – The Pen) of the Qur'an shows us that Muhammad, a Nazarenes, used to study the Holy Book with the Muslim Nazarenes, as we read the first five verses in third Sura (Al-Muzzammil – The Enshrouded One, Bundled Up). We become more convinced that Muhammad used to spend a long part of the night in praying with the Nazarenes and in reciting the "Quran" or the reading from the Holy Book (Gospel). Waking at night to pray and singing the verses from the book is not an Arab tradition, it is not Jewish, but it is a tradition of the Nazarene monks.

It is important to read the first five verses of the Muzzammil "O you who have wrapped up in your garments! Rise to pray in the night except a little. Half of it, or lessen it a little, Or add to it, and recite the Quran as it ought to be recited. Surely We will make to light upon you a weighty Word." [270]

"They are not all alike; of the followers of the Book there is an upright party; they recite Allah's communications in the nighttime and they adore (Him)." [271] It is an upright party that recites Allah's communication or "Qur'an."

---

[267] Sura Al-Baqara – (The Cow) 2: verse 143.

[268] Sura Ash-Shura – (Counsel, Consultation) 42: verse 13.

[269] Sura An-Naml – (The Ants) 27: verse 91

[270] Sura Al-Muzzammil – (The Enshrouded One, Bundled Up), 73: verses 1-5.

[271] Sura Al-Imran – (The House of Imran) 3: verse 113

CHAPTER SEVEN

The Noble Qur'an

The Noble Qur'an is "revealed" to Prophet Muhammad in both cities of Mecca (Makka) and Medina and took 23 years to complete as related to occurring events and their outcomes. The Noble Qur'an is translated to most spoken languages in the world and the reader should be aware of the fact that the translation of meanings of the Noble Qur'an falls short of conveying the wealth of the meaning of the original conveys of the Arabic text; the revelation of the Qur'an was in Arabic.

According to Muslim belief, the Qur'an is the eternal, unaltered Word of God, which has remained the same for 14 centuries. But most recently, Dr. Gerd R Puin,[272] a renowned Islamicist at Saarland University, Germany, was the head of a restoration project, commissioned by the Yemeni government, which spent a significant amount of time examining the *ancient Qur'anic manuscripts discovered in Sana'a, Yemen, in 1972*, in order to find criteria for systematically cataloging them; he says it is not one single work that has survived unchanged through the centuries. It may include stories that were written before the prophet Mohammed began his ministry and which have subsequently been rewritten.

Puin's conclusions have sparked angry reactions from orthodox Muslims and did not consider him the scholar to make any remarks on these manuscripts.

Dr. Puin is the Semitic philologist, who specializes in Arabic calligraphy and Qur'anic paleography, has been studying Sa'na manuscripts, ancient versions of the Qur'an discovered in Sa'na, the capital of Yemen. So

---

[272] *Puin, Gerd-R. (1996). "Observations on Early Qur'an Manuscripts in Sanā'". In Stefan Wild. The Qur'an as Text. Leiden, Netherlands: E. J. Brill. pp. 107–111. ISBN 978-90-04-10344-3. LCCN 95030502. OCLC 243818821.* Reprinted in *What the Koran Really Says*, ed. Ibn Warraq, Prometheus Books, 2002, ISBN 978-1-57392-945-5.

controversial are his findings that the Yemeni authorities have denied him further access to the manuscripts.

To Puin, the ancient Qur'anic manuscripts discovered in Sana'a, Yemen, in 1972 shed new light on the early development of the Qur'an as a book with a "textual history", which contradicts the fundamental Muslim belief that it is the unchanging Word of God. Any questioning of the authenticity of the Qur'anic text as the Word of God can expect a hostile reaction. The fatwa, or death sentence, is usually issued against those who are called apostate such as Suleiman Rushdie for hinting in Satanic Verses that the Qur'an may include verses from other sources - chiefly Satan.

Today, academics offering radical interpretations of the Qur'an put their lives at risk as happened in 1990 to Dr Nasr Hamed Abu Zaid.[273]

Puin believes that he will not receive the same reaction, because unlike Zaid or Rushdie he does not have a Muslim name. His claim that the Qur'an has changed since its supposed standardization, and that pre-Islamic texts have crept in, would nonetheless be regarded as highly blasphemous by Muslims. He has not yet written a book on his radical findings, but says it is "a goal to achieve" in the near future.

Furthermore, until now, there were three ancient copies of the Qur'an: one copy in the Library of Tashkent in Uzbekistan, and another in the Topkapi Museum in Istanbul, Turkey, date from the eighth century. A copy preserved in the British Library in London, known as the Ma'il manuscript, dates from the late seventh century. But the Sa'na manuscripts are even older. Moreover, the Sa'na manuscripts are written in a script that originates from the Hijaz - the region of Arabia where the prophet Mohammed lived, which makes them not only the oldest to have survived, but one of the earliest copies of the Qur'an ever.

Dr Puin's findings led him assert that the Qur'an had undergone a textual evolution. In other words, he says: "the copy of the Qur'an that we have is not the one believed to have been revealed to the prophet."

But in this book, I will continue with the traditional way of modern Muslim thinking that the Qur'an is a revealed book to Mohammad with one addition that the Qur'an carries the Nazarenes' beliefs and traditions.

---

[273] Dr. Nasr Abu Zaid (1943-2010) was formerly a lecturer in Qur'anic Studies at Cairo University, provoked a national outcry in Egypt over his book *"The Concept of the Text"*, and in 1995 he was branded an apostate by Egypt's highest court. The court forced him to divorce his wife because under Islamic law, marriage between an apostate and a Muslim is forbidden. Zaid's book argued that "the Qu'ran is a literary text, and the only way to understand, explain, and analyze it is through a literary approach".

What does the word "Qur'an" means?

Up to that point in time, in the first year of the beginning of the revelation, there was limited number of verses to recite or to "quran" for a few hours at night. Revealed verses were not enough to represent the whole revealed Noble Qur'an that took 23 years for its completion.

The Aramaic word "quran", which means "read" in Arabic, was used by Christian to start reading the Gospel. The priest before reading the Gospel announces, for example, "the quran of a chapter from the Holy Gospel is according to St. John" or any of the main four Apostles who wrote the gospels. The idiom of the Aramaic "quran" is linked with Arabic "reading" from the gospel. The term quran was dropped from the church announcement and substituted with reading out of courtesy to the Muslims who called their Holy Book the "Noble Qur'an."

The fourth revealed Sura is AL-Muddaththir (the Cloaked One, the man wearing a cloak) "O you who are clothed! Arise and warn, And your Lord do magnify, And your garments do purify, And uncleanness do shun, And bestow not favors that you may receive again with an increase, And for the sake of your Lord, be patient..." [274].

"Nay; I swear by the moon, And the night when it departs, And the daybreak when it shines; Surely it (hell) is one of the gravest (misfortunes), A warning to mankind ..." [275]

"Nay! It is surely an admonition. So whoever pleases may mind it. And they will not mind unless Allah please. He is worthy to be feared and worthy to forgive." [276]

The man wearing a cloak or Al-Muddaththir is the chosen one to preach. Oh you the one wearing a cloak (Muhammad) arise and warn. We see in the fourth Sura, the essential elements in the revelation are set to act and Muhammad is now chosen to be the Warner to warn mankind and to magnify God and to shun atrocities as a Nazarene preacher. Muhammad was chosen to warn mankind and to shun uncleanness. That was the mission given to Muhammad, no mention of being a prophet or of a messenger but a Warner. A Warner grew strong and was proclaimed to be the Prophet and the Messenger of Allah.

Reciting the fifth Sura Al-Fatihah – (The Opening), "In the name of Allah, the Beneficent, the Merciful. All praise is due to Allah, the Lord of the Worlds. The Beneficent, the Merciful, Master of the Day of Judgment. You do we serve and You do we beseech for help. Keep us on the right path. The

---

[274] Sura AL-Muddaththir – (the Cloaked One),74: verses 1-7

[275] Ibid. verses 32-36

[276] Ibid. verses 54-56

path of those upon whom You had bestowed favors. Not (the path) of those upon whom Your wrath is brought down, nor of those who go astray." [277] The Opening tells us that Muhammad asks God the Beneficent and the Merciful to keep "us" on the right path. The Fatihah (the opening) also tells about a right path of those (Nazarenes) upon whom God bestowed favors and not the path of those (Jews) upon whom God's wrath was brought down, or of those (Associators) who went astray.

It is impossible to explain "those upon whom God bestowed favors" in the first part of Al-Fatihah to the followers of Muhammad who did not exist yet. The only obvious group is the Muslim Nazarenes that Muhammad joined, as already predict in "Shall We then treat those Muslims as We treat the guilty?" [278] Or as it is mentioned in An-Naml "I am commanded only that I should serve the Lord of this city. Who has made it sacred, and His are all things; and I am commanded that I should be one of those Muslims." [279] A real surprise is found when we know to whom Muhammad request did from Allah to bestow upon the right path; those who repented with him were his people, the Muslim Nazarenes.

Clearly the right path is the belief or having faith in the light and guiding Book for those who were serving God (those were the Nazarenes) as verified in Sura Ash-Shura "And thus did We reveal to you an inspired book by Our command. You did not know what the Book was, nor (what) the faith (was), but We made it a light, guiding thereby whom We please of Our servants; and most surely you show the way to the right path:" [280]

The Nazarenes used to pray an opening that says "Oh Lord! Show me the right way in which I should walk, for to you I lift my soul ... Teach me to do your will, for you are my God. May your good spirit guide me on level ground?..." [281]

Prophet Muhammad attacks his Uncle Abi Lahab and his wife Um Jamil sister of Abi Sufyan, the wood-carrier, for not accepting his Call in the sixth Sura Al-Masadd (The Palm Fiber) "Perdition overtakes both hands of Abu Lahab, and he will perish. His wealth and what he earns will not avail him. He shall soon burn in fire that flames, And his wife, the wood-carrier, Will have upon her neck a halter of palm-fiber (strongly twisted rope)." [282]

In the seventh Sura AT-Takwir (The Overthrowing), Muhammad announces his warning based on the "Most surely it is the Word of an

---

[277] Sura Al-Fatihah – (The Opening), 1: verses 1-7

[278] Sura Al-Qalam – (the Pen), 68: verse 35

[279] Sura An-Naml – (The Ants) 27: verse 91.

[280] Sura Ash-Shura – (Consultation) 42: verse 52.

[281] Old Testament Psalm 142

[282] Sura Al-Massad – (The Palm Fiber), 111: verses 1-5

honored messenger, The processor of strength, having an honorable place with the Lord of the Dominion, One (to be) obeyed, and faithful in trust." [283]

In the eighty seventh Sura of Al-'Ala (The Most High), Muhammad declares: "Glorify the name of your Lord, the Most High, Who creates, then disposes, Who measures, then guides" [284]; "Therefore do remind, surely reminding does profit." [285] and "Most surely this is in the earlier scriptures, The Books of Abraham and Moses." [286]

Starting with eighty seventh Surah, we notice the source and the subject of Muhammad's Call. He orders the glorification of God, the Creator, in the highest, He is the One Who makes things according to a measure, then guides them to their goal. The prophecy of Muhammad was the guidance from God, and the Call of Muhammad was the guidance for his people. The guidance was to the earlier scriptures.

As the verses were revealed, we see the ethical code calling for social reform and economic adjustment. We are able to conclude that Muhammad had faith in the earlier Scripture and reminded his people of its availability and had faith in reforming the social and economic life of Muslim Arab community.

Prophet Muhammad did not start a new Book, he started by accepting the Book in the way it is revealed in "To this then go on inviting, and go on steadfastly on the right way as you are commanded. And do not follow their low desires and say: I believe in what Allah has revealed of the Book, and I am commanded to do justice between you: Allah is our Lord and your Lord; we shall have our deeds and you shall have your deeds: No plea need there be (now) between us and you: Allah will gather us together, and to Him is the return." [287]

Again, it is also revealed in "And thus have We inspired in you a Spirit of Our command. You did not know what the Scripture was, nor what the Faith. But We have made it a light whereby We guide whom We will of Our servants. And most surely you show the way to the right path" [288]

From the beginning of God's revelation to the Prophet Muhammad, Islam and Christianity still coexist in the Middle East. Knowledge of their religions is the only strength that keeps the Christian and Muslim Arabs aware of the materialistic and atheistic circumstances surrounding them.

---

[283] Sura AT-Takwir – (The Overthrowing), 81:1 verses 19-21

[284] Sura Al-'Ala – (The Most High), 87: verses 1-3

[285] Ibid. verse 9

[286] Ibid. verses 18-19

[287] Sura Ash-Shura – (Consultation) 42: verse 15

[288] Ibid. verse 52

I hope that such research matches the wisdom of God as it is revealed in "And do not dispute with the followers of the Book except by what is best, except those of them who act unjustly. And say: We believe in which has been revealed to us and revealed to you, and our Allah and your Allah is One, and to Him do we surrender." [289]

The Arab Prophet teaches wisely the unity of the revealed "Book" to all previous prophets and the unity of their message and its related revelation as the Nazarenes and Ebionites believed. The origin of the revealed books comes from one record, revealed by God. "…And with Us is a Record which speaks the truth, and they will not be wronged." [290] "God called it *"Umm Al-Kitab,"* "And verily, it is in the *Mother of the Book*, in Our Presence, high (in dignity), full of wisdom." [291] it is referred to as a guarded tablet "(Inscribed) in a Tablet Preserved!" [292]

God revealed His Book to all prophets and messengers. "…Allah sent (to mankind) prophets as bearers of good tidings and as warners. And revealed therewith the Scripture (the Book) with the truth that it might judge…" [293] Again, "… We make no distinction between any of them (the prophets), and unto Him we have surrendered." [294]

"We did send messengers (to mankind) before you, and appointed for them wives and children: and it was never the part of a messenger to bring a sign excepting as Allah permitted (or commanded). For everything there is a time prescribed (or for each period is a Book (revealed)" [295]

God revealed His Book, already prescribed in a Tablet, to all prophets as described in "He has revealed to you the Book with truth, verifying that which is before it, and He revealed the Tawrat (Moses' Law) and the Injeel (Jesus' Gospel) before this time as a guidance for the people, and He sent the Furqan." [296]

The Qur'an shows the unity of the Book and the unity of the revelation to all prophets as One. He warns those who deny any copy of the revealed Book as One in the following verses: "Those who reject the Book and that with which We have sent Our Messengers. But they will soon come to know,

---

[289] Sura Al-Ankaboot - (The Spider), 29: verse 46

[290] Sura Al-Mumenoon - (The Believers), 23: verse 62

[291] Sura Az-zukhruf – (Ornaments), 43: verse 4

[292] Sura In Al-Burooj - (Constellations), 85: verse 22

[293] Sura Al-Baqara, (The Cow), 2: verse 213

[294] Ibid. verse 136

[295] Sura Ar-Rad – (The Thunder), 13: verse 38

[296] Sura Al-Imran – (The House of Imran), 3: verse 3. Az-Zamakhshari interpreted God's reveal of the Furqan as God's heavenly books as they have the criterion of judgment distinguishing between right and wrong.

when the fetters and the chains shall be on their necks, they shall be dragged into boiling water, then in the fire shall they be burned." [297]

Reading the Holy Scripture (Gospels and Qur'an), one common and essential denominator appears in agreement and that of the belief in Allah and the Last Day. We read in the Qur'an that "It is not righteousness that you turn your faces toward East or West, but it is righteousness - to believe in Allah and the Last Day..." [298]

The same concept we find in Christianity in St. Paul Epistle to the Hebrew: "...and without faith it is impossible to please God. For Him who comes to God must believe that God exists and is a rewarder to those who seek him." [299]

Readers should faithfully convey the message that Prophet Muhammad acts as a Warner and as God's messenger to the Arabs to let them understand the Book of God in a language they know.

What is the most important knowledge contained in the 114 Sura?

The book of "Al-Bayan" has detailed counts of the 114 Sura between 6,000 to 6,236 verses and between 300,000 and 340,740 Arabic letters.[300]

I am trying to give a bird's eye view of the most important information given in the revealed verses of the entire 114 Sura in the Holy Qur'an, as follows:

The first sura is **The Opening** (Al-Fatihah) is mentioned earlier, followed with the longest second Sura **The Cow** (Al-Bakara or Al-Baqarah). It is very inclusive talking about creation, obeying and praying to God, the importance of Adam and how the angels kneeled before him, Moses and degradation of beni Israel, the story of the cow, the story of Harout and Marout, talks about magic and its kinds, the story of Um Ishmael, the building of Al-Ka'ba by Ibrahim and Ishmael and the tribe of Quraysh, the will of Ibrahim and Jacob to their children, the believe in God and his books and messengers, the pursue between Safa and Marwa, to eat Halal (Kosher), prohibiting dead meat and that of the pigs, on the necessity of fasting, the month of Ramadan, Jihad for the sake of God, pilgrimage to Mecca, the rituals and rites of pilgrimage, to enter into Islam, prohibiting fighting during the holy months, preventing making sex with infidels, divorce, the preference of Muhammad above all

[297] Sura Al-Ghafir – (The Forgiver), 40: verses 70-72
[298] Sura Al-Baqara – (The Cow), 2: verse 177
[299] St. Paul Epistle to the Hebrew, Chapter 11: verse 6
[300] "Tafseer Ibn Katheer," Volume one, Dar Al-Andalus, Beirut, 1966 page 13

115

other messengers and prophets, the story of Ibrahim and the Namroud, to story of Azeer, preventing usury, and urging honesty and the faith in Allah.

Sura 3, **The House of 'Imran** (Al-'Imran) includes talks about the religion to God is Islam, the quality of the believers, the good tidings to Mary to bring birth to 'Isa, the miracles of 'Isa, about Ka'ba as the first built for mankind, the urge to do all that is good and forbid all atrocities, victory at Badr, the provision to those who are killed in the Way to Allah, and the call for faith.

Sura 4, **Women** (An-Nisaa') deals with marriage two or three or four; but to deal justly with them or only one; and on how to treat orphans and heritage, forbidding the marriage from mothers, daughters, sisters etc., and not committing illegal sex, nor taking boy-friends, not to approach the prayer in a drunken state, and to wash whole body after sexual relations, to believe in the verses while disbelievers shall be burned in Fire; the confirmation on the family of Ibrahim a great kingdom, about greeting with greeting or better, doing righteous good deeds of male or female will make them enter paradise, and to stand firmly for justice, forbidding usury, how god have sent the revelation to Noah and the prophets after him, Ibrahim, Ishmael, Isaac, Jacob and his offspring, Moses, 'Isa, Job, Jonah, Aaron, Solomon and David, the belief in 'Isa, his death and on the Day of Resurrection, he will be a witness against the wrong-doers.

Sura 5, **The Table** (Al-Ma'idah) calls for the believers not to violate the sanctity of the Symbols of Allah, nor the Sacred Month, forbidding to eat the dead animals, blood, the flesh of the swine etc., the choice of Islam as the Muslims' religion, and how to wash the face and hands up to the elbows, rubbing the head and feet to the ankles, top purify the whole body after a sexual intercourse, if no water then perform tayammum with clean earth; followed by the story of Kabeel and Habeel because off that Allah ordained for the children of Israel that if anyone killed a person not in retaliation of murder, or to spread mischief in the land –it would be as if he killed all mankind; and to avoid strictly intoxicants and gambling, and the most important event when 'Isa asked Allah to send from heaven a table spread with food that the people can eat, to be a festival and sign from Allah to worship as mentioned in the story of The Table before.

Sura 6, **The Livestock** (Al-An'am) gives all praises and thanks to Allah; he knows what we conceal and what we reveal; and sends guardian angels over us; and to surrender to Allah; and how he showed Ibrahim the kingdoms of heavens, and bestowed upon him Isaac and Jacob, guided Noah, David, Solomon, Job, Joseph, Moses and Aaron, Zachariah, Yahiya, 'Isa, Elias, Ishmael, Elisha, Jonah, Lot that Allah has chosen them and guided them to the Straight Path. He has set the stars to guide our course through the darkness; to eat the meat on which Allah's Name has been pronounced at the time of slaughtering. And forbade the Jews to eat animals with undivided hoof, the fat of the ox and the sheep except what adheres to their backs or their entrails; and whoever brings a good deeds of obedience to Allah and his Messenger shall have ten times the like to his credit, and whoever brings an evil deed shall have the recompense of the like.

Sura 7, **The Heights** (Al-A'raf) tells that Allah told the angels to prostrate (face down) themselves to Adam except Iblis (Satan) who refused to do so; God expelled him from Paradise. The story of the Wall with Elevations stood between the dwellers of Paradise with white faces and the dwellers of Hell by their black faces. He reminds the believers that Allah sent Noah to his people to worship Allah. And told stories of Aad, the people of Hud; Thamud who were the people of Saleh of Lot, and also the people of Midian of Shu'aib. Telling the story of Moses and his relations with the Pharaoh was also included. Then, those who followed the Prophet whose name found written in the Torah and the Gospel will be successful. Encouraging the believers to show forgiveness, enjoin what is good, and turns away from the foolish and to seek refuge with Allah.

Sura 8, **Spoils of War** (Al-Anfal) urges the believers to obey Allah and his Messenger, and turn not away from him, and tells how angels smite the faces and their backs of the disbelievers as a taste for the punishment of the blazing fire. Urging the believers to fight, a hundred steadfast persons will overcome a thousand of those who disbelieve. To enjoy what you have gotten of booty in war, lawful and good, and be afraid of Allah, the most merciful.

Sura 9, **The Repentance** (Al-Taubah) encourages the killing of "*Mushrikun*" (polytheists) wherever can be found but not in the sacred months, but if they repent and perform the prayers and give "*Zakat*" (alms), then leave their way free. To fight against those who do not believe in the Oneness of Allah, or in the Last Day and those who acknowledge not the religion of truth among the people of the Scripture, until they pay the "*Jizyah*" (tribute) with willing submission and feel themselves subdued. Allah forgets those who forget him as they are promised the Fire of Hell. Allah has got ready Paradise under which rivers flow, for the believers to dwell therein forever. With every Sura coming down, the believers increase their Faith and they rejoice.

Sura 10, **Jonah** (Yunus) tells that Allah created the heavens in six days and then rose over the Throne disposing the affair of all things. He made the sun a shining thing and the moon as a light and measured out for it stages that you might know the number of years and the reckoning. How the Pharaoh followed the children of Israel across the sea till when drowning overtook him, he said: "I believe that none has the right to be worshipped but He in whom the children of Israel believe, and I am one of the Muslims"

Sura 11, **Hud** (Hud) verifies to worship none but Allah, to return to Allah who is able to do all things; how Allah blessed Noah and his people, and how Hud ordered his people to worship Allah. The story of the she-camel of Allah who sent it as a sign and called upon the people to leave her to feed in Allah's land, and touch her not with evil, to prevent torment. The story of the people of Lot and the story of the people of Midian of Shu'aib are told. Allah promised that the good deeds remove the evil deeds.

Sura 12, **Joseph** (Yusuf) tells about Joseph vision, the conspiracy of his brothers to kill him and brought his shirt stained with false blood, and how a caravan of travelers sent their water-drawer to drop the bucket and surprised to see the boy and took him as merchandise and sold him for a low price. The story of Joseph and how the wife of the man who bought tried to seduce Joseph but rejected her and ran away but she tore his shirt from the back. The women of the city started to say that the wife of Al-'Aziz sought to seduce her young man as she loved him violently, when she heard the accusation she managed to cast him prison. When the king saw in a dream seven fat cows whom seven lean ones were devouring and seven green ears of corn, and seven others dry, Joseph was the one who interpreted the dream and was set over the store-houses of the land; When Joseph brothers came and entered unto him, he recognized them. Joseph told his servants to put their money into their bags. When they returned accompanied with their brother (Benjamin), Joseph took his brother to himself and revealed himself, put the bowl of the king in his bag, then he searched and brought it out of his brother's bag. They returned without Benjamin who was accused of stealing. Jacob ordered his sons to go back and enquire about your brothers and never give up hope; They met Joseph and begged him to be charitable as they had no money to buy food, they showed mercy and confessed with their sins, so Joseph sent them with his shirt to cast it over the face of Jacob to become clear-sighted and to bring him to Joseph and all the family. When they came in before Joseph, he took his parents to himself and raised them to the throne and they fell down before him prostrate.

Sura 13, **The Thunder** (Ar-Ra'd) deals with how Allah managed and regulated all affairs. A promise to those who believed and work righteousness, Paradise is for them. Allah knows what every person earns, and the disbelievers will know who gets the good end.

Sura 14, **Abraham** (Ibrahim) reveals that Allah sent Muhammad to lead mankind out of darkness into light as sending Moses before. Allah keeps firm those who believe and cause to go away those who are wrong-doers. How Ibrahim invoked God telling him that he made some of his offspring dwell in an uncultivable valley by Allah's Sacred House to perform their prayers and to provide them with fruits so they may give thanks.

Sura 15, **Stone land** or the **Rocky Tract** (Al-Hijr) tells how the disbelievers did mock the messengers, as they were captivated people, bewitched. How Allah created man from dried clay of altered mud, and the jinn from smokeless fire. How the angels gave Ibrahim, at his old age, glad tidings to have a boy possessing much knowledge and wisdom. How Allah ordered Lot to travel in a part of the night with his family and to stay behind them in the rear, and let no one look back, and the people of the city and the dwellers of Al-Hijr, were tormented by Allah who turned upside down and rained down on them stones of baked clay.

Sura 16, **The Bee** (An-Nahl) where it is difficult to count the favors of Allah, the Most Merciful; Allah knows what men conceal and what they reveal, and He likes not the proud. Allah inspired the bees to take their habitations in the mountains and in the trees and in what they erect; and what comes forth from their bellies, a drink of variable colors healing for men. Allah has preferred some of the men above others in wealth and properties, and made for men wives, sons and grandsons to worship Allah or no others beside Him. To those who disbelieved and hinder from the Path of Allah, for them Allah will add torment to the torment because they used to spread corruption. Allah enjoins justice and benevolence to kinship and forbids all evil deeds and forbidden things; not to make one's oaths a means of deception. Allah awards whoever works righteousness whether male or female. And the Day when every person will come up pleading for himself, and everyone will be paid in full for what he did and they will not be dealt with unjustly. Allah chose Ibrahim and guided him to a Straight Path and sending Mohammad the revelation to follow the religion of Ibrahim Hanif who was not of the polytheists. Truly, Allah is with those who fear Him and those who are good-doers.

Sura 17, **The Night Journey** (Al-Israa') glorifies be to He Who took His slave for a journey by night from Al-Masjid-al-Haram to Al-Masjid-al-Aqsa, the neighborhood whereof Allah have blessed, in order that Allah might show him. How Allah gave Moses the Scripture; and whoever goes right, then he goes right only for the benefit of his oneself. And whoever goes astray, and then he goes astray to his own loss. No one laden with burdens can bear another's burden. And tells how many generations have Allah destroyed after Noah. And concerning the Ruh (the spirit) which is one of the things, the knowledge of which is only with Allah. And none of mankind and the jinn together could not produce the like of the Qur'an. The nine signs that Allah gave to Moses to Pharaoh to turn the children of Israel out of the land.

Sura 18, **The Cave** (Al-Kahf) tells about the people of the cave and the Inscription was a wonder among Allah's Signs. The story of the two men that Allah had given two gardens of grapes, surrounding both with date-palms; and had put between them green crops. The story of Moses asking to follow the teaching of the knowledge that Khidr had been taught. The reciting of the story is about Dhul-Qarnain that was known.

Sura 19, **Mary** (Maryam) starts with the story of Zachariah. It was followed by the story of Maryam and her withdrawal into seclusion from her family and the good tidings that Allah's Ruh appeared before her and announced the gift of a righteous son. Again, it was followed by the repetition of stories of Ibrahim, Moses, Ishmael, and Idris. Those who followed lusts will be thrown in Hell; those who repent and believe, and work righteousness will enter Paradise and they will not be wronged.

Sura 20, **Taha** (Ta-Ha) includes the story of Moses with the Pharaoh.

Sura 21, **The Prophets** (Al-Anbiyaa') tells the stories of Ibrahim and his people, the stories of David and Solomon, of Job and that of Yunis.

Sura 22, The Pilgrimage (Al-Hajj) How Allah proclaims to mankind the Hajj. They will come to the site of the Sacred House on foot and on every lean camel; they will come from every deep and distant mountain highway. Allah is able to give the believers victory and protection.

Sura 23, **The Believers** (Al-Mu'minum) shows how Allah created man out of an extract of clay and made him as a *Nutfah* in a safe lodging and made the *Nutfah* into a clot and the clot into a little lump of flesh and bones, clothing the bones with flesh, and brought it forth as another creation. Blessed is Allah, the Best creators.

Sura 24, **Light** (An-Nur) tells about the punishment of the sinners by stating that the fornicates and the fornicator should each of them flog with a hundred stripes, and of married persons commit it, the punishment is to stone them to death. The believing men and women should lower their gaze, and protect their private parts. To marry those among who are single and pious, slaves and maid-servants; if they were poor, Allah will enrich them out of His Bounty. Allah is the Light of the heavens and the earth. Light upon Light, Allah guides to His Light whom He wills, and sets forth parables for mankind, and Allah is All-Knower of everything. To remember the name of Allah in houses which Allah has ordered to be raised?

Sura 25, **The Criterion** (Al-Furqan) is to differentiate between virtues and vice and between believers and disbelievers, good and bad, it includes all the qualities of those who worship Allah.

Sura 26, **The Poets** (Ash-Shu'raa') includes the story of Moses and Pharaoh, the story of Ibrahim and his people, Noah and his people, Hud and his people, Lot and his people, Shu'aib and his people.

Sura 27, **The Ants** (An-Naml) continues in telling the stories of Moses and the Pharaoh, David and Solomon, Saleh and his people. The story of a beast that Allah shall bring out of the earth for the people to speak to them because mankind believed not with certainty in Allah's *Ayaat* (verses).

Sura 28, **The Stories** (Al-Qasas) recites some of the news of Moses and Pharaoh, and that of Qarun who was of Moses' people, but he behaved arrogantly toward them.

Sura 29, **The Spider** (Al-'Ankaboot) recites some of the news of Noah and his people and that of Ibrahim.

Sura 30, **The Byzantines** (Ar-room) includes the verses that glorify Allah and His revealed Signs

Sura 31, **Luqman** (Lukmaan) includes Luqman's will to his son advising him not to join in worship others with Allah.

Sura 32, **The Prostration** (As-Sajdah) gives description to the qualities of the believers in Allah's verses.

Sura 33, **The Clans** (Al-Ahzaab) emphasizes that the Prophet is closer to the believers than their own selves, and his wives are their mothers. And blood relations among each other have closer personal ties in the Decree of Allah than the believers and the *Muhajirun* (emigrants), except that you do kindness to those brothers. Allah has taken from the prophets a strong covenant. Indeed, in the Messenger of Allah you have a good example to follow for him who hopes for Allah and the Last Day, and remember Allah much. Allah asked the Prophet to tell his wives if they desire the life of this world, and its glitter, he will makes provision for them and set them free in a handsome manner; but if they desire Allah and His Messenger, and the home of the Hereafter, then Allah has prepared for *Al-Muhsinat* (good doers) among them an enormous reward. And to those who believe should remember Allah with much remembrance. The believers should not enter the Prophet's houses, unless permission is given for a meal and not wait for its preparation. But when invited enter, and take the meal and disperse without sitting for a talk and should not annoy the Prophet who is shy, but Allah is not shy of the truth. And when you ask for anything you want, ask them from behind a screen: that is purer for your hearts and for their hearts. The believer should never to marry the Prophet's wives after him. Verily, with Allah that shall be an enormity. Allah sends His *Salat* (graces) on the Prophet and also His angels. Send your Salat on him and greet him the Islamic way of greeting. Allah asks the Prophet to tell his wives and his daughters and the women of the believers to draw their cloaks all over their bodies, better that to be annoyed.

Sura 34, **Sheba** (Saba') starts with Allah subjecting the wind and the jinn to his orders and let them work as he desired. The story of *Saba'* (Sheba) and the sign in their dwelling-place – two gardens on the right and one on the left; and Allah has not sent the Prophet except as a giver of glad tidings and a warner of all mankind, but most men know not.

Sura 35, **The Angels** (Fatir) says that all the praises and thanks are to Allah, the Originator of the heavens and earth. Who made the angels messengers with wings, two or three or four? The talk about how mankind stands in need of Allah. But Allah is rich Worthy of all praise. Those who recite the Book of Allah and perform *As-Salat*, and spend out of what Allah has provided for them, they hope for a trade-gain that will never perish.

Sura 36, **Yaseen - Yasin** (Yaseen) puts forward to them a similitude, an example of the dwellers of the town, when there came Messengers to them. When Allah intends a thing, is only that He says to it, "Be!" – And it is!

Sura 37, **Those Ranged in Ranks** (As-saffat) encourages destroying idols made of sticky clay. The attempt of Ibrahim to slaughter his son as seen in a dream was about to fulfill when both submitted themselves to the will of Allah, Allah called Ibrahim that he fulfilled the dream and ransomed the son with a great sacrifice.

Sura 38, **The Letters** (Saad) has Allah's calling on the Prophet to be patient of what the disbelievers say, and to remember Allah's slave David who was endured with power and was ever Oft-Returning in all matters and in repentance. Allah made the mountains to glorify His Praises with David in the morning and evening; and the birds assembled: all obedient to him, made his kingdom strong and gave him the wisdom and sound judgment in speech and decision.

Sura 39, **The Troops** (Az-Zumar) tells how Allah has put forth for men, in the Qur'an every kind of similitude in order that they may remember. And to the worshipers who have transgressed against themselves not to despair of the Mercy of Allah who forgives all sins, and turning in repentance and in obedience with true Faith to Allah and submit to Him before the torment comes. Those who kept their duty to Allah will be led to Paradise in groups, till, when they reach it, and its gates will be opened and its keepers will say *Salamun 'Alaikum*, you have done well, so enter here to abide therein.

Sura 40, **The Forgiver** (Ghafeer) addresses those who disbelieve that Allah's aversion was greater towards them than their aversion towards one another, when they were called to the Faith but they used to refuse saying that Allah made them die twice and given them life twice, so they confess their sins, and ask for any way to get out. About Joseph who did come in times gone by, with clear signs, but the disbelievers ceased not to doubt in that which he did bring to them, and after them they thought that no Messenger will Allah send after him. And when the Pharaoh called upon Haman to build him a tower that he may arrive at the ways of the heavens and may look upon the God of Moses, but he was a lire and was made fair-seeing, in Pharaoh's eyes, the evil of his deeds, and was hindered from the Path; and the plot of Pharaoh led to nothing but loss and destruction. And the man who believed said that he will guide the people to the way of right conduct. Allah gives life and causes death, and when He decided upon a thing He says to it only: Be, and it is. Those who deny the Book and that with which Allah sent His Messengers they will come to know when iron collars will be rounded over their necks and the chains, they shall be dragged along in the boiling water, and then they will be burned in the Fire.

Sura 41, **Spelled Out** (Fussilat) shows the Book, a revelation from Allah, has verses detailed in the Qur'an in Arabic for people to know. Giving glad tidings and warning, but most of the people turn away, so they hear not. Who is better in speech than he who invites to Allah's, and does righteous deeds and says: "I am one of the Muslims."

Sura 42, **Consultation** (Ash-Shura) tells those who take as *Auliya'* (guardians) others besides Allah, Allah is the Protector over them and the Prophet Muhammad is not a *Wakil* (disposer of their affairs).

Sura 43, **The Gold Ornaments** (Az-Zukhruf) states that were it not that mankind would have become of one community, Allah would have provided for those who disbelieve in Allah, silver roofs for their houses, and elevators whereby they ascend, and for their houses, doors and thrones on which they could recline, and adornments of gold.

Sura 44, **Smoke** (Ad-Dukhan) tells about waiting for the Day when the sky will bring forth a visible smoke, covering the people: this is a painful torment. Allah promised the *Muttaqun* (the Pious) a place of Security, among Gardens and springs, and dressed in fine silk. Allah shall marry them to *Hur* (fair females) with wide, lovely eyes.

Sura 45, **Crouching** (Al-Jaathiyah) shows that whosoever does a good deed, it is for his oneself. And whosoever does evil, it is against. Then to Allah they will be made to return. How each nation humbled to their knees and is called to its Record to be recompensed for what they used to do.

Sura 46, **The Dunes** (Al-Ahqaf) tells that Allah sent towards the Prophet a group of the jinn, listening to the Qur'an. When they stood in the presence thereof, they said: "Listen in silence" and when it was finished, they returned to their people, as warners saying that they heard a Book sent down after Musa, confirming what came before it, guides to the truth and to the Straight Path.

Sura 47, **Muhammad** (Muhammad) tells that those who are killed in the Way of Allah, He will never let their deeds be lost, and admit them to Paradise which Allah has made known to them. While those who disbelieve enjoy themselves and eat as cattle eat; and the Fire will be their abode.

Sura 48, **The Victory** (Al-Fathh) addresses those who give *Bai'ah* (pledge) to the Prophet they are giving pledge to Allah. The Hand of Allah is over their hands. Then whosoever breaks his pledge, breaks it only to his own harm; and whosoever fulfils he has covenanted with Allah. Allah will bestow on him a great reward. Had there not been believing men and believing women whom the Prophet did know, and may kill them and on those account a sin would have been committed without knowledge, that Allah might bring into His Mercy whom He wills – if they had been apart, Allah would have punished those of them who disbelieved with painful torment. Indeed Allah shall fulfil the true vision which He showed to His Messenger is very truth, and to enter AL-Masjid-al-Haram, if Allah wills, secure, having your heads shaved, and having your head hair cut short, having no fear.

Sura 49, **The Dwellings** (Al-Hujuraat) shows that those who lower their voices in the presence of Allah's Messenger, they are the ones whose hearts Allah has tested for piety. For them are forgiveness and a great reward. Verily those who call from behind the dwellings, most of them have no sense. The believers are nothing else than brothers. So make reconciliation between brothers, and fear Allah to receive mercy.

Sura 50, **The letter Q** (Qaaf) has the Sentence that comes from Allah cannot be changed, and He is not unjust to the slaves. Allah knows best what people say and the Prophet is not the one to force them. But warn by the Qur'an; him who hears Allah's Threat.

Sura 51, **The Winnowing Winds** (Adh-Dhariyat) has a reference to Moses whom Allah sent to Pharaoh with a manifest authority, but turned away accused of being a sorcerer, so Allah took Pharaoh and his hosts, and dumped them in the sea, for he was blameworthy. And in A'ad when Allah sent against them the barren wind. The wind spared nothing that it reached, but blew it into broken spreads of rotten ruins.

Sura 52, **The Mount** (At-Toor) starts with verily the Torment of Allah will surely come to pass, byte Toor, and by the Book Inscribed, in parchment unrolled, and by *AL-Bait-ul-Ma'mur* and by the roof raised high and by the sea kept filled.

Sura 53, **The Star** (An-Najm) tells that by the star when it goes down, the Prophet has neither gone astray nor has erred, nor does he speak of desire; it is only a Revelation revealed.

Sura 54, **The Moon** (Al-Qammar) has the Hour drawn near, and the moon has been divided and split. The Day that the caller will call will lead to a terrible thing.

Sura 55, **The Beneficent** (Ar-Rahman), Ar-Rahman has taught the Qur'an, created man, and taught him eloquent speech. Is there any reward for good other than good?

Sura 56, **The Event** (Al-Waqi'ah) tells when the Event befalls, and there can be no denial of its befalling, bringing low exalting when the earth will be shaken with a terrible shake, and the mountains will be powered to dust, so that they will become floating dust particles.

Sura 57, **The Iron** (Al-Hadeed) states that Allah have sent His Messengers with clear proofs, and revealed with them the Scripture and the Balance that mankind may keep up justice. And Allah brought forth iron wherein is mighty power, as well as many benefits for mankind, that Allah may test who it is that will help Him and His Messengers in the unseen Verily, Allah is All-Strong, All- Mighty.

Sura 58, **The Woman Who Disputes** (Al-Mujadilah) tells that Allah has heard the statement of her with the Prophet and complains to Allah. And Allah hears the argument. And that secret counsels are only from Satan, in order that he may cause grief to the believers. But Satan cannot harm them in the least, except as Allah permits. And in Allah let the believers put their trust.

Sura 59, **The Gathering** (Al-Hashr) ends with the verse that Allah is the Creator, the Inventor, of all things, the Bestower of forms. To Him belong the Best Names. All that is in the heavens and the earth glorify Him And He is the All-Mighty, the All-Wise.

Sura 60, **The Woman to be examined** (Al-Mumtahanah) tells when believing women come to the Prophet as emigrants, examine them; Allah knows best as to their Faith, then if the Prophet ascertains that they are true believers sent them not back to the disbelievers. They are not lawful for the disbelievers nor are the disbelievers lawful for them. But give them that which they have sent to them. And there will be no sin to marry them after paying their *Mahr* to them. Likewise hold not the disbelieving women as wives. And if any of the Prophet's wives have gone from him to the disbelievers, then he went out for a *Ghazwah* (military expedition) gained booty; then pay from the booty to those whose wives have gone, the equivalent of what they had spent. Allah called upon the prophet when believing women come to you to give you the pledge, that they will not associate anything in worship with Allah that they will not steal, that they will not commit illegal sexual intercourse, not killing their children and not utter slander, not forging falsehood, and do not disobey. Then, accept their pledge and ask Allah to forgive them.

Sura 61, **The Rank** (As-Saff) shows how Allah loves those who fight in His Cause in rows as if they were a solid structure.

Sura 62, **Friday** (Al-Jumu'ah) is to those who believe when the call is proclaimed for the prayer on Friday, come to the remembrance of Allah and leave off business.

Sura 63, **The Hypocrites** (Al-Munafiqoon) deals with the hypocrites when they come to the Prophet they say that they bear witness that Muhammad are indeed the Messenger of Allah. Allah knows that Muhammad is indeed His Messenger, and Allah bears witness that the hypocrites are liars indeed.

Sura 64, **Mutual Disillusion** (At-Taghaboon) is about the Day when Allah will gather all on the Day of Gathering, that will be the Day of *At-Taghabun* ((mutual loss and gain), and whosoever believes in Allah and performs righteous good deeds. In Allah the believers put their trust.

Sura 65, **The Divorce** (At-Talaq) tells the Prophet when divorcing women; divorce them at their *'Iddah* (prescribed periods) and count their 'Iddah. And turn them not out of their homes nor shall they leave, except in the case they are guilty of some open illegal sexual intercourse.

Sura 66, **The Prohibition** (At-Tahrim) starts with Allah asking the Prophet why you forbid that which Allah has allowed to you, seeking to please your wives. And Allah is Oft-Forgiving, Most Merciful. Believers should turn to Allah with sincere repentance. The Prophet should strive hard against the disbelievers and the hypocrites, and be severe against them; their abode will be Hell. Allah sets forth an example for those who disbelieve the wife of Noah and the wife of Lot. Allah sets forth an example for those who believe the wife of Pharaoh and Maryam, the daughter of "Imran.

Sura 67, **The Sovereignty - Dominion** (Al-Mulk) starts with blessing is to Allah in Whose Hand is the dominion; and He is Able to do all things.

Sura 68, **The Pen – letter N** (Al-Qalam – Noon) has the first verse saying: By the pen and what they write.

Sura 69, **The Reality –The Inevitable** (Al-Haqqah), starts with the question: what is the Inevitable? And what will make the Inevitable known? Thamud and A'ad people denied the *Qari'ah* (the striking hour of Judgment). As for Thamud they were destroyed by the awful cry. And as of A'ad, they were destroyed by a furious violent wind.

Sura 70, **The Way of Ascent** (Al-Ma'arij) is from Allah, the Lord of the Ways of Ascent. The angels and the Ruh ascend to Him in a Day the measure whereof is fifty thousand years, so be patient with a good patience.

Sura 71, **Noah -Nuh** (Nooh) tells that Allah sent Noah to his people warning them before there comes to them a painful torment. Because of their sins they were drowned, then were made to enter the Fire.

Sura 72, **The Jinn** (Al-Jinn) starts with Allah saying that it has been revealed to Him that a group of jinn listened and said that they verily they have heard a wonderful Recitation that guided them to the Right Path.

Sura 73, **The Enshrouded One** (Al-Muzzammil) calls upon who wrapped in garments to stand all night, except a little, half of it or a little less than that, or a little more. And recite the Qur'an in a slow style.

Sura 74, The Cloaked One – The One Enveloped (Al-Muddaththir) calls upon the one enveloped in garments to arise and warn and magnify Allah, and purifies your garments, and keeps away from idols, and gives not a thing in order to have more, and be patient for the sake of Allah.

Sura 75, **The Resurrection** (Al-Qiyamah) tells that on the Day of Resurrection man will be informed of what he sent forward and what he left behind. Man will be a witness against himself though he may put forth his excuses.

Sura 76, **The Man** (Al-Insaan) has there not been over man a period of time, when he was not a thing worth mentioning? Remember the Name of Allah every morning and afternoon and during night, prostrate to Him and glorify Him a long night through.

Sura 77, **The Emissaries – those Sent Forth** (Al-Mursalaat) starts by the winds sent forth one after another, and by the winds that blow violently, and by the winds that scatter clouds and rain. And by the Verses that separate the right from the wrong, and by the angels that bring the revelations to the Messengers.

Sura 78, **The Tidings – The Great News** (An-Naba') opens with the question: What are they asking about? It is asking about the great news, about which they are in disagreement.

Sura 79, **Those Who Pull Out** (An-Nazi'aat) begins with by those who pull out with great violence. By those who gently take out and by those that swim along, and by those that press forward as in a race, and by those angels who arrange to the Commands of their Lord.

Sura 81, **Wound Round and Lost its Light** (At-Takweer) opens when the sun is wound round and the light is lost and is overthrown.

Sura 82, **The Cleaving** (Al-Infitaar) starts when the heaven is cleft asunder (split apart), and when the stars have fallen and scattered, and when the seas are burst forth. And when the graves are turned upside down, a person will know what he has sent forward and left behind.

Sura 83, **Defrauding Those Who Deal in Fraud** (Al-Mutaffifin) commences with Woe to Al-Mutaffifun, those who, when they have to receive by measure from men, demand full measure, and when they have to give by measure or weight to men, give less than due. Do they nit think that they will be resurrected.

Sura 84, **Splitting Open** (Al-Inshiqaaq) is when the heaven split opens, and listens to and obeys its Lord, and it must do so. And when the earth is stretched forth, and has cast out all that was in it and become empty.

Sura 85, **Constellations – The Big Stars** (Al-Burooj) kicks off by the heaven holding the big stars, and the Promised Day and by the Witnessing day, and the Witness Day. Cursed were the people of the Ditch, of fire fed

127

with fuel, and they witnessed what they were doing against the believers. And they had no fault except that they believed in Allah, the All-Mighty, Worthy of all Praise.

Sura 86, **The Night-Comer** (At-Tariq) opens with the heaven, and *Al-Tariq* (the night comer), and what will make you to know what *Al-Tariq* is? It is the star of piercing brightness' there is no human being but has a protector over him, so let man see from what he is created.

Sura 87, **The Most High** (Al-A'laa')starts with glorify the Name of your Lord, the Most High, who has created, and then proportioned, and Who has measured; and then guided, and Who brings out the pasturage, and then makes it dark stubble. We shall make you to recite, so you shall not forget, except what Allah may will. He knows what is apparent and what is hidden.

Sura 88, **The Overwhelming** (Al-Ghaashiyah) has there come to you the narration of the overwhelming? Some faces, that Day will be humiliated, laboring, and weary.

Sura 89, **The Dawn** (Al-Fajr) commences with by the dawn; by the ten nights, and by the even and the odd. And by the night when it departs, there is indeed in them sufficient proofs for men of understanding.

Sura 90, **The City** (Al-Balad) begins by I swear by the city; and you are free in this city. And by the begetter and that which he begot. Verily, Allah has created man in toil. Does he think that none can overcome him?

Sura 91, **The Sun** (Ash-Shams) is by the sun and its brightness. By the moon as it follows it. By the day as it shows up brightness. By the night as it conceals it. By the heaven and Him who built it. By the earth and Him who spread it.

Sura 92, **The Night** (Al-Lail) is by the night as it envelops. By the day as it appears in brightness. By Him Who created male and female. Certainly, your efforts and deeds are diverse; as for him who gives and keeps his duty to Allah and fears Him.

Sura 93, **The Morning Hours –The Forenoon – After Sunrise** (Ad-Duhha) starts with by the forenoon, and by the night when it darkens, Allah has neither forsaken you nor hates you, and indeed the Hereafter is better for you than the present, and verily, Allah will give you so that you shall be well-pleased.

Sura 94, **The Opening Forth** (Ash-Sharh) says: "Have We not opened your breast for you? And removed from you your burden, which weighed down your back? And have **We** not raised high your fame? Verily, along with every hardship is relief, so when you have finished, devote yourself for Allah's worship; and to your Lord turn intentions and hopes."

Sura 95, **The Fig** (At-Teen) says: "By the fig and the olive, by Mount Sinai, by this city of security, verily **We** created man in the best stature;

then **We** reduced him to the lowest of the low. Save those who believe and do righteous deeds. Then they shall have a reward without end. Then what causes you to deny the Recompense? Is not Allah the Best of judges?"

Sura 96, **The Clot** (Al-'Alaq) begins with read in the Name of your Lord Who has created man from a clot. Read and your Lord is the Most Generous, who has taught by the pen and has taught man that which he knows not. Nay! Man does transgress because he considers himself self-sufficient…

Sura 97, **The Fate** (Al-Qadr) says: "Verily, **We** have sent it down in the night of *Al-Qadr*, and what will make you know what the night of *Al-Qadr* is? The night of *Al-Qadr* is better than a thousand months; therein descend the angels and the *Ruh* by Allah's Permission will all Decrees, there is Peace until the appearance of dawn."

Sura 98, **The Clear Evidence** (Al-Bayyinah) starts with those who disbelieve from among the people of the Scripture and *Al-Mushrikun*, were not going to leave until there came to them clear evidence. A Messenger from Allah, reciting purified pages, wherein are correct and straight laws from Allah. The disbelievers will abide in the Fire of Hell, and the believers will be rewarded with Allah's 'And Paradise underneath which rivers flow. They will abide therein forever…

Sura 99, **The Earthquake** (Az-Zalzalah) says: "When the earth is shaken with its earthquake, and when the earth throws out its burdens, and man will say: 'What is the matter with it?' That Day it will declare its information because Allah will inspire it. That Day mankind will proceed in scattered groups that they may be shown their deeds. So whosoever does good equal to the weight of an atom shall see it; and whosoever does evil equal to the weight of an atom shall see it."

Sura 100, **Those That Run** (Al-'Adiyat) says: "By that run with panting, striking sparks of fire and scouring to the raid at dawn, and raise the dust in clouds the while, and penetrating forthwith as one into the midst; verily, man is ungrateful to his Lord, and to that he bears witness, he is violent in the love of wealth, knows he not that when the contents of the graves are poured forth, and that which is in the breasts is made known? The day their Lord will be Well-Acquainted with them."

Sura 101, **The Calamity – The Striking Hour** (Al-Qaari'ah) says: "*Al-Qaari'ah*, what is *Al-Qaari'ah*? And what will make you know what *Al-Qaari'ah* is? It is the Day whereon mankind will be like moths scattered about, and the mountains will be like carded wool; then as for him whose balance will be heavy, he will live a pleasant life, but as for him whose balance will be light, he will have his home in *Hawiyah* (pit), and what will make you know what it is? It is a fiercely blazing Fire."

Sura 102, **The Rivalry - The piling Up** (At-Takaathur) says: "The mutual rivalry diverts you until you visit the graves, nay! You shall come to know. Again nay! You shall come to know. Nay! If you knew with a sure knowledge, you shall see the blazing Fire, and again, you shall see it with certainty of sight; then on that Day you shall be asked about the delights."

Sura 103, **The Declining Day** (Al'Asr) says: "By *Al-'Asr,* man is in loss except those who believe and do righteous good deeds, and recommend one another to the truth and one recommend one another to patience."

Sura 104, **The Slanderer** (Al-Humazah) says: "Woe to every slander and backbiter who has gather wealth and counted it. He thinks that his wealth will make him last forever. Nay! Verily, he will be thrown in the crushing Fire. And what will make you know what the crushing Fire is? The fire of Allah kindled, which leaps up over the hearts, and it shall be closed upon them in pillars stretched forth."

Sura 105, **The Elephant** (Al-Feel) says: "Have you not seen how Allah dealt with the owners of the Elephants? Did He not make their plot go astray? And He sent against them birds in flocks, striking them with stones of *Sijjil* (baked clay), and He made them like stalks."

Sura 106, **Quraysh** (Quraish) says: "For the protection of the Quraish, the caravans to set forth safe in winter and in summer, so let them worship the Lord of this House Who has fed them against hunger, and has made them safe from fear."

Sura 107, **The Small Kindnesses** (Al-Maa'oon or Al-Ma'un) says: "Have you seen him who denies the Recompense? That is he who repulses the orphan, and urges not on the feeding o *Al-Miskin* (the Poor). So woe unto those performers of Salat. Those who delay their Salat. Those who do good deeds only to be seen, and prevent *Al-Ma'un.*"

Sura 108, **A River in Paradise** (Al-Kauthar) says: "Allah has granted you *Al-Kauthar.* Therefore turn in prayer to your Lord and sacrifice for he who hates you, he will be cut off."

Sura 109, **The Disbelievers** (Al-Kafirun) says: "Say: O *Al-Kafirun,* I worship not that which you worship, nor will you worship that which I worship. And I shall not worship that which you are worshiping, nor will you worship that which I worship. To you be your religion, and to me my religion."

Sura 110, **The Succour, The Help** (An-Nasr) is about when there comes the Help of Allah and seeing the people enter Allah's religion in crowds, so glorify the Praises of Allah and ask His forgiveness.

Sura 111, **The Palm Fiber** (Al-Masad) tells to perish the two hands of Abu Lahab and perish him, his health and his children will not benefit him and he will be burnt in a Fire of blazing flames; and his wife, too, who carries wood, in her neck, is a twisted rope of *Masad.*

Sura 112, **Sincerity or The Purity** (Al-Ikhlas or At-Tauhhid) says Allah is the one, *Allah-us-Samad*, begets not, nor was He begotten, and there is none co-equal or comparable unto Him.

Sura 113, **The Daybreak** (Al-Falaq) is to take refuge with the Lord of the daybreak, from the evil of what He has created, and from the evil of the darkening as it comes with its darkness, and from the evil of those who practice witchcraft when they blow in the knots, and from the evil of the envier when he envies.

Sura 114, **Mankind** (An-Naas) is the last Sura with six verses that Allah is the Lord of mankind, the King of mankind, the God of mankind, and from the evil of the whisperer who withdraws, and who whispers in the breasts of mankind, and of jinn and men.

The Correct Explanation Corresponding to "Beni Israel" in the Qur'an

The Jews of "Beni Israel" stood as enemies to the Call of the Qur'an in Mecca and Al-Medina, except the Nazarenes who insert the Israeli dogma into Islam. Should we be satisfied with approximately the verse which says: "Do not argue with the People of the Book unless it is in the finest manner, except for those of them who do wrong; SAY: "We believe in what has been sent down to us and what has been sent down to you. Our God and your God is [the same] One and we are committed before Him to [observe] peace (to be Muslims)" [301].

Then, "who do wrong" from the people of the Book, and it is possible to argue with them not in the finest manner? Yes. They are the Jews as expressed clearly and in absolute frankness in the Qur'an: "Those who are laden with the Torah, yet do not carry it out may be compared to a donkey that is carrying scriptures. It is such a dreadful way to have to compare people who reject God's signs! God does not guide such wrongdoing folk. (5). SAY: "You who are Jews, if you claim to be God's adherents ahead of [other] people, then long for death if you are so truthful." They will never long for it because of what their hands have already done. God is Aware as to who are wrongdoers." [302]

---

[301] Ibid. Sura Al-Ankabout (the Spider), 29: verse 46.

[302] Ibid. Sura Al-Jum'a (Friday), 62: verse 6.

It is also said: "We forbade those who became Jews what We have already told you about; We did not harm them, but they harmed themselves." [303] The Jews in Mecca and in Al-Medina were called "the oppressors" because they disbelieved in Muhammad as they disbelieved in Christ… But the Nazarenes are the ones that should be argued with, in the finest manner, they are the ones who believe in one God, one revelation and one unity in Islam between the Nazarenes and the followers of Muhammad. The oppressors, the Jews are the ones who deserve vilification since the "Children of Israel, remember My favor which I have shown you, and fulfill My agreement! I shall fulfill your covenant. I am the One you should revere! Believe in what I have sent down to confirm what you already have, and do not be the first to disbelieve in it. …" [304].

It is sufficient to go over this testimony: "You will find the most violently hostile people towards those who believe are the Jews, and those who associate [others with God]; while you will find the most affectionate of them towards those who believe, are those who say: "We are Nazarenes." That is because some of them are priests and monks; they do not behave so proudly." [305]

Notice the strong language that "the Jews", with no exception, are number one enemies of Islam. That is why the Qur'an considers the Jews as the first Disbelievers [306] and in "Those People of the Book who disbelieve as well as the associators will remain in Hell fire; those are the worst creatures." [307]

In Mecca as well as in Medina, the Qur'an's nearly specify the Jews of Beni Israel as Disbelievers in Muhammad and his Call. The Qur'an considers the Nazarenes of Beni Israel, on the other hand, alone as the Believers in both Jesus ('Isa) and Muhammad. The Qur'an supports the Nazarenes of Beni Israel against the Jews of Beni Israel as shown in "… A faction from Beni (the Children) of Israel believed (the Nazarenes), while another faction disbelieved (the Jews). We assisted the ones who believed against their enemy, till they held the upper hand." [308]

The Umma or Uma (nation) that Muhammad orders his followers to be guided by is not the nation of the Jews, and it is not the Christian nations, but the Nazarenes of Beni Israel. "Those are the ones to whom We have given the Book, (and Al-Hukm) along with discretion and Prophet-hood; if such men should disbelieve in it, then We will entrust it to a folk who will not disbelieve in it. Such are the ones whom God has guided, so copy their

---

[303] Ibid. Sura Al-Nahl (Bees), 16: verse 118.

[304] Ibid. Sura of Al-Bakara (the Cow), 2: verses 40-41.

[305] Ibid. Sura Al-Ma'ida (the Table), 5: verse 82.

[306] Ibid. Sutat Al-Bakara, (the Cow), 2: verse 41.

[307] Ibid. Sura Al-Bayyinat (Evidence), 96: verse 6.

[308] Ibid. Sura Al-Suff (Battle Array), 61: verse 14.

guidance...." [309]. The term Al-Hukm is Hebrew in origin, it means wisdom, and reflects the Gospel. It is clarified in "He will teach him the Book and Wisdom, the Torah and the Gospel." [310] Those who perform the commands of the Torah and the Gospel are not the Jews, and not the Christians, but the Nazarenes of Beni Israel that Muhammad orders to copy their guidance.

"We gave Moses the Book, so do not be in any doubt about meeting it. We granted it to the Children of Israel for guidance. We even set some of them up as leaders to guide [people] at our command...". The Nazarenes of Beni Israel are intended in "setting up some of them as leaders" [311], and not the scholars Jews who are "the first Disbelievers in it, (the Qur'an)" [312]. The Nazarenes are "Out of Moses' folk [there grew] a nation who guided by means of the Truth and dealt justly by means of it." [313]

In the Qur'an "SAY: 'People of the Book, you will not make any point until you keep up the Torah and the Gospel, as well as anything that has been sent down to you by your Lord...'" [314]. Those who keep up the Torah and the Gospel are not the Jews, and not the Christians, but the Nazarenes of Beni Israel.

The Qur'an decrees that the religion of Moses and 'Isa as one religion. "He has instituted the religion for you ...and which We have inspired in you and recommended for Abraham, Moses and Jesus to maintain the religion and do not stir up any divisions within it..." [315] Again, this is not the religion of the Jews, nor that of Christians. It is the religion of the Nazarenes who join Moses and 'Isa in one religion. Not to differentiate among prophets is another principle in the Qur'an "SAY: "We believe in God...and what was given Moses and 'Isa and what was given the prophets by their Lord. We do not discriminate against any one of them and are committed [to live] in peace (Muslims) to Him. If they believe the same as you believe, then they are guided, while if they turn elsewhere, they will only fall into dissension..."[316] Same emphasis in "SAY: "We believe in God... and what was given Moses, 'Isa and the prophets by their Lord. We do not differentiate between any one of them, and we are committed to [live at] peace (Muslims) with Him." [317]

---

[309] Ibid. Sura t Al-Ina'am, 6: verses 89-90.

[310] Ibid. Sura Al-Imran (the House of Imran), 3: verse 48.

[311] Ibid. Sura Al-Sajadat (Worship or Adoration), 32: verses 23-24.

[312] Ibid. Sura of Al-Bakara (the Cow), 2: verses 41

[313] Ibid. Sura Al-A'raf (The Heights), 7: verse 159.

[314] Ibid. Sura Al-Ma'ida (The Table), 5: verse 68.

[315] Ibid. Sura Al-Shura (the Consultation), 42: verse 13.

[316] Ibid. Sura Al-Bakara (Cow), 2: verses 136-137.

[317] Ibid. Sura House of Imran, 3: verse 84.

Muslims indeed believe in both Moussa and 'Isa, and respect their codes, and only the Nazarenes of Beni Israel who have the same believe that Muhammad commanded his followers to copy their guidance.

Those who interpreted the Qur'an were ignorant of the role of the Nazarenes of Beni Israel in Hijaz before Islam. They rallied round the Call and dispersed in the Qur'an and were stuck with the interpretation of the reference of the Qur'an to Beni Israel. Every support or testimony given to the people of the Book was for the Nazarenes of Beni Israel; and every suspicion in the people of the Book or in Beni Israel was towards the Jews. In "...A witness from Beni Israel has testified concerning something similar to it...."[318] This witness from Beni Israel is not a Jew. He is a Nazarene from Beni Israel. No one of the Jews, who are "the first Disbelievers in it", testifies that they have something similar to the "Qur'an", or else they have to testify for Christ or for Muhammad! This never happened and will never happen to any Jew. A Jew who witnesses to testify for Christ or for Muhammad is a non-Jewish Jew and not a Jew anymore, according to Judaism as is considered converted to either Christianity or Islam.

Is the Qur'an a Work of Multiple Hands?

This question has been around and made hesitate to mention or comment, but I felt that readers would like what some historians and researchers points of view. Muslims believe that the Qur'an is from God. Skeptics of Islam tend to assume that it is the work of Muhammad. However, there is no real basis for accepting one single origin of the book, divine or human. For example traditional Jewish and most Christians believe that the Torah was authored by one person – Moses. Secular scholarship however considers the Torah to be a compilation of multiple different traditions with different authors, all brought together far later than Moses' supposed lifetime.

Concerning the Qur'an, some secular scholarship finds out that it exhibits many similarities to the Torah – multiple stories about the same thing. For example to Crone and Cook, "the Qur'an is strikingly lacking in overall structure, frequently obscure and inconsequential in both language and content, perfunctory in its linking of disparate materials, and given to the repetition of whole passages in variant versions. On this basis it can plausibly be argued that the book is the product of belated and imperfect editing of materials from a plurality of traditions." [319] While Salmon Reinach says: that

---

[318] Ibid. Sura Al-Ahkaf (the Dunes), 46: verse 10.

[319] Patricia Crone and Michael Cook, Hagarism: The Making of the Islamic World, (Cambridge, 1977) p. 18

"from the literary point of view, the Qur'an has little merit. Declamation, repetition, puerility, a lack of logic and coherence strike the unprepared reader at every turn. It is humiliating to the human intellect to think that this mediocre literature has been the subject of innumerable commentaries and that millions of men are still wasting time absorbing it". [320]

After reading the Noble Qur'an, I wondered why the same statement needs to be said over and over again if it is coming from a single source. What is worse, many of these duplicate statements differ in context and wording. Such ambiguity let historians like Reinach, Warraq, Katz and Bernard to profess that once the reader becomes aware of repletion, a lack of logic and coherence it becomes easier to understand their theory that the Qur'an is a work of multiple hands.[321]

---

[320] Reinach, Salomon, Orpheus: *A History of Religion*, (New York, 1932), p. 176

[321] Warraq, *Quest for the Historical Muhammad*, p. 9, and Katz, Bernard, *The Ways of an Atheist*, (Prometheus, 1999), p. 145

CHAPTER EIGHT

Islam Today

Islam is an Arabic word. It means "submission to God", or "acceptance of God's guidance". It is the name used to identify monotheistic religions spread before Islam in Syria and the Arabian Peninsula. The followers of Prophet Muhammad are also called Muslims belonging to Islam, the religion of Islam that related its origin to the traditions of Abraham, as Judaism and Hebrew Christian Nazarenes.

Today, Islam has a global following of approximately 1.4 billion adherents, accounting for 23.5 percent of the world population.[322] Today, the vast majority of Muslims are not Arabs and the largest Muslim population is that of Indonesia, estimated at 210 million.

The Basic Forms of Islam

Islam started as a religion but with more emphasis on statehood called Uma ruled by a Caliph. Disagreements over the choice of a new leader after the death of Prophet Muhammad resulted in the emergence of three basic forms of Islam:

The Sunnites

The 'Sunnites' (meaning 'traditional') represent those Muslims who did not question the legitimacy of the 'caliphs' (or 'successors' to the Prophet) who headed the Uma from the time of the Prophet's death.

---

[322] According to estimates published by the World Conference on Religion and Peace, New York, 1999

1. The Sunnites Islam recognizes four different schools of jurisprudence, each bearing the name of its founder.
2. The Hanifite (founded by Abu Hanifa Al-Nu'man who died in 767AD),
3. The Malikite (founded by Malik ibn Anas who died in 795 AD),
4. The Shafiite (founded by al-Shafi who died in 819 AD), and
5. The Hanbalite (founded by Ibn Hanbal who died in 855 AD).

A Sunni Muslim may choose to follow any of these four schools singly or in combination. In general, the Hanafite is seen as the most liberal, while the Hanbalite is considered the strictest. The Muslims of Turkey have been historically Hanafite and, in the Arab world, the Malikites predominate in North Africa and the Sudan, the Hanbalites in Saudi Arabia as well as the adoption of the Wahhabi movement, and the Shafiites in Egypt, Syria and other adjacent countries.

The Sunnites adhere to the observance of Ash-Sharia, the law of God. They have the following twelve Imams (Khalifas): [323]

1. Abu Bakr
2. Umar
3. Uthman
4. Ali
5. Mu'awiya
6. Yazid bin Mu'awiya
7. Abdul Malik bin Marwan
8. Walid bin Abdul Malik bin Marwan
9. Sulayman bin Abdul Malik bin Marwan
10. Umar bin Abdul Aziz
11. Yazid bin Abdul Malik bin Marwan
12. Hisham bin Abdul Malik bin Marwan

The Shiites

The 'Shiites' (meaning 'partisans') and according to a Sunni scholar Al Muhaddith Shah 'Abd al-'Aziz Dehlavi in his discussion of hadith relating to Ali and his Shiites writes: [324] "The title Shia was first given to those

---

[323] Taken from Sharra Fiqa Akbar, by Mulla Ali Qari, p 176 (publishers Muhammad Saeed and son, Qur'an Muhalla)

[324] Taken from "Tuhfa Ithna 'Ashariyyah," (Gift to the Twelvers) (Farsi edition p 18, publishers Sohail Academy, Lahore, Pakistan)

Muhajireen and Ansar who gave allegiance (bay'ah) to Ali [325] (Shiites add "may Allah enlighten his face" whenever his name is mentioned). They were his steadfast faithful followers during Ali's caliphate. They remained close to him; they always fought his enemies, and kept on following Ali's commands and prohibitions. The true Shi'as (Shiites) is those who came in 37 Hijri" (37 Hijri -the year Imam Ali fought Mu'awiya at Sifeen).

Shiites follow Imam Ja'far al-Sadiq whom they consider the teacher of the two Sunni Imams: Abu Hanifa al-Nu'man, and Malik Ibn Anas. The Shiites' school of Islam is called "the Jafari School" of Imam Ja'far al-Sadiq, who was born in 83 Hijriah and died in 148.

The Shiites follow the path of members of the house (Ahl-al-Bayt), which include Imam Ali, Fatima, al-Hasan and al-Husain who were all contemporaries of the Prophet and nurtured in his House.

Shiites pray "in the Name of Allah, the compassionate, the all-merciful Greeting of Allah be upon Muhammad and the pure members of his House" (Ahl-al-Bayt).

Shiites hold that both the Qur'an and Ahl-al-Bayt to be on the right path. Shiites have grasped the Qur'an, which sets their religion, and the Imams from Ahl-al-Bayt. They recite "Verily Allah intends to keep off from you every kind of uncleanness O' People of the House (Ahl-al- Bayt), and purify you a perfect purification." [326]

According to Shiites, they seek the truth and consider Sunnites unable to produce any argument to show them which of the four different jurists - the Hanafis, the Shafi'is, the Malikis and the Hanbalis - to follow. Shiites believe that the jurists were all acclaimed as very great and honest and just men. But they were aware that jurists' capacity, honesty, justice and greatness are not monopoly of these four persons only. Therefore, Shiites question how can it be "compulsory" to follow them only?

Clearly, the disagreements between the Shiites and the Sunnites are confined in two main areas:

1. The Caliphate (successor ship/leadership), which the Shiites believe, is the right of the Imams of Ahlul-Bayt –the people of the House. And

---

[325] Ali was the first cousin of the Prophet Mohammed and the husband of his eldest surviving child, Fatima. According to Shiite belief, he was designated by the Prophet as his successor, and endowed with divine guidance so that the community of Muslims would not go astray. In 662 AD, Ali was murdered and was buried at the city of Najaf in Iraq to become the most important Shiite shrine city and a Shiite religious center.

[326] Taken from (Sura Al-Ahzab- the clans 33:33), the last sentence of the verse.

2. The Islamic rule when there is no clear Qur'anic statement, nor is there a Hadith upon which Muslim schools have agreed.

The Shiites have adopted a creed that differs from that of the Ash'arites as far as the fundamental beliefs are concerned, and differs from the four schools of Sunni jurists as far as the laws, rites, and observances are concerned. The Shiites contemplate that it is rather the theological reasoning and not any sectarianism or prejudice which led them to adopt the creed of those Imams who belong to Ahl-al-Bayt of Prophet Muhammad, the Messenger of Allah.

The Shiites came to be organized into different communities, each developing special doctrines and rites. The majority Shiite group today, called the Twelver. Shiites Twelvers is the overwhelming majority of Shiites in the present day.

Shiites believe that a succession of Imams, each appointed by his predecessor from the line of Ali, possesses the same infallibility that Ali possessed. After Ali, only the third of these Imams, Ali's son Hussein made a bid to be an actual political ruler, and he was murdered in 680 AD, and was buried at the city of Karbala in Iraq to become the second most important Shiite shrine city.

In 941 AD, Shiite leaders declared that the 12th Imam had disappeared to return at the end of time. Around 1057 AD, a leading Shiite scholar called Tusi, migrated from Baghdad, where Sunnis had burned his house and books, to Najaf, where he began systematic teaching of Shiite learning. By the end of the 10th century, those qualified Shiite mullahs/scholars within the learned area or a seminary community within Najaf was referred to as "Al-Hawza" had already developed systems of theology and jurisprudence based on natural law, and established norms of behavior for the ordinary Shiite believers.

The Twelver refers to the twelve Imams of Ahl-al-Bayt. The Twelvers are:

1. Imam Abul-Hasan Ali ibn Abi Talib (al-Murtadha)
2. Imam Abu Muhammad al-Hassan (al-Mujtaba)
3. Imam Abu Abdallah al-Hussain bin Ali (Sayyid al-Shuhada)
4. Imam Abu Muhammad Ali bin al-Hussain (Zainul-'Abideen)
5. Imam Abu Ja'far Muhammad bin Ali (al-Baqir)
6. Imam Abu Abdallah Ja'far bin Muhammad (al-Sadiq)
7. Imam Abu Ibrahim Musa bin Ja'far (al-Kazim)
8. Imam Abu al-Hasan Ali bin Musa (al-Redha)
9. Imam Abu Ja'far Muhammad bin Ali (Taqi al-Jawaad)
10. Imam Abul-Hasan Ali bin Muhammad al-Hadi al-Naqi
11. Imam Abu Muhammad al-Hasan bin Ali (al- Askari)

12. Imam Abul-Qasim Muhammad bin al-Hasan (al-Mahdi)

Other important groups of Shiites are the Zaydi community of Yemen, and the Ismaili communities now headed by the Aga Khan Offshoots of such Shiite groups include the Druze, principally found in Lebanon, and the Alawites (or Nusayris) of the coastal mountains of Syria. The Shiites disagree with Sunnites in the observance of Ash-Sharia as the law of God. They maintain their own interpretations of this law.

Today, the Shiites are still those who pledged their allegiance to Ali, remained close to him, followed his orders and fought his enemies.

The Kharijites

The 'Kharijites' (meaning 'dissidents') are those Muslims who dissented from both the Sunnis and the Shiites by maintaining that the leaders of the Uma after the Prophet Muhammad should be elected, and that any believing and capable Muslim were eligible for election. Today, the Ibadi Muslims of Oman and some parts of North Africa represent the Kharijites. The Kharijites like the Shiites maintain their own interpretation of Ash-Sharia, the law of God.

Between the Dogma and the Law

From my point of view, there is no dispute between the people of the Book and the people of the Qur'an in Dogma (Al'Aqida), but the dispute are in the Law (Ash-Sharia').

The dogma is a religion - a faith in God's religion – and the Law is based on ceremonial rituals and tribal symbols combined to form a unique system of distinguishing behaviors reflected in social and political activities of the different human races. Such facts are clearly expressed in God's words as expressed in An-Nahl "And if Allah please, He would certainly make you a single nation. But He causes to err whom He pleases and guides whom He pleases; and most certainly you will be questioned as to what you did." [327]

God want us to be diversified to compete in doing what is just and useful to mankind and He will question us on our actions. He never made the diversification in His religious dogma. As revealed in Al-Ma'eda, "...for every one of you did we appoint a law and a way, and if Allah had pleased He would have made you (all) a single people. But that He might try you in what He gave you, therefore strive with one another to hasten to virtuous

---

[327] Sura An-Nahl – (The Bees), 16: verse 93.

deeds; to Allah is your return, of all (of you), so He will let you know that in which you differed." [328]

The major lessons that the Muslims should not forget are taught in the following verse: "Surely Allah has bought of the believers their persons and their property for this, that they shall have the garden. They fight in Allah's way, so they slay and are slain, a promise which is binding on Him in the Torah and the Gospel (Injeel) and the Qur'an, and who is more faithful to his covenant than Allah? Rejoice therefore in the pledge, which you have made, and that is the mighty achievement." [329]

---

[328] Sura Al-Mae'da –(The Table) 5: verse 48.

[329] Sura At-Tawba –(Repentance) 9: verse 111.

CHAPTER NINE

The Qur'an according to God's Holy Book

"...He has chosen you, and has imposed no difficulties on you in religion; it is the cult of your father Abraham. It is He Who has named you Muslims, both before and in this (Revelation); that the Messenger may be a witness for you, and ye are witnesses for mankind! So establish regular Prayer, give regular Charity, and hold fast to Allah! He is your Protector - the Best to protect and the Best to help!" [330]

It is clearly stated that those who believed in the One God, the monotheists, are called Muslims before the Prophet's revealed message of Islam. "Our Grand-Father" Abraham surrendered to God, and all successors, Prophets and Messengers, were Muslims. They surrendered their lives to God.

The Noble Qur'an called for the belief in one God. A call guided by the written Book of God. The Qur'an refers to the Holy Book as One inscribed in a guarded and preserved Tablet. Therefore, the Noble Qur'an is not an independent book. It is revealed from the Holy Book that already been known in the Torah and the Gospels.

Those who read the Noble Qur'an, according to the sequence of the revelation as organized in Al-Qur'an Al-Amiri, can observe the phenomenon of its development. In Mecca, the revealed verses were based on the pure teachings of the Gospels. In Al-Medina, a shift toward the Hanifa's national approach was observed, while sticking to the same creed and the written monotheistic Call that Muslims and the people of the Book share and believes in.

---

[330] Sura Al-Hajj – (The Pilgrimage) 22: verse 78.

Islam as revealed in Mecca

The Prophet Muhammad preaches in Mecca the belief in Allah and the Last Day wisely and gravely for 12 years from 610 AD to 622 AD. His Call was according to the Book in all its aspects: the source, the subject, the method, and the related stories. For twelve years, Muhammad was preaching to convince his tribe and the Arabs and the unbelievers without going into any religious, political or national fight of any kind with the people of the Book in all of the 86 Chapters of the Qur'an revealed upon him in Mecca. The only truth revealed shows the faith in the holy unity of the people of the Book.

In the early phase of Islam in Mecca is based on the environment, the chapters (Al Suwar) are short full of pledges and request for preparing themselves for the Judgment Day by our acts and good behaviors. "Did He not find you an orphan and give you shelter? And He found you wandering, and He gave you guidance. And find you in want and make you to be free from want?" [331] Notice the close similarity to the teaching in Christianity in the Judgment Day, the Lord will accept those who did it for one of these, the least of my brethren, you did it for me; "for I was hungry and you gave me to eat; I was thirsty and you gave me to drink; I was a stranger and you took me in; naked and you covered me; sick and you visited me ..." [332]

The middle phase of Islam in Mecca is limited between the immigration to Ethiopia and the Prophet personal immigration to At-Tae'f between 615 AD and 620 AD. The chapters have the rhetoric approach in presenting the stories about earlier prophets as good examples to his people, using Allah's name as "Ar-Rahman" (the Beneficent). "Say: Call upon Allah or call upon, Rahman (the Beneficent Allah); whichever you call upon, He has the best names; and do not utter your prayer with a very raised voice nor be silent with regard to it, and seek a way between these." [333] Later on, the term Rahman was never used in Al-Medina.

The last phase of Islam in Mecca is limited to the period between the immigration to At-Tae'f (620 AD) and the great immigration to Al-Medina (622 AD). It is the period of curiosity and hesitation to explore the creation of a new national identity and independence from the people of the Book.

---

[331] Sura Ad-Dhuha – (The Morning Hours) 93: verses 6-8.

[332] The New Testament, St. Mathrew Chapter 25, verses 35-36, The Holy Bible, Rembrandt Edition, Abradale Press Inc., New York, 1959

[333] Sura Al-Isra' – (The Night Journey) 17: verse 110

"Verily, this brotherhood (nation) of yours is a single brotherhood (nation), and I am your Lord, so serve Me." [334]

The source:

The Qur'an considers itself as a copy of the Holy Book revealed in an Arabic tongue. "And this is in the Books of the earliest (Revelation). The Books of Abraham and Moses" [335] "Nay, is he not acquainted with what is in the Books of Moses - And of Abraham who fulfilled his engagements?" [336] "They say: "Why does he not bring us a sign from his Lord? Has not a Clear Sign come to them of all that was in the former Books of revelation?" [337] "Verily this is a Revelation from the Lord of the Worlds: With it came down the spirit of Faith and Truth."[338]

I copied some of the verses that show the source of the Prophet's inspiration, the Holy Book, as revealed in "And thus did We reveal to you an inspired book by Our command. You did not know what the Book was, nor (what) the faith (was), but We made it a light, guiding thereby whom We please of Our servants; and most surely you show the way to the right path." [339] Again, "And they say: Why are not signs sent down upon him from his Lord? Say: The signs are only with Allah, and I am only a plain warner."[340]

The subject:

After specifying the source, the subject becomes obvious a Call to believe in God and the Last Day. It is stated in the verse: "Those were the (prophets) who received Allah's guidance: Copy the guidance they received; Say: "No rewards for this do I ask of you: This is no less than a message for the nations." [341] Then we observe a clear reference to the Book of Moses "And before this, was the Book of Moses as a guide and a mercy: And this Book

---

[334] Sura Al-Anbyia – (The Prophets) 21: verse 92. (The verse is also repeated in Al-Mu'menoon – The Believers 23:52).

[335] Sura Al-Ala - The Most High) 87: verses 18-9.

[336] Sura An-Najm - (The Star) 53: verses 36-7.

[337] Sura Taha 20: verse 133.

[338] Sura Ash-Shu'ara - (The Poets) 26:192.

[339] Sura Ash-Shura -(Consultation) 42: verse 52.

[340] Sura Al-Ankaboot - (The Spider) 29: verse 50.

[341] Sura Al-Anaam - Cattle or Livestock 6:90).

confirms (it) in the Arabic tongue; to admonish the unjust, and as Glad Tidings to those who do right." [342]

Again "Can they be (like) those who accept a Clear (Sign) from their Lord and whom a witness from Himself does teach, as did the Book of Moses before it, - a guide and a mercy? They believe therein; but those of the Sects that reject it, - the Fire will be their promised meeting-place. Be not then in doubt thereon: for it is the truth from thy Lord: yet many among men do not believe!" [343] Strongly the Qur'an announces "Who does more wrong than such as forge a lie against Allah, or deny His Signs? But never will prosper those who sin." [344]

The Method:

Now by looking at the method that the revelation called for was based on mixing religion with social rectification. The truth was that the social alteration as the real reason for the religious adjustment. Muhammad started preaching the Gospel in Arabic in Arabia in the same way that St. John Chrysostom, "golden-mouthed" [345] used to do two centuries before him and as well as St. Afram the Syrian who was preaching in Aramaic in Syria.

Jesus Christ started roaming the Palestinian villages preaching the people "to repent because the Kingdom of God is getting near," and we read in the Qur'an a call on the people "Surely to your Lord is the return." [346] "But ye prefer the life of the world. Although the Hereafter is better and more lasting" [347]

The Gospel of Jesus Christ starts by the Sermon on the Mount "... Blessed are you poor, for yours in the kingdom of God. Blessed are you who hunger now, for you shall be satisfied. Blessed are you who weep now, for you shall laugh …. But woe to you rich! For you are now having your comfort, Woe to you who are filled! For you shall hunger. Woe to you who laugh now! For you shall mourn and weep. Woe to you when all men speak well of you! In the selfsame manner their fathers used to treat the prophets." [348]

Following the same pattern, Muhammad preaches: "Woe to every (kind of) scandalmonger and-backbiter, Who piled up wealth and laid it

---

[342] Sura Al-Ahqaf – (The Dunes) 46: verse 12.

[343] Sura Hood – (Hud) 11: verse 17.

[344] Sura Yunus - (Jonah) 10: verse 17

[345] So called on account of his eloquence

[346] Sura Al-Alaq – (the Clot) 96:verse 8

[347] Sura Al-Ala – (The Most High) 87: verses 16-7

[348] The New Testament according to St. Luke chapter 6 verses 20-26, The Holy Bible, Rembrandt Edition, Abradale Press Inc., New York, 1959

by," [349] "Therefore, as for the orphan, do not oppress (him). And as for him, who asks; do not chide (him)" [350] "Have you considered him who calls the judgment a lie? That is the one who treats the orphan with harshness," [351] "Ah, woe unto worshipers. Who are heedless of their prayer; Who would be seen (at worship), Yet refuse small kindnesses!" [352] "Woe to the defrauders, Who, when they take the measure (of their dues) from men take it fully, But when they measure out to others or weigh out for them, they are deficient." [353] Prophet Muhammad made it clear that his message in Mecca does not differ from the earliest revelation. He stresses the fact that God's Words can't be changed: "They shall have good news in this world's life and in the hereafter; there is no changing the words of Allah; that is the mighty achievement." [354]

To those who are in doubt of Muhammad's revelation, the prophet refers them to the earlier Book. "But if you are in doubt as to what We have revealed to you, ask those who read the Book before you; certainly the truth has come to you from your Lord, so be in no wise of those in doubt." [355]

Prophet Muhammad accepts the friendship of Christians and shows his doubt in trusting the Jews as revealed in the following verse: "Certainly you will find the most violent of people in enmity for those who believe (to be) the Jews and those who are poly theists. And you will certainly find the nearest in friendship to those who believe (to be) those who say: We are Christians; this is because there are priests and monks among them and because they do not behave proudly." [356]

The Prophet came to teach the people in Arabia the Book that they did not read before for their ignorance of the prevailing languages at that time: the Aramaic, Syriac and Greek. The following verses qualify our statement: "And most surely this is a revelation from the Lord of the worlds. The Faithful Spirit has descended with it, Upon your heart that you may be of the warners, in simply Arabic language. And most surely the same is in the scriptures of the ancients." [357] Again in "I swear by the Book that makes things clear: Surely We have made it an Arabic Qur'an that you may understand." [358]

---

[349] Sura Al-Humaza – (The Traducer) 104: verses 1-2

[350] Sura Ad-Dhuha – (The Morning hours) 93: verses 9-10.

[351] Sura al-Maun - (Almsgiving) 104: verses 1-2

[352] Ibid. verses 4-6

[353] Sura Al-Mutaffifin - (Defrauding) 83: verses 1-3

[354] Sura Yunus – (Jonah) 10: verse 64

[355] Ibid. verse 94

[356] Sura Al-Maeda – (The Table 5: verse 82

[357] Sura Ash-Shu'ara – (The poets) 26: verses 192-6.

[358] Sura Az-Zukhruf – (Ornaments) 43: verses 2-3

The Arab prophet believes that Jesus Christ was supported by the Holy Spirit and with the direct revelation of the Gospel. "Those messengers We endowed with gifts, some above others: To one of them Allah spoke; others He raised to degrees; And We gave clear proofs (miracles) to Isa son of Maryam, and strengthened him with the Holy Spirit. ...." [359] And in the verse, "And in their footsteps We sent Isa son of Maryam, confirming the Law that had come before him. We sent him the Gospel therein was guidance and light, and confirmation of the Law that had come before him: guidance, and an admonition to those who fear Allah." [360]

The newly born child Baby Jesus spoke in the Qur'an, and said: "I am indeed a servant of Allah: He has given me revelation and made me a prophet..." [361] The Gospel teaches the worship of Allah, the Only God. It is revealed in the Qur'an Jesus saying: "(I have come to you), to attest the Law which was before me. And to make lawfully to you part of what was (Before) forbidden to you; I have come to you with a Sign from your Lord. So fear Allah, and obey me. It is Allah Who is my Lord and your Lord; then worships Him. This is a Way that is straight." [362]

Clearly, the Arab Prophet recognizes the earlier Book and directs his audience to Allah for guidance and "Allah would explain to you and guide you by the examples of those who were before you, and would turn to you in mercy. Allah is All-Knowing, All-Wise." [363] The Prophet Muhammad honors equally the Law of Moses, the Gospel of Jesus, and his Qur'an as it is revealed "that they shall have the garden (of Paradise) ... a promise which is binding on Him in the Torah (Law) and the Injeel (the Gospel) and the Qur'an..." [364] Indeed, it is always true to say that Jesus' Gospel was and still is a guidance and light, as it is seen stated in the Qur'an.

Islam as revealed in Al-Medina

In 622 AD, Prophet Muhammad relocated from Mecca to Al-Medina after signing the 'Aqaba military agreement. The date of the prophet's immigration starts the first year of the Islamic Calendar (As-Sana Al-Hujriah). In Al-Medina, a new direction appears in the prophet's intention, a shift from the religious Call in Mecca to a Call for State building in Al-Medina. The new

---

[359] Sura Al_Baqara – (The Cow) 2: verse 253.

[360] Sura Al-Mae'da – (The Table) 5: verse 46

[361] Sura (Maryam – (Mary) 19: verse 30.

[362] Sura Al-E-Imran – (The House of 'Imran) 3: verses 56-7

[363] Sura An-Nisa – (Women) 4: verse 26

[364] Sura At-Tawba – (Repentance) 9: verse 111.

development is to transfer to statehood by laying the foundation of Islam from within through decrees and from without by declaring the holy Jihad.

The first phase in Al-Medina

The first phase in Al-Medina starts with year 622 AD or 1 Hijriah and ends with the Al-Hadibia agreement in 628 AD or 6 H. The atmosphere of that phase was best described in chapter Al-Hadid or Al-Hadeed. "... and We have made the iron, wherein is great violence and advantages to men (in matters of war). And that Allah may know who helps Him and His apostles in the secret; surely Allah is Strong, Mighty." [365] And a middle creed is "The Religion before Allah is Islam (submission to His Will). And those to whom the Book had been given did not show opposition but after knowledge had come to them, out of envy among themselves; and whoever disbelieves in the communications of Allah then surely Allah is quick in reckoning." [366] And middle in legislating ways and means, "Allah desires to explain to you, and to guide you into the ways of those before you, and to turn to you (mercifully), and Allah is Knowing, Wise." [367]

The prophet sets the plan for his new direction to establish a "middle (in-between) Nation" and goals, "Thus We have appointed you a middle nation, that you may be witnesses against mankind, and that the messenger may be a witness against you. And We appointed the kiblah, which you formerly observed only that We might know him who followed the messenger, from him who turned on his heels. In truth it was a hard (test) save for those whom Allah guided. But it was not Allah's purpose that your faith should be in vain, for Allah is Full of Pity, Merciful toward mankind." [368]

Contrary to what Muhammad started in Mecca, where he was working closely with the people of the Book. Due to political reasons, the prophet decides to separate between the infidel Arabs and those who have the Book, by accepting the creed of the people of the Book and most of the traditions of the infidel Arabs who believe in many gods. A middle nation is between the Nazarenes and the Hebrews too, neither Christian nor Hebraic. Indeed, the new religion is from both Hebraic and Christianity. It is in-between both accepting Isa and Isa's teachings and considering them an extension to Moses' prophecy and the other prophets' messages after him.

---

[365] Sura Al-Hadid – (The Iron) 57: verse 25.

[366] Sura Al-E-Imran – (The House of 'Imran) 3: verse19

[367] Sura An-Nisa – (The Women) 4: verse 26

[368] Sura Al-Baqara – (The Cow) 2: verse 143

A middle nation will not be "Nazarene-Christian" so that it will not dissolve in the Christian Roman Empire, but a unique Arab Nation with new declared "Nazarene-Islamic" characteristics.

The new religion does not accept the divinity of Isa as "claimed" by Christians and does not deny Isa as the Hebrew do. Prophet Muhammad never denies the revelation of God to Isa as the Hebrew insists upon that denial. In his way, Prophet Muhammad sees a unification of religions through the unification in God.

Therefore we conclude that Islam started in Mecca as a "Religion", and it became a "State" in Al-Medina. And so, the main components of the Nation are both the religion and the state. The middle nation that was brought out to the people in Al-Medina is the newly established religious community of Islam.

The second phase in Medina

The second phase in Al-Medina was characterized by establishing the State of Islam and to direct the military attacks in all directions after conquering of Al-Hadibia until the death of the Prophet. In this phase, the Prophet was calling on the people of the Book to come to an agreement, "Say: 'O People of the Book! Come to common terms as between us and you: That we worship none but Allah; that we associate no partners with him; that we erect not, from among ourselves, Lords and patrons other than Allah.' If then they turn back, say: "Bear witness that we (at least) are Muslims (bowing to Allah's Will)." [369]

The New Religion in Al-Medina: Dispute with the Hebrews

The majority of the people in Al-Medina were Hebrews, with a Nazarenes minority. "Al-Medina was a caravan city located some 280 miles north of Mecca." [370] Al-Medina's population was more than in Mecca for both Hebrews and Christians. "The influential Jewish presence in the city played a decisive role in the power struggle there." [371] The new prophet has to define his position from the beginning. "According to traditions, it was

---

[369] Sura Al-E-Imran – (The House of 'Imran) 3: verse 64

[370] Barbara Ann Kipfer, ed,. "Encyclopedia of Archaeology," New York: Kluwer Academic/Plenum, 2000, pp. 342-43.

[371] John A. Garraty and Peter Gay, eds., "The Colombbia History of the World," New York: Harper &Row, 1972, p.260.

the Arab people of Medina who invited Muhammad to make their city his headquarters and to mediate among them." [372]

Sura Al-Baqara (The Cow) has kept for us the early relationship between Muhammad and the Hebrews of Al-Medina. We notice that the dialogue that took place in the verses was addressed to the Hebrews of the Book directly, with no relations to the Nazarenes except accidentally. It seems that the Arab Hebrews in Al-Medina were apprehensive to accept Muhammad who tried to convince them to accept his message similar to the Hebrews in Mecca. The Qur'anic verse: "And believe in what I reveal, confirming the revelation which is with you, and be not the first to reject Faith therein..." [373] This verse verifies the hesitancy of the Hebrews.

Then we observe Muhammad warning his followers from the Hebrews in: "Do you then hope that they would believe in you, and a party from among them indeed used to hear the Word of Allah, then altered it after they had understood it, and they know (this)." [374] The supporters of Muhammad and those believers at that time in the oneness of the religion, they tried to bring the Arab Hebrew tribes to their side to strengthen their cause. But the Hebrews isolated themselves and started in criticizing the new teaching of Muhammad.

Friction started and different opinions surfaced to express enmity. Muhammad argued their opinions by the revealed verses: "Woe, then, to those who write the book with their hands and then say: This is from Allah, so that they may take for it a small price. Therefore woe to them for what their hands have written and woe to them for what they earn. And they say: Fire shall not touch us but for a few days, Say: Have you received a promise from Allah, then Allah will not fail to perform His promise, nor do you speak against Allah what you do not know?" [375]

Fire is never meant to be for the people of the Book, because God promises them to inherit Paradise. Muhammad felt that the Hebrews were willing to fight against the Muslims, but Muslims were encouraged by the revealed verse: "They shall by no means harm you but with a slight evil. And if they fight with you they shall turn (their) backs to you, then shall they not be helped." [376]

So, the prophet challenges the Hebrews, "Say: 'If the last Home, with Allah, be for you specially, and not for anyone else, then seek you for death,

---

[372] Al-Sayyed Abd el-Aziz Salem, "Tarikh al-Dawlah al-Arabiyyah," [History of the Arab Nation] Beirut: Dar al-Nahdah al-Arabiyyah, pp. 228-38.

[373] Sura Al-Baqara – (The Cow) 2: verse 41.

[374] Ibid. verse 75

[375] Ibid. verses 79-80

[376] Ibid. verse 111

if you are sincere."' [377] But the Hebrew insists on being the chosen people to inherit Paradise. We observe a number of verses identify the Hebrews' conspiracies that Islam warns of. The Hebrews rejected Islam after they were told about its true revelation "Surely the (true) religion with Allah is Islam, and those to whom the Book had been given did not show opposition but after knowledge had come to them, out of envy among themselves; ..." [378] It is stated that: "...Allah gives the kingdom to whomsoever He pleases and takes away the kingdom from whomsoever He pleases, and He exalts whom He pleases and abases whom He pleases in His hand is the good ..." [379]

The Hebrews tried to deceit the Muslims as revealed in "A party of the followers of the Book desire that they should lead you astray, and they lead not astray but themselves, and they do not perceive. O followers of the Book! Why do you disbelieve in the communications of Allah while you witness (them)?" [380]

"O followers of the Book! Why do you confound the truth with the falsehood and hide the truth while you know? And a party of the followers of the Book says: Avow belief in that which has been revealed to those who believe, in the first part of the day, and disbelieve at the end of it, perhaps they go back on their religion. And do not believe but in him who follows your religion. Say: Surely the (true) guidance is the guidance of Allah-- That one may be given (by Him) the like of what you were given; or that they would contend with you by an argument before your Lord. Say: Surely, grace is in the hand of Allah. He gives it to whom He pleases; and Allah is Ample-giving, Knowing." [381]

So Prophet Muhammad warns his followers from the attempts of the Hebrews as revealed in "O you who believe! If you obey a party from among those who have been given the Book, they will turn you back as unbelievers after you have believed." [382]

Muhammad urges his followers to hold to Islam as the right path: "But how can you disbelieve while it is you to whom the communications of Allah are recited, and among you is His Messenger? And whoever holds fast to Allah, he indeed is guided to the right path." [383]

The Hebrews tried to compete with God's revealed verses to the limit of throwing lies on Him. This verse reveals that in "Most surely there is a

---

[377] Ibid. verse 94

[378] Sura Al-E-Imraan – (The House of 'Imraan) 3: verse 19

[379] Ibid. verse 27

[380] Ibid. verses 69-70

[381] Ibid. verses 71-73

[382] Ibid. verse 100

[383] Ibid. verse 101

party amongst those who distort the Book with their tongue that you may consider it to be (a part) of the Book. And they say, It is from Allah, while it is not from Allah, and they tell a lie against Allah whilst they know." [384]

Muhammad repeats with warning his followers to beware from the Jews as revealed in "O you who believe! Do not take for intimate friends from among others than your own people; they do not fall short of inflicting loss upon you; they love what distresses you; vehement hatred has already appeared from out of their mouths, and what their breasts conceal is greater still. Indeed, We have made the communications clear to you, if you will understand. Lo! You are they who will love them while they do not love you, and you believe in the Book (in) the whole of it; and when they meet you they say: We believe, and when they are alone, they bite the ends of their fingers in rage against you. Say: Die in your rage; surely Allah knows what is in the breasts. If good befalls you, it grieves them, and if an evil afflicts you, they rejoice at it; and if you are patient and guard yourselves, their scheme will not injure you in any way; surely Allah comprehends what they do." [385]

Through such continuous arguments and warnings against the Hebrews, those who followed Isa Bin Maryam or His priests were excluded as revealed in "They are not all alike; of the followers of the Book there is an upright party; they recite Allah's communications in the nighttime and they adore (Him). They believe in Allah and the last day, and they enjoin what is right and forbid the wrong and they strive with one another in hastening to good deeds, and those are among the good. And whatever good they do, they shall not be denied it, and Allah knows those who guard (against evil)." [386] Nazarenes/ Christians are proud of the credentials that the Prophet Muhammad bestowed upon them through the ages. He witnesses the righteousness of the faith in Christianity and their Gospel that they behold in their hands during the prophet's period.

Islam is the Religion of Abraham

The arguments between Prophet Muhammad and the Hebrews turned into conflict and dispute. Chapters Al-Baqara, Al-E-Imran, An-Nisa and Al-Ma'eda confirm and analyze the dialogue and arguments that took place between the Hebrews and the Prophet. The Qur'an of Prophet Muhammad cleverly withdrew Abraham from being a Hebrew to being a Muslim. "And when his Lord tried Abraham with certain words, he fulfilled them. He

---

[384] Ibid. verse 78

[385] Ibid. verses 118-20

[386] Ibid. verses 113-15

said: Surely I will make you an Imam of mankind. Ibrahim said: And of my offspring? My covenant does not include the unjust, said He." [387] The Qur'an made it clear that the Jews are the unjust offspring of Abraham.

"Our Lord! Make us both submissive (Muslims) to You and (raise) from our offspring a nation submitting to You, and show us our ways of devotion and turn to us (mercifully), surely You are the Oft-returning (to mercy), the Merciful. Our Lord! And raise up in them a Messenger from among them who shall recite to them Your communications and teach them the Book and the wisdom, and purify them; surely You are the Mighty, the Wise." [388]

The Noble Qur'an competently presented the sect of Abraham as Islam before the Hebrew considers Abraham as their father. "And who forsakes the religion of Abraham but he who makes himself a fool, and most certainly We chose him in this world, and in the hereafter he is most surely among the righteous." [389]

In the Holy Qur'an, Ismail (the grandfather of the Arabs) came first before Isaac to give his offspring the heredity of his religion and nations and the right of prophecy that shaped Prophet Muhammad. "Say: We believe in Allah and (in) that which had been revealed to us, and (in) that which was revealed to Abraham and Ismail and Isaac and Yaqoub and the tribes. And (in) that which was given to Musa and Isa, and (in) that which was given to the prophets from their Lord, we do not make any distinction between any of them, and to Him do we submit." [390]

Again the Qur'an shows that Al-Ka'ba in Mecca is the only House of Abraham. "And when We made the House a pilgrimage (Mecca) for men and a (place of) security, and: Appoint for yourselves a place of prayer on the standing-place of Abraham. And We enjoined Abraham and Ismail saying: Purify My House for those who visit (it) and those who abide (in it) for devotion and those who bow down (and) those who prostrate themselves. And when Ibrahim said: My Lord, make it a secure town and provide its people with fruits, such of them as believe in Allah and the last day. He said: And whoever disbelieves, I will grant him enjoyment for a short while, then I will drive him to the chastisement of the fire; and it is an evil destination. And when Abraham and Ismail raised the foundations of the House: Our Lord! Accept from us; surely You are the Hearing, the Knowing:" [391]

The in-between (medium) nation merges to become an independent nation away from Judaism and the strong influence of the Jews in Al-Medina

---

[387] Sura Al-Baqara – (The Cow) 2: verse 124

[388] Ibid. verses 128-29

[389] Ibid. verse 130

[390] Ibid. verse 136

[391] Ibid. verses 125-27

manifested mainly in the shift of direction of prayer to the East (Al-Kiblah). The following verses explicitly tell us that "The fools among the people will say: What has turned them from their Kiblah that they had? Say: The East and the West belong only to Allah. He guides whom He likes to the right path. And thus We have made you a medium nation that you may be the bearers of witness to the people and (that) the Messenger may be a bearer of witness to you. And We did not make that which you would have to be the Kiblah but that We might distinguish him who follows the Messenger from him who turns back upon his heels. And this was surely hard except for those whom Allah has guided aright; and Allah was not going to make your faith to be fruitless; most surely Allah is Affectionate, Merciful to the people." [392]

The verse "Allah has certainly heard the saying of those who said: Surely Allah is poor and we are rich. I will record what they say, and their killing the prophets unjustly, and I will say: Taste the chastisement of burning" [393] was revealed after the battle of "Uhhud" to indicate its impact and the impact of the dispute. The Hebrews revealed their true feelings towards the Arab Prophet in the verse "(Those are they) who said: Surely Allah has enjoined us that we should not believe in any messenger until he brings us an offering that the fire consumes. Say: Indeed, there came to you messengers before me with clear arguments and with that which you demand; why then did you kill them if you are truthful?" [394]

And in the verse "But if they reject you, so indeed were rejected before you messengers who came with clear arguments (miracles) and scriptures and the illuminating Book." [395] The conflict became obvious in the verse "You shall certainly be tried respecting your wealth and your souls, and you shall certainly hear from those who have been given the Book before you and from those who are polytheists much annoying talk. And if you are patient and guard (against evil), surely this is one of the affairs (which should be) determined upon." [396]

That dispute causes the division between the Jews and the followers of Prophet Muhammad. It was based on tribal politics and sects but not on religion or dogma. It was related to a group of those tribes and it never reflected the conditions among all.

The last revealed verses in the House of 'Imran chapter states: "And most surely of the followers of the Book there are those who believe in Allah and (in) that which has been revealed to you and (in) that which has been revealed

---

[392] Ibid. verses 142-43

[393] Ibid. verse 182

[394] Ibid. verse 183

[395] Ibid. verse 184

[396] Ibid. verse 186

to them, being lowly before Allah. They do not take a small price for the communications of Allah; these it is that have their reward with their Lord; surely Allah is quick in reckoning." [397] And "O you who believe! be patient and excel in patience and remain steadfast, and be careful of (your duty to) Allah, that you may be successful." [398]

---

[397] Sura Al-E-Imraan – (The House of 'Imraan) 3: verse 199
[398] Ibid. verse 200

CHAPTER TEN

Jesus Christ in the Qur'an

Jesus is called in Greek Usus. In Iraq, Christians translated it into Arabic as 'Isu, and referred to it also as 'Isa. Nestorius, Bishop of Constantinople, as shown in the previous chapter, believed and taught that the Virgin Mary gave birth to a man, Jesus Christ, not God, the "Logos" ("The Word," Son of God). Consequently, the Virgin Mary should be called "Christotokos," "Mother of Christ" and not "Theotokos," "Mother of God."

Nestorius over emphasized the human nature of Christ at the expense of His divine nature. He called, The Lord Jesus Christ, as one person, not two separate "people": the Man, Jesus and the Son of God, Logos. And this is how the term "Jesus Son of Mary or 'Isa Bin Maryam" came to existence before the birth of Islam.

While the Orthodox Catholic Church through its councils decreed that the Lord Jesus Christ, the Son of God (Logos), is complete God and complete man, with a rational soul and body. The Virgin Mary is "Theotokos" because she gave birth not to man but to God who became man. The union of the two natures of Christ took place in such a fashion that one did not disturb the other.

The following attempt analyzes the verses, in relation to The Lord Jesus Christ, as revealed in the Noble Qur'an.

'Isa Bin Maryam is a Sign at His Birth

"She said: How can I have a son when no mortal has touched me, neither have I been unchaste? He said: Even so; your Lord says: It is easy to Me: and that We may make him a sign to men and a mercy from Us and it is a matter which has been decreed."[399]

---

[399] Sura Maryam (Mary) 19: verses 20-21

The Qur'an describes the birth of Jesus as the greatest miracles of God, "He only says to it, 'Be,' and it is!" God sends His Angel to Virgin Maryam with the good tidings to have her pure son without being touched by a mortal. She said: "O my Lord! How shall I have a son when no man has touched me?" He said: "Even so: Allah creates what He pleases: When He has decreed a plan, He only says to it, 'Be,' and it is!" [400]

Jesus' pure and unique birth is from God's Spirit as stated clearly in the following verse: "And she who guarded her chastity, so We breathed into her of Our Spirit and made her and her son a sign for the peoples." [401] Precisely referred to Jesus in "...His word which He conveyed unto Mary and a spirit from Him..." [402]

The Qur'an confesses that Jesus is a unique prophet by birth. The newly born Jesus speaks in defense of His Mother and of His prophecy. "And the throes (of childbirth) compelled her to betake herself to the trunk of a palm tree. She said: Oh, would that I had died before this, and had been a thing quite forgotten!" "Then (the child) called out to her from beneath her: Grieve not, surely your Lord has made a stream to flow beneath you; And shake towards you the trunk of the palm tree, it will drop on you fresh ripe dates:

"So eat and drink and refresh the eye. Then if you see any mortal, say: Surely I have vowed a fast to the Beneficent Allah, so I shall not speak to any man today. And she came to her people with him, carrying him (with her). They said: O Maryam! surely you have done a strange thing.

"O sister of Haroun! your father was not a bad man, nor, was your mother an unchaste woman. But she pointed to him. They said: How should we speak to one who was a child in the cradle? He said: Surely I am a servant of Allah; He has given me the Book and made me a prophet; And He has made me blessed wherever I may be, and He has enjoined on me Prayer and Charity so long as I live;" [403]

The above verses are self-explanatory to show the most miraculous and uniqueness birth of Jesus Christ as revealed to the Arab Prophet in Mecca.

'Isa Bin Maryam is a Sign during His Early Life

The Qur'an did not specify where Jesus spent his childhood except in the following verse. To distinguish the location from being a desert, the verse describes the place by a high ground, a place of flocks and furnished with

---

[400] Sura Al-E-Imran – (The House of 'Imran) 3: verse 47

[401] Sura Al-Anbiya – (The Prophets) 21: verse 91

[402] Sura An-Nisa – (Women) 4: verse 171

[403] Sura Maryam – (Mary) 19: verse 23-31

water springs. "And We made the Son of Maryam and his mother a Sign, and We gave them a shelter on a lofty ground having meadows and springs." [404] At Jesus' birth, Allah gave Him the Perfect and Complete Revelation of the Book. Jesus was more than human and more than a prophet, we hear Him at the moment of His Birth saying, "...He has given me revelation (the Book) and made me a prophet..."

By the inspiration of the Holy Spirit Jesus' life is stimulated, and by God's permission Jesus performs miracles. "When Allah will say: O Isa Bin Maryam! Remember My favor on you and on your mother, when I strengthened you I with the Holy Spirit, you spoke to the people in the cradle and I when of old age. And when I taught you the Book and the wisdom and the Tawrat and the Injeel; And when you determined out of clay a thing like the form of a bird by My permission, then you breathed into it and it became a bird by My permission. And you healed the blind and the leprous by My permission; and when you brought forth the dead by My permission. And when I withheld the children of Israel from you when you came to them with clear arguments, but those who disbelieved among them said: This is nothing but clear enchantment." [405]

'Isa Bin Maryam is a Sign by His Message

"We have made some of these messengers to excel the others among them are they to whom Allah spoke, and some of them He exalted by (many degrees of) rank. And We gave clear miracles to Isa son of Maryam, and strengthened Him with the Holy Spirit..." [406] We also have seen another reference to "Isa" and the Holy Spirit in Al-Ma'eda's verse above.

No doubt that the Qur'an verifies the inspiration of the Holy Spirit of God to Jesus "Isa Bin Maryam" in His message that we celebrate and believe in.

The concept of Spirit in the Qur'an is vague as we observe in "...And they ask you about the Spirit. Say: The Spirit is one of the commands of my Lord, and you are not given at all of knowledge but a little." [407] But, we have a feeling that by calling the power of the Spirit associated with 'Isa Bin Maryam alone as Holy gives it a different meaning from any other spirit that relates to the other prophets. The term Holy denotes God's Spirit and not a reference to an angel such as Jebreel (Gabriel). Because the power of the Holy Spirit

---

[404] Sura Al-Mumenoon – (The Believers) 23: verse 50

[405] Sura Al-Maeda – (The Table) 5: verse 110.

[406] Sura Al-Baqara – (The Cow) 2: verse 87

[407] Sura Al-Isra' – (The Night Journey) 17: verse 85

given to 'Isa from Allah "gave clear miracles to Isa son of Maryam..." And with the power of the Holy Spirit, 'Isa made miracles.

Using the Qur'an's above verse "...you spoke to the people in the cradle and I when of old age ... You determined out of clay a thing like the form of a bird ... then you breathed into it and it became a bird...You healed the blind and the leprous ... and brought forth the dead..." [408]

How great is 'Isa's message in the Qur'an? "We sent Isa the son of Maryam, confirming the Law that had come before him. We sent him the Injeel (Gospel) therein was guidance and light. ..." [409]

Jesus Christ, 'Isa Bin Maryam, taught the Christians to surrender to Allah, or Islam to God. 'Isa taught his message that we best described as a Muslin-Christian teaching or the belief in God and the Last Day as we understand it from the verse "I have come to you with a Sign from your Lord therefore be careful of (your duty to) Allah and obey me. It is Allah Who is my Lord and your Lord; then worships Him. This is a Way that is straight." [410]

Christ 'Isa spends his life preaching the wisdom and the belief in One God, in His unification. It is enough to conclude 'Isa's message with the following verse. "And when Isa came with Clear Signs, he said: I have come to you indeed with wisdom and that I may make clear to you part of what you differ in. So be careful of (your duty to) Allah and obey me." [411] God reveals this Christian-Muslim teaching to the Disciples of Jesus. The following serve tells us the Disciples of Christ surrendered to Him as Muslims. "... When I withheld the children of Israel from you when you came to them with Clear Signs, but those who disbelieved among them said: This is nothing but clear enchantment (magic). And when I revealed to the disciples, saying, Believe in Me and My messenger, they said: We believe and bear witness that we have submitted ourselves (surrendered unto Thee) "we are Muslims". [412]

The followers of Christ believed in Him, while the rest of the Jews disbelieved. "But when Jesus became conscious of their disbelief, he cried: Who will be my helpers in the cause of Allah? The disciples said: We will be Allah's helpers. We believe in Allah, and bear witness that we have surrendered (unto Him). Our Lord! We believe in what Thou hast revealed and we follow the messenger, so write us down with those who bear witness." [413] The Disciples, apostles and all the followers of Christ believed in His miracles and His message.

---

[408] Sura Al-Maeda – (The Table) 5: verse 110.

[409] Ibid. verse 46

[410] Sura Al-E-Imran – (The House of Imran) 3: verses 50-51

[411] Sura AZ-Zukhruf – (The Ornament of Gold) 43: verse 63

[412] Sura Al-Maeda – (The Table) 5: verse 110-11

[413] Sura Al-E-Imran – (The House of Imran) 3: verses 52-53

The world bear witness to those miracles as clearly states in the Qur'an. "They said: We desire that we should eat of it and that our hearts should be at rest, and that we may know that you have indeed spoken the truth to us and that we may be of the witnesses to it. Isa the son of Maryam said: O Allah, our Lord! Send down for us a table spread with food from heaven, which should be to us an ever-recurring happiness, to the first of us and to the last of us, and a Sign from Thee, and grant us means of subsistence, and Thou art the best of the Providers. Allah said: Surely I will send it down to you, but whoever shall disbelieve afterwards from among you, surely I will chastise him with a chastisement with which I will not chastise, anyone among the nations." [414]

'Isa Bin Maryam is a Sign by the End of His Life

"And when Allah said: O Isa, I am going to terminate the period of your stay (on earth) and cause you to ascend unto Me and purify you of those who disbelieve and make those who follow you above those who disbelieve to the day of resurrection…" [415] The termination of 'Isa's life on earth or His death, His Resurrection and His Ascend to God's throne" is the core of the Christians' faith.

History books recorded six hundred years before Islam that the Jews used to spread the news and never denied repetitively that they did commit the crime of killing Jesus Christ. They boasted about the killing of Jesus wherever they went and still do.

Who can figure out one reason not to believe what the Jews admitted that they killed Jesus Christ? None before the coming of Islam doubted or rejected the act what the Jews performed against Christ. The Gospel tells us that "They all said: 'Let him be crucified!' The procurator said to them, 'Why, what evil has he done?' But they kept crying out the more, saying 'Let him be crucified!' Now Pilate, seeing he was doing no good but rather a riot was breaking out, took water and washed his hands in sight of the crowd, saying, 'I am innocent of the blood of this just man; see to it yourselves.' And all the people answered and said, 'His blood is on us and on our children.'" [416]

---

[414] Sura Al-Maeda – (The Table) 5: verse 113-15

[415] Sura Al-E-Imran –(The House of Imran) 3: verse 55

[416] The Holy Gospel of Jesus Christ according to ST. Matthew, chapter 27 verse 23-25. The Holy Bible, Rembrandt Edition, Abradale Press Inc., New York, 1959.

The Qur'an conveys a strong message of blasphemy that the Hebrews committed against Jesus Christ: "And their saying: Surely we have killed the Messiah, Isa son of Maryam...." [417]

Muslim scholars were under pressure how to deny a historic fact that Muslims got from the continuation of the same verse "....and they did not kill him nor did they crucify him, but it appeared to them so (like Isa) and most surely those who differ therein are only in a doubt about it; they have no knowledge respecting it, but only follow a conjecture, and they killed him not for sure." [418]

Ar-Razi, the famous Muslim scholar, has interpreted this verse to what is equivalent to saying that: "the great number of the Nazarenes (Christians), in the western and eastern parts of the world and with their extravagance in their devotion and love to Christ, inform us seeing Christ dead on the cross. If we deny that, we will be contesting what has been told in succession. Contesting what is frequently repeated as a fact, means we are contesting the revelation of Allah to Muhammad, to Isa and to all the prophets". [419]

There are a good number of verses in the Qur'an refer to the death of Christ as stated in Sura Maryam "Peace on me the day I was born, and the day I die, and the day I shall be raised alive!" [420]

This verse talking to the Jews implies the slaying of Isa "whenever then a messenger came to you with that which your souls did not desire, you were insolent so you called some liars and some you slew." [421]

The same implication applies to this verse "there came to you messengers before me with clear arguments and with that which you demand; why then did you kill them if you are truthful?" [422]

The death of Isa was referred to: "And when Allah will say: O Isa son of Maryam! ... and I was a witness of them so long as I was among them, but when You did cause me to die, You were the watcher over them, and You are witness of all things." [423]

If an apparent denial of Christ's death is comprehended, then in-depth truth related to the death repeatedly referenced in the Qur'an is undeniable. And without any doubt whether Isa Bin Maryam, was dead or alive, he was ascended to heaven and is still alive with God until the coming of the

---

[417] Sura (An-Nisa – (Women) 4: verse 157

[418] Ibid.

[419] Taken from the book of Imam Abi Al-Fadel Ahmad Ar-Razi "Hujaj Al-Qur'an leejamee' Ahl almilal wa ala'dian"

[420] Sura Maryam – (Mary) 19: verse 33

[421] Sura Al-Baqara - (The Cow) 2: verse 87

[422] Sura Al-E-Imran – (The House of Imran) 3: verse 183

[423] Sura Al-Maeda - (The Table) 5: verses 116-17

Last Day. As we read in the verse that "...Allah said: O Isa, I am going to terminate the period of your stay (on earth) and cause you to ascend unto Me. ..." [424]

We repeat that, at least, one third of the total Christians' Dogma, as written in the Gospel, is devoted to reflect the mystery of Jesus' Death and His Resurrection. Therefore, it is not possible to accept one condensed verse to represent the Spirit and the Faith of Christianity.

'Isa Bin Maryam is a Sign at the Judgment Day

In the Qur'an, Isa the only one who has the superior role at the Judgment day, no other prophet has ever given that privilege. "And (Jesus) shall be a Sign (for the coming of) the Hour (of Judgment): therefore have no doubt about the (Hour), but follow Me: this is a Straight Way." [425] This verse teaches us about the Second Coming of Christ when the Hour of Judgment arrives. It reflects what St. Paul, the Apostle, in his epistle to the Hebrews says: "And just as it is appointed unto men to die once and after this comes the judgment. So also was Christ offered once to take away the sins of many; the second time with no part in sin he will appear unto the salvation of those who await him." [426]

No one has the power of give forgiveness or to meditate in the Qur'an, except Christ, not even the prophet Muhammad. "Ask forgiveness for them (O Muhammad) or do not ask forgiveness for them; even if you ask forgiveness for them seventy times, Allah will not forgive them; this is because they disbelieve in Allah and His Messenger, and Allah does not guide the transgressing people." [427] The Qur'an reveals when the angels said: "O Maryam! Allah gives you glad tidings of a Word from Him: his name will be Christ Jesus, the son of Maryam, held in honor in this world and the Hereafter and of (the company of) those nearest to Allah;" [428] This verse shows that Jesus is the only one who is illustrious and is worthy of regard in the World and the Hereafter. Thus, the Qur'an does agree with St. Paul when he says: "For Jesus has not entered into the Holies made by hands, a mere copy of the true, but into heaven itself, to appear now before the face of God on our behalf;" [429]

---

[424] Sura Al-E-Imran – (The House of Imran) 5: verse 55

[425] Sura Az-Zukhruf –(Ornaments) 43: verse 61

[426] St. Paul's Epistle to the Hebrews, Chapter 9 verses 27-28

[427] Sura At-Tawba – (Repentance) 9: verse 80

[428] Sura Al-E-Imran – (The House of Imran) 9: verse 45

[429] St. Paul, the Apostle, his Epistle to the Hebrews 9:24

Again, "Therefore he (Jesus) is able at all times to save those who come to God through him, since he lives always to make intercession for them." [430]

Jesus Christ Divine Quality in the Noble Qur'an

The three unique qualities given to Jesus Christ alone and not to any of all prophets, messengers, angels and those nearest to God are the followings. They are expressed in one part of a verse that "...the Messiah, Isa Son of Maryam, was a messenger of Allah, and His Word which He conveyed unto Mary, and a Spirit from Him (Allah)...." [431]

'Isa Son of Maryam is the Messiah

The Messiah is a name for Isa son of Maryam and not a nickname as stated in the previous verse "...O Maryam! Allah gives you glad tidings of a Word from Him: his name will be Messiah..." Messiah is a divine name revealed by Allah directly. The name is witnessed in the Torah and in the Gospel to indicate that He is the expected, the extreme unction and blessed One.

'Isa Son of Maryam is a Word from God

The Word is best understood as expressed by St. John "In the beginning was the WORD, and the WORD was with God; and the WORD was God. He was in the beginning with God. All things were made through him, and without him was made nothing that had been made. In he was life, and his life was the light of men..." [432] "And the WORD was made flesh, and dwelt among us..." [433] The Qur'an does not openly admit the divinity of Isa, but all the meanings are implied whenever we read the Qur'an religiously.

'Isa Son of Maryam is the Spirit of God

"...And they ask you about the Spirit. Say: The Spirit is one of the commands of my Lord, and you are not given at all of knowledge but a

---

[430] Ibid. Chapter 7, verse 25

[431] Sura An-Nisa – (Women) 4: verse 171

[432] The Holy Gospel of Jesus Christ according to St. John, Prologue: 1-4. The Holy Bible, Rembrandt Edition, Abradale Press Inc., New York, 1959.

[433] Ibid. Prologue: 14.

little." [434] To those who try to interpret the term spirit as a person such as the angel Jibreel, or a part of something, the above verse tells what the Prophet Muhammad confesses that such knowledge of spirit was not given to him. Therefore we have to take the Prophet's recommendation: when in doubt go to the Clue (Remembrance) from the earlier source "The Book", "And We did not send before you any but men to whom We sent revelation -- so ask the followers of the Reminder if you do not know." [435] or "Which the True Spirit has brought down." [436] Furthermore Allah ordered Muhammad if on doubt to ask those read the Book. "But if you are in doubt as to what We have revealed to you, ask those who read the Book before you; certainly the truth has come to you from your Lord, therefore you should not be of the challengers (disputers)." [437]

The trinity in the Qur'an is the true representation of unification in God. It is reflected in Allah, His Word and His Holy Spirit. Anyone who does not have faith in the trinity surely he is an infidel.

---

[434] Sura Al-Isra' – (The Night Journey) 17: verse 85

[435] Sura An-Nahl – (the Bees) 16: verse 43

[436] Sura Ash-Shuara' – (the Poets) 26: verse 193

[437] Sura Yunis 10: verse 94

CHAPTER ELEVEN

The Prophet's Political Environment

"Times of Ignorance"

In his anxiety to wean the people of Al-Hijaz from pre-Islamic religious ideas, particularly from idolatry, The Prophet Muhammad declared that the new religion was to wipe out that gone before it, by calling the era before him age of "Jajiliyah", Times of ignorance. "And stay quietly in your houses, and make not a dazzling display, like that of the former Times of Ignorance; and establish regular Prayer, and give regular Charity; and obey Allah and His Messenger...." [438] The reference to that age is also reflected in: "When those who disbelieve had set up in their hearts zealotry, the zealotry of the Age of Ignorance. Then Allah sent down His peace of reassurance upon His messenger and upon the believers and imposed on them the word of self-restraint, and they were entitled to it and worthy of it. And Allah is Aware of all things." [439]

Al-Hujrah

Ibn Hisham [440] considers the greatest event in the Prophet's life and his Call is the immigration (Al-Hujrah) to Yathreb (Al-Medina); and that immigration was not a hidden and a sudden one similar to that of Al-Ta'ef. Prophet Muhammad took him more than two years in accurate preparation and negotiation.

Since the start of the declaration of Muhammad's Qur'anic message in Mecca, the Prophet was met with obstacles. The continuous prosecution of

---

[438] Sura Al-Ahzab – (The Clans) 33: verse 33
[439] Sura (Al-Fat-H – (Victory) 48: verse 26
[440] Ibn Hisham, "Al-Sirah", Egypt 1936, 2:73, 81, 93

Muhammad in Mecca created personal crisis within him that urged him to flee from that horrible environment. It is best reflected in the verse "Say: O my servants who believe! be careful of (your duty to) your Lord; for those who do good in this world is good, and Allah's earth is spacious; only the patient will be paid back their reward in full without measure." [441]

The attitude of the tribe of Quraysh toward the Prophet was best described in "Their purpose was to scare you off the land, in order to expel you; but in that case they would not have stayed (therein) after you, except for a little while." [442]

Darwaza's book "Sirat Al-Rassoul" [443] reflects on the Prophet tense crisis from those who believed and later disbelieved, and on his eagerness to immigrate. Events revealed in the following verses: "He who disbelieves in Allah after his having believed, not he who is compelled while his heart is at rest on account of faith, but he who opens (his) breast to disbelief. On these is the wrath of Allah, and they shall have a grievous chastisement. These are they on whose hearts and their hearing and their eyes Allah have set a seal, and these are the heedless ones. No doubt that in the hereafter they will be the losers. Yet surely your Lord, with respect to those who fly after they are persecuted, then they struggle hard and are patient, most surely your Lord after that is Forgiving, Merciful." [444]

After the return of the Prophet from Al-Ta'ef to Yathreb, events went fast. The following summary explains Muhammad's despair from his people and the people of the Book.

In Ethiopia

In the beginning Prophet Muhammad associated himself with the Nazarenes, and his followers immigrated to Ethiopia, the Arabs used to respect the Christian King there, who was in alliance with Caesar. Ethiopia at that time was powerful, and history tells us that Ethiopia had occupied Al-Yemen several times, and tried to invade Mecca and Al-Hijaz in the year of the Elephant. But due to the rough communication with Ethiopia, the limited number of the Nazarenes in Mecca and to their military weakness, in comparison to the idolatry believers among the members of Quraysh and the other tribes of Hijaz. They could not give enough support to the Prophet.

---

[441] Sura Az-Zumar – (The Troops) 39: verse 10

[442] Sura Al-Isra – (The Night Journey) 17: verse 76

[443] Darwaza, *"Sirat Al-Rassoul"* (The Life of the Prophet), 1:262

[444] Sura Al-Isra – (The Night Journey) 17: verse 76

In Ta'ef

Then, the Prophet tried to approach the Hebrews who were controlling both Al-Ta'ef and Yathreb, and to their influence was spread from Najran to Al-Hirra. Muhammad's immigration to Al-Ta'ef requesting the Hebrews' support and the Arab tribe of Beni Thaqeef but they did not listen and did not give Muhammad any support. Muhammad was convinced that it was difficult for him to join the Hebrews who were monopolizing most of the resources of the area and are in collaboration with the imperialist the infidel Persians. The Persians were laying siege to Al-Hijaz from the south and the north. The Prophet approached Yathreb for social, political and religious reasons and draw near the Arabs from Al-Yemen there.

Historically, hostility was deeply rooted between the people of Yemen and of those in Hijaz. The leaders of Yemen managed to control Hijaz and the people of Yemen who were the first to build their colonies in Hijaz. Yathreb was an example of such colonies. The people of Yemen had their own kingdom in Najd with the tribe of Kinda, and small statehood in the north with the tribe of Lakham in Al-Hirra and with the Ghassan's tribe in Busra. But, in the fifth and sixth centuries, the people of Al-Hijaz revolted and managed to get rid of the ruling family in Najd, the tribe of Kinda, and managed to regain the commercial superiority of Yathreb. Next to controlling the caravan routes within Hijaz, the tribe of Quraysh took over the international commercial routes between the north and the south and between the east and the west.

Physically, Al-Hijaz is standing like a barrier between the uplands of Najd and the low coastal region of Tihamah. Major cities of Al-Hijaz are Ta'ef, Yathreb and Mecca with its Al-Ka'ba, which attracts pilgrimage from all tribes yearly.

In Yathreb (Al-Medina)

In Yathreb, two of its quarters were dwelled by the Arab tribes of Al-A'ws and Al-Khazraj who came from Yemen after the disastrous destruction of Ma'reb Dam. While there was three outsized quarters dwelled with the influential Jewish tribes of Bani Qurayzah, Bani Al-Nadhir and Bani Qinqaa'. Those areas had their own traditions based on religious background that influenced their way of life and affected most of the inhabitants of Yathreb. A number of verses from Sura Al-Baqara (the Cow) [445] deal with social traditions and sexual relationships between men and women who lived there.

---

[445] Sura Al-Baqara (the Cow) 2: verses 220-241

In Yathreb, the general religious, cultural, political and economic leadership were in the hands of the Hebrews, making the non-Jewish Arabs frustrated and ready to rise up whenever the opportunity comes about to take control of the city from the Jews. So the Arabs in Yathreb welcomed the emigrants coming from Mecca with a new Prophet to help them achieve their objective.

One of the first steps that Prophet Muhammad took is create a rapport with the Jews and sign a "Pledge of Peaceableness" ('Ahd Al-Muwada'ah). According to Ibn Hisham this pledge states that "the Jews and the Believers are one nation: Jews have their own religions and the Believers have their own. Jews and Believers support each other as they fight together. Jews promote themselves as Believers do. They both will be winning over those who will fight the people of this declaration. None of the merchants of Quraysh or their supporters will overcome, and both will be victorious over anyone to attempt to raid Yathreb." [446]

The Arabs of Yathreb (Al-Ansar) supported and accommodated the Emigrants in their own homes. But, such accommodation did not last long, as the instinct of the Bedouins' raid and invasion of other tribes took over.

Ghazwat Badr

It started with the "Nakhleh detachment" followed by the Ghazwat Badr, the raid near Badr, located 85 miles southwest of Al-Medina (Yathreb), and 15 miles away from the Red Sea coast. The Ansar (the supporters of Muhammad) intercepted a summer caravan on its return from Syria to Mecca, striking at the heart of the commercial vital life of the City of Mecca. The leader of the caravan, Abi-Sufyan, sent for reinforcement from Mecca, but the Ansar intercepted it at Badr, resulted in a complete victory to 300 Muslims over one thousand Meccans who were riding on one thousand camels [447]. Ghazwat Badr laid the foundation of Prophet Muhammad's progressive power.

It is true that the Meccans under Abi-Sufyan avenged at Uhud their defeat and even wounded the Prophet, but their triumph was not to endure. The Prophet and his supporters recovered and made Islam to pass on gradually from the defensive to the offensive, and Islam's proliferation seemed always assured. "And fight with them until there is no more persecution and religion should be only for Allah..." [448]

---

[446] Ibn Hisham, "Al-Sirah", Egypt 1936, 2:148

[447] Farroukh, Omar "Al-Arab wal Islam" p. 45

[448] Sura Al-Anfal - (Spoils of War) 8: verse 39

In 627 AD, the tribe of Quraysh and its allies attacked Al-Medina, but the new warfare tactic of digging a trench round Al-Medina forced the besiegers to withdraw after a month of despair. The Jews sided with the allies, and Muhammad conducted his campaign against them. First, came the evacuation of Bani Qinqaa' who were forced to leave after confiscating their properties and possessions. As it is revealed in the verses "For the worst of beasts in the sight of Allah are those who reject Him: They will not believe. Those with whom you make an agreement, then they break their agreement every time and they do not guard (against punishment); therefore if you overtake them in fighting, then scatter by (making an example of) them those who are in their rear, that they may be mindful. And if you fear treachery on the part of a people, then throw back to them on terms of equality; surely Allah does not love the treacherous." [449]

The rest of the Jewish tribes, who conspired against the Prophet, were attacked and more than 600 of Bani Qurayzah were killed, and Bani Al-Nadhir was sent to exile. Revealed verses reflect the event and it starts with glorying God "All that is in the heavens and all that is in the earth declares the glory for Allah, and He is the Mighty, the Wise." [450] Then the rest 23 verses went on reflecting the attack on Bani Al-Nadhir, starting with: "He it is Who caused those who disbelieved of the followers of the Book to go forth from their homes at the first banishment. You did not think that they would go forth, while they were certain that their fortresses would defend them against Allah. But Allah came to them whence they did not expect, and cast terror into their hearts; they demolished their houses with their own hands and the hands of the believers; therefore take a lesson, O you who have eyes! And had it not been that Allah had decreed for them the exile, He would certainly have punished them in this world, and theirs in the hereafter they shall have chastisement of the fire. That is because they were opposed to Allah and His messenger; and whoever acts in opposition to Allah, then surely Allah is severe in reprisal...." [451]

History tells us that Prophet Muhammad started his worship following the steps of the people of the Book. He fast 'Ashura' turned in prayer to the direction of Al-Sham (Jerusalem). Those who read "Al-Sirah" of Ibn Hisham read details of growing pressure on the Prophet toward independence and separation[452]. He places the time for the development of the concept of independence to take its form to the middle of February 624 AD, since the revelation of Sura Al-Baqara (The Cow), until the revelation of Al-Jumua'

---

[449] Ibid. 8: verses 55-58

[450] Sura Al-Hashr – (The Exile or Banishment) 59: first verse

[451] Sura Al-Hashr – (The Exile or Banishment) 59: verses 2-4

[452] Ibn Hisham "Al-Sirrah" 2:276-272 & 3:51-60

(Friday) where the prayer for the Islamic republic is set. "Oh you who believe! When the call is made for prayer on Friday, then hasten to the remembrance of Allah and leave off trading; that is better for you, if you know." [453]

According to Hitti, Islam "had been a religion within a state; in al-Medina, after Badr, it passed into something more than a state religion — it itself became a state. Then and there Islam came to be what the world has ever since recognized it to be — a militant polity." [454]

According to Al-Tabari[455], Prophet Muhammad started in Mecca as a religious leader and a prophet of Islam; he roused in Medina to political leadership. He quickly started consolidating the ranks of Muslims and getting rid of his enemies from the Arabs whether they were Jews or pagan. It is in Medina that Islam became both religion and state.

---

[453] Sura Al-Jumua' (Friday) 62: verse 9

[454] Hitti, Philip K., "History of the Arabs", Macmillan & Co. Ltd. London, eighth edition, St. Martin's Press, New York, 1964, p. 117

[455] Al-Tabari, "Tarikh al-Ummam wal Muluk," [History of Nations and Kings], Beirut: Dar al-Fikr, 1987, p. 3:1

CHAPTER TWELVE

The Prophet's Phases of Change

Both the treaty of Al-'Aqaba and the Prophet's immigration to Yathreb have forced new changes in the Prophet's personality and in his message. It started after the failure of Muhammad in making his message acceptable in Mecca. But later on, The Arabs in Yathreb supported the Prophet, and the new spirit of Islam replaced their tribalism by surrendering to Allah and accepting the message of Muhammad.

Rebellion in the Prophet's life and personality

Muslim historians notice the deep change in the character of the Prophet. Haykel [456] shows how the political role of Muhammad starts, a role none of the prophets played before. According to Haykel, "Muhammad is the messenger of Allah, the politician, the freedom fighter (Mujahidin) and the Conqueror."

In Mecca, Muhammad used to say, "Say: I am not the first of the messengers...." [457] Or, as the British scholar Abdullah Yusuf Ali translates it: "Say: I am no bringer of new-fangled doctrine among the messengers..." We must note that each of the translations of the Qur'an is actually an interpretation that has been translated by qualified people. This verse shows the controversy in what Hussein Haykel tells us about the new-fangled doctrine that Muhammad started in Al-Medina. Haykel's interpretation leads us to ask whether we are before a prophet who brings a new celestial religion, a message from heaven, or a prophet who comes to establish a state on earth.

---

[456] Haykel, Hussein, "Hayat Muhammad" (Life of Muhammad) p.190
[457] Sura Al-Ahqaf – (The Dunes) 46: verse 9

Rebellion in "The Revelation"

The Meccan Qur'an is a call to believe in One God (Allah) and the Day of Judgment. Every verse of the revelation in Mecca inspires righteousness and asks people to prepare for the eternal life by discarding earthly belongings based on selfishness and jealousy. For example, "Nor strain your eyes in longing for the things We have given for enjoyment to parties of them, the splendor of the life of this world, through which We test them: but the provision of your Lord is better and more enduring. And enjoin upon your people worship, and be constant therein. We ask not of you a provision: We provided for you. And the sequel is for righteousness." [458] In Al-Medina, the Call of the Prophet shifted from preaching the denouncement of worldly pleasures, and preparing for the enjoyment of "the Last Day", to the enjoyment of "the Present Day". The verse "O you people! Eat of that which is lawful and wholesome in the earth," [459] reflects this concept.

Again, "They ask you as to what is allowed to them. Say: The good things are allowed to you, and what you have taught the beasts and birds of prey, training them to hunt. You teach them of what Allah has taught you. So eat of that which they catch for you and mention the name of Allah over it; and be careful of (your duty to) Allah; surely Allah is swift in reckoning." [460]

The Prophet's worldly enjoyment is best described in the following verse. "O Prophet! Surely We have made lawful to you your wives whom you have given their dowries. And those whom your right-hand possesses out of those whom Allah has given to you as prisoners of war; and the daughters of your paternal uncles, and the daughters of your paternal aunts, and the daughters of your maternal unless and the daughters of your maternal aunts who fled with you. A believing woman if she gave herself to the Prophet, if the Prophet desired to marry her-- especially for you, not for the (rest of) believers. We know what We have ordained for them concerning their wives and those whom their right hands possess in order that no blame may attach to you; and Allah is Forgiving, Merciful." [461]

Rebellion from Religion to State

Going back to the Bedouin environment in Al-Hijaz, we realize that Bedouins never understood any religious concept outside their own clans,

---

[458] Sura Taha 20: verses 131-32

[459] Sura Al-Baqara – (The Cow) 2: verse 168

[460] Sura Al-Ma'eda – (The Table) 5: verse 4

[461] Sura Al-Ahzab – (The Clans) 33: verse 50

tribes and power. Best described in "Mukadamat Ibn Khaldoun" - (Ibn Khaldoun' Introduction to his History book) -. Ibn Khaldoun is the founder of the Principles of Arab Civilization; he says, "The Arabs will never have a society except within a religious understanding. This is a result of their monstrous insulting characters and they are the most difficult people to have someone from within to lead them, because of their pride and their competition for leadership." [462] Currently, there is a saying "no hens among the Arabs, they are all roosters fighting for leadership."

Mixing between religion and statehood is deeply rooted in any Arab society. Islam ends up becoming a reflection of that primitive attitude that no one can politically express it without such a mix. Therefore, for any government to succeed in Al-Hijaz is to have its foundation based on religion? It becomes obvious that religion in Al-Medina becomes "and we have made the iron (Al-Hadid or Al-Hadeed), wherein is great violence and advantages to men (in matters of war)."

Rebellion in the approach to Islam – The Jihad

Clearly stated "Islam in Mecca was a religious call, Islam in Medina became a religious state after it started as a religion only... For that purpose, the Prophet took the approach of preparing his followers spiritually and ethically to the acts of Al-Jihad." [463] "Permission (to fight) is given to those upon whom war is made because they are oppressed, and most surely Allah is well able to assist them; those who have been expelled from their homes without a just cause except that they say: Our Lord is Allah. And had there not been Allah's repelling some people by others, certainly there would have been pulled down cloisters and churches and synagogues and mosques in which Allah's name is much remembered; and surely Allah will help him who helps His cause; most surely Allah is Strong, Mighty." [464] (These are the first two verses that the Prophet gives permission to fight (in Medina) after he prevented it in over seventy other verses (in Mecca).

How fighting is allowed in "Fighting is prescribed for you, and you dislike it. But it may happen that you hate a thing, which is good for you, and that you love a thing, which is bad for you. But Allah knows, and you know not." [465] The believers dislike fighting, but the Prophet made them understand that "it is a good thing for them". "They ask you concerning

---

[462] Ibn Khaldoun "Mukadamat", Dar Al-Kitab Al-Lubnani, Beirut, p.269

[463] Farroukh, Umar, "Al-Arab wal Islam", (The Arabs and Islam), Beirut, pages 42-45

[464] Sura Al-Hajj – (The Pilgrimage) 22: verses 39-40

[465] Sura Al-Baqara - (the Cow) 2: verse 216

fighting in the Prohibited Month. Say: "Fighting therein is a grave (offense); but graver is it in the sight of Allah to prevent access to the path of Allah, to deny Him, to prevent access to the Sacred Mosque, and drive out its members. Tumult and oppression are worse than slaughter. Nor will they cease fighting you until they turn you back from your faith if they can. And if any of you turn back from their faith and die in unbelief, their works will bear no fruit in this life and in the Hereafter; they will be companions of the Fire and will abide therein." [466]

"And fight in the way of Allah with those who fight with you, and do not exceed the limits, surely Allah does not love those who exceed the limits. And slay them wherever you catch them, and turn them out from where they have turned you out; for tumult and oppression are worse than slaughter; but fight them not at the Sacred Mosque, unless they (first) fight you there; but if they fight you, slay them. Such is the reward of those who suppress faith." [467]

The reference to the following verses is self-explanatory, it shows how death is becoming acceptable for state building and establishing Allah's will, and for Allah we belong and to Him we return. "And do not speak of those who are slain in Allah's way as dead; nay, (they are) alive, but you do not perceive. And We will most certainly try you with somewhat of fear and hunger and loss of property and lives and fruits; and give good news to the patient. Who say, when afflicted with calamity: "To Allah We belong, and to Him is our return?" [468]

From now on, we do not hear from the Qur'an in Al-Medina except the thundering sounds of war, and the new call becomes to "fight in the way of Allah, and know that Allah is Hearing, Knowing." [469]

It is also true to keep in mind that "There is no compulsion in religion. Truly the right way has become clearly distinct from error; therefore, whoever disbelieves in the Shaitan and believes in Allah he indeed has laid hold on the firmest handle, which shall not break off, and Allah is Hearing, Knowing." [470]

Al-Jihad, apart from its being a meritorious act serves the good of Islam and the Muslims. Two verses indicate their being a voluntary effort; six others suggest that it can involve material sacrifice as well as personal effort. In three verses, the Prophet Muhammad is urged to undertake and press jihad against his opponents, again without specifying the nature of the action. Jihad, as a war effort, is no more than voluntary military service to the community when it is in danger.

---

[466] Ibid. verse 217

[467] Ibid. verses 190-91

[468] Ibid. verses 154-56

[469] Ibid. verse 244

[470] Ibid. verse 256

Prophet Muhammad Military Strategy:

The Prophet executed his military strategy in Al-Medina in two phases: defense and attack.

The phase of military defense starts with Al-Hujrah in 622 AD, until the time for the preparation for the Hodeibieh campaign in 628 AD. For over five years and during that period, the tribe of Quraysh attacked Al-Medina twice: The day of Uhud and the day of Al-Khandaq.

In this period 12 chapters (suwar) were revealed. They are: Al-Baqara –The Cow, Al-Anfal –Spoils of War, Al-E-'Imran – The House of 'Imran, Al-Hashr – Banishment, An-Nisa' – Women, Muhammad, Al-Ahzab – The Clans, Al-Talaq – Divorce, Al-Bayyinna – Evidence, Al-Munafiqoon – The hypocrites, Al-Muhadila –The Pleading Woman, An-Noor –The light.

The second phase of military attack was from the year 628 AD to the death of the Prophet in 632 AD. For five years and during that period, Muslims attacked Mecca twice: the year of Hodeibieh and the year of the Great Victory (Al-Fateh Al-Akbar). Again, in this period 12 chapters (suwar) were revealed. They are: Al-Hajj – The Pilgrimage, At-Tahrim – Banning, Al-Taghabun – Haggling, Al-Jumua – Friday, Al-Fathh – Conquest, Al-Mumtahina – Examining Her, Al-Hujraat – The Inner Apartments, As-Saff – Battle Array, Al-Maeda – The Table, Al-Hadid – The Iron, At-Tawba – Repentance, An-Nasr – Divine Support.

Prophet Muhammad proved to be a military genius, one of the world greatest commanders in his planning strategy and execution. He made the Jihad a holy mission and the foundation for building the religious nation of Islam. He gave the Arabs the incentive to die in war for the spread of the Islamic cause, fulfilling the will of Allah that will allow them to inherit heaven and to live forever in paradise; furthermore, they can enjoy also the spoils of war to their advantage on earth.

Prophet Muhammad himself masterminded and led the battles and forces his way against the plans of his commanders and showed his brave decisions to what he did with the prisoners of Badr, the Treaty of Al-Hadidiah or the invasion of Tabouk. Because of his heroism stand after the defeat at Uhd and the siege of Al-Medina Islam would never survived. The same applies to Prophet Muhammad at his brave stand in the battle of Hanin that made him conquer Mecca and brought victory to Islam.

The personality of Prophet Muhammad

To those who are involved with the history of religions wonder how great was Prophet Muhammad? One of the famous historic figures that had a similar experience that Muhammad went through was the Prophet and King, David, the son of Jesse, as we read about him in the Hebrew Bible. Both Muhammad and David had same background of loneliness and poverty and both fought their ways up to defeat their enemies and conquer their religious capitals to rule in the name of a monotheist God Who kept by their sides to support and protect. David spent years in fighting wars of attrition to defend himself "And David wasted all the land and left neither man nor women alive: and took away the sheep and the oxen, and the asses, and the camels, and the apparels and returned..." [471]

David used to consult God to set a war strategy: "Another time also the Philistines made an eruption and spread themselves abroad in the valley. And David consulted God again. And God said to him: Go not up after them, turn away from them, and come upon them over against the pear trees... And David did as God had commanded him, and defeated the Philistines slaying them from Gabaon to Gezera. And the name of David became famous in all countries, and the Lord made all nations fear him." [472] Another reference to David was made in the Acts of the Apostles: "The (God) raised David to be their king, and to him he bore witness and said, 'I have found David, the son of Jesse, a man after my heart, who will do all that I desire.'" [473]

We also read in the Noble Qur'an God's helping and blessing Muhammad. "Surely We have given to you a clear victory that Allah may forgive your community their past faults and those to follow and complete His favor to you and keep you on a right way. And that Allah might help you with a mighty help." [474] And even "prays" upon him. "Surely Allah and His angels bless the Prophet; O you who believe! call for (Divine) blessings on him and salute him with a (becoming) salutation. [475] Accordingly Allah and Muhammad share the same respect: "Those who annoy Allah and His Messenger - Allah have cursed them in this World and in the Hereafter, and has prepared for them a humiliating Punishment." [476].

Both David and Muhammad were blessed and privileged to marry many wives. Even Allah forced the followers to respect Muhammad's wives as their mothers. The revealed verse says: "The Prophet has a greater claim on the faithful than they have on themselves, and his wives are (as) their mothers. And the possessors of relationship have the better claim in the ordinance of Allah to inheritance, one with respect to another, than (other) believers, and

---

[471] Old Testament, 1Kings 27:9

[472] Paralipomenon 14:13-17

[473] New Testament, Acts 13: verse 22

[474] Sura Al-Fathh – (Victory) 48: verses1-3

[475] Sura Al-Ahzab – (The Clans) 33: verse 56

[476] Ibid. 33: verse 57

(than) those who have fled (their homes), except that you do some good to your friends; this is written in the Book." [477].

And again, "O you who believe! Do not enter the houses of the Prophet unless permission is given to you for a meal, not waiting for its cooking being finished. But when you are invited, enter, and when you have taken the food, then disperse, not seeking to listen to talk; surely this gives the Prophet trouble. But he forbears from you, and Allah does not forbear from the truth and when you ask of them (ladies) any goods, ask of them from behind a curtain. This is purer for your hearts and (for) their hearts; and it does not it right for you that you should give trouble to the Messenger of Allah; or that you should marry his wives after him ever; surely this is grievous in the sight of Allah." [478]

Furthermore, besides being a military genius, Prophet Muhammad had combined in his personality a collection of mastermind activities helped him to build the Uma or nation of Islam, combining religion and worldly affairs from nothing, qualities not seen in any other leader through history. He was a real world genius in his religious aspiration, in politics, in diplomacy, in administration, in legislation and in literature.

In Religion

Prophet Muhammad had an intrinsic religious nature. Besides being a merchant, He used to retreat and spent time in prayer and in monotheistic speculation. He spent about 13 years in calling for reforming his surrounding religious life but he was ridiculed and treated with mockery, prosecution and attempts of assassination. But with perseverance, he managed within the next 10 years to introduce the concept of Jihad and enforce it and changes the Arabia Peninsula into a "volcanic" turmoil and crowned his religious life by bringing the Arabs to the worship of Allah the Only monotheistic God.

In Politics and Diplomacy

Prophet Muhammad was both a successful politician and very diplomatic. He knew how to bring together his followers and how to negotiate and when to wage war or to accept a truce. His main political success was in monopolizing the primitive Bedouin life and changed it into a religious nation. He emigrated from Mecca to Al-Medina to gather supports and invade Mecca successfully. He managed to change the direction of prayer

---

[477] Ibid. 33: verse 6

[478] Ibid. 33: verse 52

from Jerusalem to Mecca, and the reorganization of pilgrimage (Al-Hajj) to become a Muslim duty to visit the conquered Mecca. He made Friday, a day for prayer too after it was a market day only. He successfully made himself surrounded by all of his followers waiting for his command. His diplomatic approach made all Arab tribes acknowledge Muhammad's sovereignty and leadership as a real Prophet from God to be obeyed and followed.

In Administration

Prophet Muhammad administrative power was reflected in the way he organized the religious, social, political and military affairs that brought victory to his plans. His strength was in molding the Arab tribes and managed to have their leaders accept a state consultative council to solve their problems. The revealed verse "The response of the believers, when they are invited to Allah and His Messenger that he may judge between them is only to say. We hear and we obey; and these it is that are the successful" [479] indicates that the followers of the Prophet must listen and obey him.

The followers of the Messenger must ask his permission to leave was very important to Muhammad to strengthen his administration and control or else Allah would punish those who evade his orders backed up by the revealed verses "Only those are believers who believe in Allah and His Messenger, and when they are with him on a momentous affair (requiring collective action) they go not away until they have asked his permission. Surely they who ask your permission are they who believe in Allah and His Messenger; so when they ask your permission for some affair of theirs, give permission to whom you please of them and ask forgiveness for them from Allah; surely Allah is Forgiving, Merciful. Make not the calling of the messenger among you as your calling one of another. Allah knows those of you who steal away, hiding themselves. And let those who conspire to evade orders beware lest grief or painful punishment befall them." [480]

Allah sent to the Arabs His Messenger as a bearer of good news and as a warner who should be obeyed, aided and revered. It was a genius administrative and far-reaching controls, "Surely we have sent you as a witness and as a bearer of good news and as a warner. That you may believe in Allah and His Messenger and may aid him and revere him; and (that) you may declare His glory, morning and evening." [481]

---

[479] Sura An-Noor – (The Light) 24: verse 51
[480] Ibid. 24: verses 62-3
[481] Sura Al-Fathh – Victory 48:8-9)

In Legislation

Prophet Muhammad legislative genius dealt with the nullifying and the nullified flexibility as a basis for the legislation development according to the reasons given for the revelation. Muhammad started establishing his legislation in Mecca after being inspired with the revealed verse, "He has made plain to you of the religion what He enjoined upon Noah and that which We have revealed to you and that which We enjoined upon Ibrahim and Musa and Isa that keep to obedience and be not divided therein; hard to the unbelievers is that which you call them to; Allah chooses for Himself whom He pleases, and guides to Himself him who turns (to Him), frequently." [482] Such verse paved the religious way before the Prophet Muhammad.

In Literature

Only poetry was the most famous literature in the period before Islam. With the spread of Islam, prose, poetry and oratory flourished. Prophet Muhammad was the most famous literary genius since the seventh century AD. Translating the verses of the Noble Qur'an to any other language than Arabic will lose its rhetoric. But reading the verses in Arabic, the in-depth eloquence that Muhammad mastered perfectly reflects itself and elates the audience. He was well known to be a speaker and an orator. The Noble Qur'an describes the universe and the Judgment Day in prosaic poetry, and fine literature in relating stories, events and in presenting the personal status. The Arabic Literature exploded in it its rhetoric power and oratory in dialogues, conversations and communications dealing with religious, social, political, economic, art and scientific subjects.

The Independence of Islam from the people of the Book:

"The Medium Nation"

The separation between Islam under the leadership of Muhammad and the people of the Book (the Nazarenes and the Hebrews) starts with the revelation of Sura Al-Baqara (the Cow) as a result of the intensification of the conflict between the Prophet and the Jewish tribes in Al-Hijaz.

The essence of this new religious movement grew stronger with the specification of the "kiblah", that was the turning of the direction of the

---

[482] Sura Ash-Shoura – (The Consultation) 42: verse 13

Muslim in prayer from Jerusalem toward the Ka'aba in Mecca. The emphasis of Ka'aba for Islam is based on considering as the center of the pilgrimage since Abraham, the first of God's prophets to mankind. To Prophet Muhammad, Abraham was a Hanafi and he was the grandfather of Ismail and the Arabs of Al-Hijaz. So the Prophet considered Abraham's faith the basis for his Call.

The arguments that the Noble Qur'an present before the Jews echoed the arguments that Christianity present to the Jews through St. Paul who argues in his epistles that Abraham was not justified by the works of the Law, but by faith. In his message to the Romans, St. Paul says: "For not through the Law but through the justice of faith was the promised made to Abraham and to his posterity that should be heir to the world. For if they who are of the Law are heirs, faith is made empty, the promise is made void. For the Law works wrath, for where there is no law, neither is there a transgression. Therefore the promise was the outcome of faith, that it might be a favor, in order that it might be secure for all the offspring. Not only of those who are of the Law, but also those who are of the faith of Abraham, who is the father of us all; as it is written. "'I have appointed thee the father of many nations.'" [483]

Furthermore, we read in St. Paul's message to the Galatians that justifies the independence of Abraham by saying: "Know therefore that the men of faith are the real sons of Abraham. And the Scripture, foreseeing that God would justify the Gentiles by faith, announced to Abraham beforehand, 'In thee shall all the nations be blessed.' Therefore the men of faith shall be blessed with faithful Abraham." [484]

The Prophet presented his message to create an independent religion and a medium nation between Christianity and Judaism. A situation presented in "Abraham was not a Jew nor yet a Nazarene; but he was true in Faith, and bowed his will to Allah's (Which is Islam), and he joined not gods with Allah. Without doubt, among men, the nearest of kin to Abraham, are those who follow him, as are also this Prophet and those who believe: And Allah is the Protector of those who have faith." [485]

And in the verse "Who can be better in religion than one who submits his whole self to Allah, does good, and follows the way of Abraham the true in Faith? For Allah did take Abraham for a friend." [486] Clearly the tendency is to show Islam as the religion that follows "the way of Abraham". It is the right and true way for the value of the new religion in an independent state, as revealed in "And they have been commanded no more than this. To worship Allah, offering Him sincere devotion, being true (in faith);

---

[483] The Epistle of St. Paul the Apostle to the Romans 4: verses 13-17

[484] The Epistle of St. Paul the Apostle to the Galatians Chapter 3: verses 7-9

[485] Sura Al-E-'Imran - (the House of 'Imran) 3: verses 67-68

[486] Sura An-Nisa' – (Women) 4: verse 125

to establish regular prayer; and to practice regular charity; and that is the Religion Right and Straight." [487]

Muhammad Subayhh wrote, "one third of the Qur'an was in reality revealed in defense of Prophet Muhammad's dogma and faith against the accusation of the Jews. The revelation's other mission besides fighting the Jews, is to expose the "liars" with numerous verses in the long chapters." [488]

The Prophet attacks on the Jews are best summarized in the following verses: "O Children of Israel! Remember My favor wherewith I favored you and how I preferred you to (all) creatures." [489] The Prophet reminds the Jews of God' Covenant with them, "O children of Israel! Remember My favor which I bestowed on you and be faithful to (your) covenant with Me, I will fulfill (My) covenant with you; and of Me, Me alone, should you be afraid. And believe in what I reveal, confirming the revelation which is with you, and be not the first to reject Faith therein, nor sell My Signs for a small price; and fear Me, and Me alone." [490]

"When it is said to them, 'Believe in what Allah has sent down,' they say, 'we believe in what was sent down to us:' yet they reject all besides, even if it be Truth confirming what is with them. Say: 'Why then have you slain the prophets of Allah in times gone by, if you did indeed believe?'" [491]

"And when there comes to them a Book from Allah, confirming what is with them. Though before that they were asking for a signal triumph over those who disbelieved; When there comes to them that which they (should) have recognized, they refuse to believe in it but the curse of Allah is on those without Faith (the Disbelievers)." [492]

The Death of Muhammad and the Apostasy Wars

The greatest crisis in the history of Islam took place with the death of the Arab Prophet. The desert Arab Bedouins, who supported Muhammad out of fear, thought that by Muhammad's death, the message and the messenger had seized and deserted Islam, while the Ansar – the supporters of the Prophet - decided to finish what Prophet Muhammad started.

---

[487] Sura Al-Bayyina – (Evidence) 98: verse 5

[488] Muhammad Subayhh, "A'an Al-Qur'an" (About the Qur'an), pp. 64-5.

[489] Sura Al-Baqara – (The Cow) 2: verse 47

[490] Ibid. 2: verses 40-1

[491] Ibid. 2: verse 91

[492] Ibid. 2: verse 89

The Death of the Prophet

On the 25th of Zhee Al-Qa'da of the 10th Hijra year, (March of 632 AD), Prophet Muhammad made his last pilgrimage to Mecca after converting over 100,000 Arab follower to his way of belief. The pilgrimage was a spectacle event for a great Arab Prophet who led the Arab liberation movement based on national faith, a faith that unified the Arabs nationally and religiously. That day was best manifested in that part of the verse "…This day have I perfected your religion for you, completed My favor upon you, and have chosen for you Islam as your religion…" [493] That verse sets the foundation or the starting points for the growth and expansion of Islam after the death of the Arab Prophet.

The death of the Prophet came after he left to Al-Medina and spent there the months of Zhi Al-Hijah, Muharram and Safar. During that period, he managed to appoint Osama Bin Zayd Bin Harithah ruler the land of Al-Sham (Syria) and to prepare his people to invade Palestine. The best source of information about that period is written in Al-Sirra for Ibn Hisham, volume four. It seemed that the Prophet plan was not to attack the Roman Empire directly. He preferred to weaken the Romans' allies by invading the areas bordering Al-Hijaz and Al-Sham where the Nazarenes had control to it. The Prophet also seemed aware of Monk Abu Amer travel to Caesar of Rome asking for help against the Muslim ruler of Al-Hijaz who was prosecuting the expansion of the Nazarenes in Al-Hijaz area.

Prophet Muhammad found refuge in the house of his most preferred wife, Ayesha. He had tense headache[494]. The Prophet died on Monday 13th of Rabi' Al-Awal in the year 11 Hijriah or on June 8, 632 AD. Omar Ibn Al-Khattab and Abu Bakr were the first to take to the audience. Abu Bakr famous words are, "Oh people, anyone among you who worshipped Muhammad, should know that Muhammad died! But those who worshipped Allah, Allah is alive, and does not die!" Then Abu Bakr recited the following verse: "And Muhammad is no more than a messenger; the messengers have already passed away before him; if then he <u>dies or is killed</u> will you turn

---

[493] Sura Al-Ma'eda – (The Table) 5: verse 3

[494] The details for the Prophet's last days roaming among his wives and friends are described in a number of resources mainly in "Sahhih" Al-Bukhari and in "Tabakat" Ibn Saad, the Kazweeni in "Imtina' Al-Assmaa'" and in Abu Al-Fida in this "History" book. As well as in Hussein Haykal's book "Hayat Muhammad" and that of Mohamad Al-Samman's "Muhammad, the Human Prophet"

back upon your heels? And whoever turns back upon his heels, he will by no means does harm to Allah in the least and Allah will reward the grateful." [495]

I have underlined the words "dies or is killed" to acquaint the readers with a certain vagueness involved around the death of the Prophet. Did he die as a result of his wound in the battle of Uhud? As a rumor was proliferate. Or he died from painful headache in a location that writers differ in pinpointing it? Some said that he died in the house of his wife Um Habibah under his Uncle Abu Al-Abbas' care while others said that he died in the house of his son-in-law Ali Bin Abi Taleb, husband of the Prophet's daughter Fatima. Muhammad's body was left three days without burial and according to 'Aeesha, without her knowledge and the others the body was buried in the middle of the night of Wednesday.

The Apostasy wars

The desert dweller Arab Bedouins, who pledge allegiance to follow Islam, felt that the Prophet's death released them from their pledge believing in Muhammad's tribal leadership rather than in his prophecy. Prophet Muhammad was aware of the mentality of the desert Arab dwellers. It is revealed in the verse that: "The Arabs of the desert are the worst in unbelief and hypocrisy, and most fitted to be in ignorance of the command which Allah has sent down to His Messenger..." [496]

Abu An-Nasr wrote "In the beginning, what attracts attention is that the inhabitants of the Arabian Peninsula, mainly the desert dwellers Arab tribes, did not accept Islam willingly and out of sincerity. That is why their strong desertion took place immediately after the announcement of the Prophet's death and disagreements among the Muslim Arabs followed. The Ansar of Muhammad rejected to come under the rule of the Emigrants and decided to elect a leader from among them. Banu Hashim rejected at the same time to be ruled by a "foreign" leader not from their tribe. While the latest Nazarenes and Jews who accepted Islam refused to pay taxes (Al-Jiziah), some revolted against the Islamic government and some rejected Islam totally." [497]

The Apostasy war started when the first Caliph Abu Bakr had his army march in all directions to bring back the Arabs into Islam and under his leadership. Numerous battles took place and a number of persons pretended to be prophets, and played the role of the prophet in spreading their teachings such as Maslamah Bin Habib of Bani Hanifah, and Sujahh among Bani

---

[495] Sura Al- Emraan – (The House of Imran) 3: verse 144

[496] Sura Al-Tawba – (The Repentance) 9: verse 97

[497] Translated from Omar Abu An-Nasr "Al-Hhadhara Al-Amawiya Al-Arabia fi Dimashk" pp. 132 and 142

Tameem and Taghleb, and Talhhah of Bani Assad. But it took the Caliph Abu Bakr approximately two years to put an end to such abandonment and to reunite the Arabian Peninsula, nationally and politically, and to prepare the Arabs to invade the world under the leadership of the Rashideen Caliphate.

Without the apostasy wars, the Arabs would not have returned to Islam and those who pretended prophecy could have divided the land of Arabian Peninsula into tribal counties without any Arab national and religious unity that Islam provided for them.

What did the apostasy wars and pretended prophecies mean? Obviously such events show that the Arabs used to look at Islam as a nation more than a religion. Islam desertion of the Arabs and their return by force into Islam in the apostasy wars revealed that they surrendered to the Nation of Islam more than to the Religion of Islam, as they found out a regime forced upon them rather than a religion offered to them.

It is also important to observe that the contention of the Sahhabat (Companions of the Prophet) on the caliphate succession and the rush to the apostasy wars show that the people of the Arabian Peninsula saw a nation in the message of Muhammad more than a prophecy. That is why the Caliph was called Amir Al-Mou'meneen (Prince of the Believers) and not Imam Al-Muslimeen (The Imam of the Muslims).

CHAPTER THIRTEEN

The Miracle of Victorious
Wars led by the Arabs

Omar Farroukh states: "Arab conquests were based on diverting their energy to attack the surrounding enemies on the boarders of the Peninsula rather than fighting each other. They had to enforce the Arab boarders facing the Persian on one side and the Roman on the other side who started to be annoyed by the Arabs call for Islam." [498]

Starting with the invasion of the Fertile Crescent to the North of the Peninsula, the Arabs of the desert used to have a continuous dream to emigrate and live in the fertile land of Syria. Through history various waves of emigration took place from the desert to the Fertile Crescent and the greatest took place with the conquest of Islam. Such a conquest was a real Arabian miracle that the world witnessed. It is obvious that the Prophet Muhammad Islam message was based on the Nazarene teachings and beliefs in Isa Bin Maryam led the Arab Nazarene Muslims into victory.

These conquests took place in three phases: military, religious and cultural.

The Military Phase

In few years, the followers of the Prophet were able to destroy the two greatest empires of Greece and Persia that ruled the world at that time. The Christian Nestorian and the Jacobite were the majority of the population in Syria, Palestine and Egypt and were subjected for the second time to Heracle's despotism in 626 AD, after having Persia liberating them before. After eight years of having the Christians surrendering to the despot religious

---

[498] Omar Farroukh "*Al-Arab fi Al-Islam*", p.58

185

persecution and heavy taxation, they were eager to revolt and were happy to receive the Arabs as their liberators and conquerors.

The Yarmouk battle on the 20th of August 636 AD (the 11th of Rajab in the year 15 Hijriah), allowed the Arabs to put an end to the Byzantine' rule in Syria. The Arabs won the battle because they were united and were supported by the Arabs of Syria and the Romans lost the battle because of the growing conflict among them and being hated by the Arabs of Syria as aggressors and occupiers.

The Yarmouk battle was very decisive. It opened the door of Syria to the Arabs of the desert and it showed the power of the Arabs in waging and winning wars outside their territories similar to the battle of Badr that showed the power of the Arabs in winning internal fights.

Without much efforts, the Arabs led by The Caliph Omar invaded the Byzantine Syria and Palestine and conquered the land in 634 AD. In 637 AD, the Arabs managed to crush the Persian army and ruined Al-Mada'en, the capital of the Sassanedae dynasty of Persia. The Arabs conquered Egypt too in 643 AD.

The Nazarenes of Syria welcoming the Arab conquests showed that the Arabs started with a military conquest rather than a religious conquest. The division among the Muslims and their conflict upon the caliphate revealed that the Arab conquests wanted Islam to impose a nation building rather than to present a religion.

The Rashedeen Caliphs era was a period of loyalty and martyrdom in Islam. Unfortunately, the deadly conflict on the caliphate mutilated the growing face of Islam with blood and caused the assassination of all the Rashedeen caliphs expect Abu Bakr.

A Christian, Abu Lou'lou' Ghoulam Al-Maghira Bin Sha'bat assassinated the second Caliph Omar Bin Al-Khattab. Abdullah Bin Abu Bakr murdered Othman Bin Affan, the third Caliph. And the fourth Caliph, Ali Bin Abi Talib was killed by Abed Al-Ruhman Bin Maljem of the Khawarij (the dissenters). Clearly, assassination is a political act and religion has nothing to do with it.

A closer looks at the disagreement about the caliphate and the monopolization of power had divided the Muslims since the dawn of Islam into Sunni, Shiite and Khawarij/dissenters. Religion did not divide the Muslims, but politics and power did divide them. According to Omar Farroukh, when Abu Bakr entrusted the caliphate to Omar Bin Al-Khattab, "it increased the desolation between the Emigrants (Al-Muhajereen) and the Supporters (Al-Ansar). And between Bani Hashim and the rest of the

Muslims and so it forced Ali Bin Abi Talib to declare that the designation of Omar prevented him from becoming a Caliph for the second time." [499]

The caliphate ignited the traditional religious and national leadership competition between Bani Umaya and Al Hashim in Mecca and Al-Hijaz. Such dispute could be the real reasons for mutilating Islam since the development of Islam in Al-Hejira (migration) to Al-Medina and the shift from religion to a religious state. The same reasons applied for the division of Muslims into sects and for the relocation of the caliphate from Al-Medina to Damascus. It followed by the transfer of the caliphate from an Emirate over the believers to a kingdom by inheritance over the Muslim world.

In short, the Arab tribal competition led to division of the Muslim World into an Abbassid Empire in Baghdad (the Abbasid empire was famous with its great literature, philosophy, architecture, science and medicine. It was an Iraqi contribution that is still the basis for Arab culture) and an Amawi Empire in Al-Andalusia and Al-Fatimieh in Egypt. The end result of such divisions and competition led to their decline, extinction and dissolution. [500]

The Religious Phase

The religious phase started 200 years after the military conquests mainly after the Amawi regime came to an end. The Amawi caliphates turn the Arab religious state into a real Syrian Empire based on their intellectual way of thinking without tribalism and Christians in major official ministerial positions, making Damascus the capital of the Orient.

The greatness of the Amawi regime made the people enjoy their life and follow the religion of their beloved Muslim leaders and accepted Islam. Such religious conquest had followed the military conquests.

The Cultural Phase

The cultural phase is based on the spread of the Arabic language as the main language in all countries that constituted the Islamic nation. It is a fact of life that the language used in prayers and the official language of the Islamic Empire is Arabic. Arabic competed with other local nationalist languages and with time, Arabic became the language of the people. And

---

[499] Ibid. p. 60

[500] We recommend the reading of the introduction of the second edition of Hussein Haykal book "Hayat Muhammad" to grasp the decline caused by the tension, competition and conflicts among Arab leadership, it may also explain current dispute among the leading Arab states.

so, after 200 years in active contact with local cultures, the Arabic language and Arabic culture engaged all other cultures and languages. The cultural invasion of the Arabs proved to be stronger than both the military and the religious invasions even after considering the end result that allowed the absolute conquest of the Islamic religion.

CHAPTER FOURTEEN

The major difference between the originators of Islam and Christianity

In Mecca, Prophet Muhammad failed at the start of his call to spread his message. So, he went through spiritual crisis and decided to emigrate and change his religious call into a state building endeavor. Prophet Muhammad leaves Islam struggling within a mixture of religion with statehood.

The Gospel tells us that Christ ran away for the worldly and state affairs and preserved the purity of God's religion. He did that through three phases in his life. In the beginning, Christ surmounted the attempt of the devil against all the pleasures of the world as the Gospel tells us according to St. Matthew "Again, the devil took him to a very high mountain, and showed him all the kingdoms of the world and the glory of them. And he said to him 'All these things will I give thee, if thou wilt fall down and worship me.' Then Jesus said to him, 'Begone, Satan! For it is written, 'The Lord thy God shalt thou worship and him only shalt thou serve.' Then the devil left him; and behold, angels came and ministered to him." [501]

At the peak of preaching his message, Christ succeeded in running away from the endeavors of the zealous people to crown him their king. St. John tells us: "When the people, therefore, had seen the sign which Jesus had worked, they said, 'This is indeed the Prophet who is come into the world.' So when Jesus perceived that they would come to take him by force and make him king, he fled again to the mountain, himself alone." [502]

At the end of his days, Christ entered the City of Jerusalem, the capital of the State of Palestine, as conquerors welcomed by the people as the Gospel

---

[501] From the Holy Gospel of Jesus Christ according to St. Matthew, Chapter 4, verses 8-11

[502] From the Holy Gospel of Jesus Christ according to St. John, Chapter 5, verses 14-15

according to St. Mark tells us: "And those who went before him, and those who followed, kept crying out, saying, and 'Hosanna! Blessed is he who comes in the name of the Lord. Blessed is the kingdom of our father David that comes! Hosanna in the highest!'" [503]

At every phase of his life, Christ prefers religion instead of statehood. Christ prefers martyrdom instead of immigration. Christ believes that the authenticity and the credentials of death are more honorable than the credential of power and the authenticity of the sword. Christ believes that his bloodshed is more effective in the hearts and souls of human beings. Christ leaves Christianity in a pure religion form away from statehood.

How does Christianity look at Islam today?

Before discussing this section, it is very important to warn both Christians and Muslims about the newest conspiracy of Zionism against both Christianity and Islam. They have created most recently as part of their effort to disfigure history, a new group calling themselves: "The Ebionite Jewish Community" declaring "**Jesus is not Lord! Jesus was not the Messiah! Jesus did not die as blood atonement! He is not a savior! He was not divine! He was not a Christian and you cannot follow him by being one! There is no reason for the existence of Christianity! He was better than that; he was a man--no more, no less.**" [504]

Islam came 622 years after the spread of Christianity. Christianity accepted Islam as a natural extension of the early Christianity of the Nazarene Church giving respect to Jesus Christ.

The vitality in showing the basic difference between Islam and Christianity

Islam accepts the teachings of Jesus as being no less divinely revealed than the Qur'an, although the Qur'an is believed to be God's final, complete,

---

[503] From the Holy Gospel of Jesus Christ according to St. Mark, Chapter 11, verses 9-10

[504] The Ebionite Jewish Ebionite Community is established in 1985, a Zionist movement claiming that they are restoring the way of the ancient Evyonim, Yahwism, and renewed covenant. Their objective is "to **help deprogram Jews once lost to the Messianic Christian cult to restore their souls to the God of Israel**". They promote their believe that the gentiles (including Christians) will turn away from their idolatry and sin to acknowledge God and His servant Israel.

unadulterated and authoritative revelation, while Christianity believes that Jesus is Divine. He is the Face of God on earth.

Islam considers Jesus as a virgin-born prophet of special pre-eminence, in whom the Word and Spirit of God were manifested. Prophet Muhammad is regarded by Muslims as the last of God's messengers and, hence, 'the seal of the prophets'. Arab Christians consider Prophet Muhammad as the most eminent Arab Leader who polished the Arab traditions and revived the Arab culture and heritage. They are proud to call him the greatest Arab political, social and religious Leader ever born up to date in the Arabian Peninsula. He is the Arab Prophet who brought dignity and prestige to the Arabic language and strengthened the Arab Nationalistic aspiration and made it prevail in the Middle East.

Islam considers Mary, the mother of Jesus, especially holy and is, in fact, the only woman mentioned by name in the Qur'an "Mary" (Arabic, Maryam) being the name of one of the Qur'an's most often-read chapters. Christianity gives Mary the absolute respect to carry the divine Child.

Following Arab traditions, before the Arab Prophet was born, the five 'Pillars', or basic foundations of Islam, that Islam teaches Muslims are:

1. The testimony that there is no deity other than God, and added that Muhammad is God's messenger.
2. The five daily prayers should be followed with its set rites.
3. The daytime fast during the holy month of Ramadan (the ninth of the Hijra calendar) is required.
4. The annual payment of a proportion of one's wealth for charitable and communal use; and
5. The pilgrimage to the holy city of Mecca during the last month of the Hijra year, made at least once in a lifetime, if possible.

Arab Christians believe that the basic foundations in Islam sprung from early Arab Christianity with Nazarenes traditions. They believe that there is no deity other than God Jesus, and that Muhammad is God's Arab messenger to the Arabs in the Arabian Peninsula using the Arab tongue.

Both Christian and Muslim Arabs obey the ethical code that religion teaches the equality of all believers. Both believe the encouragement of communal solidarity, truth, honesty and justice in dealings among human beings. They believe in the ethical code of modesty, humility and clemency; honoring parents and caring for the family; caring for the poor and the stranger; kindliness and love, especially toward neighbors; and patience in the face of adversity.

The code also commands Arab believers to encourage virtue and discourage wrongdoing, and warns against aggression, corruption, pride, avarice, greed, envy and waste.

Islam deviates from Christianity because there is no Muslim equivalent to the Christian Church as a religious institution, nor Muslim sacraments or an ordained Muslim clergy. In principle, Muslims, guided by the Qur'an and the Sharia, that is responsible for their religious lives and for the performance of their religious duties.

Each Muslim, man or woman, is considered individually accountable before God. In practice, however, religious guidance may be sought from any scholar with a specialized knowledge of Islam. The Mufti is a recognized expert qualified to give considered opinions on points of law concerning all aspects of life; when a Muslim has a question, it may be submitted to the mufti, who gives a legal opinion. However, the mufti's opinions are not binding and other expert opinions on the same legal point may, in fact, be sought.

Islam has the Mosque the place where Muslims meet and worship. Any believer may lead Muslims' prayers, although a professional Imam, or prayer-leader, normally fills that role.

Do Arab Muslims relate to Arab Christians?

In principle, the Muslim community, or Ummat Al-Islam, is indivisible and is headed by a caliph. The caliphate as an institution lasted up to the end of World War One and after the crumbling of the Ottoman Empire in 1924.

No one denies that among most Muslims in the Arab countries, real or professed allegiance to Ummat Al-Islam normally comes first, though not to the exclusion of other allegiances that is equally real, to country, for example, or to the sense of Arab community and Arab national unity.

Judging by social and political behavior, and no matter the theory, Muslim Arabs seem distinctly able to identify and have compassion more with Christian Arabs and compatriots than with non-Arab Muslims. Likewise, Christian Arabs, being proud of their culture and heritage and the importance of the Noble Qur'an in preserving the Arab language, normally identify more with Muslim Arabs than they do with Christians elsewhere. Christian Arabs sympathy for Islam is often go beyond the Arab world to all the neighboring countries in the Middle East.

CHAPTER FIFTEEN

What should the Arabs do next?

The Arabs need to establish a clear understanding between Christianity and Islam after observing the extent to which Muslims living in the US and other Western countries have come to be politically and culturally integrated into Western society. Regardless of the degree to which Muslims continue to practice Islam or remain conscious of being Muslim.

Most studies, so far, have been focused upon Muslims in the West who have had problems with integration. Faced with such problems, or with real or imagined discrimination (i.e., "when push comes to shove"), minority groups in any society, no matter how integrated, tend to react by reasserting their sense of ethnic or communal identity. In this respect, Muslims are no exception.

If, on the other hand, America succeeds in striking a balance between its own interests and those of democracy, it would then be possible to integrate the Arab world (and the entire Muslim world) into the globalize order smoothly and with the minimum amount of aggravation.

Listening to Rev. Pat Robertson describing Prophet Muhammad was a warrior who led the jihad against the infidels and that Islam is not a peaceful religion [505] will disturb this democratic balance. It also disturbs the Christian Arab Americans when such preachers take quotes from the noble Qur'an out of its proper historical context to justify their interpretation that Islam is a violent faith.

Christianity is a faith of love and peace. But what response should we have to those who misinterpret the quote from St. Matthew "Do not think I have come to send peace upon the earth; I have come to bring a sword, not

---

[505] From an interview with Rev. Pat Robertson with George Stephanopoulos, ABC News, "This Week", Sunday, December 1, 2002.

peace" [506] How do Christians feel when such quotations from the Gospel are taken out of context to describe Christianity also as a religion of violence?

Democracy is the answer, but democracy cannot be imported and imposed from without, it must come from within. There is no doubt that homegrown democracy is more acceptable than the other variety, yet there is a growing realization in the Arab world that change from within is impossible because Arab regimes - which perceive democracy as a threat to their monopoly on power - are so well-entrenched and so oppressive.

This fact led many Arab intellectuals to admit defeat in their attempts to instigate change from within, and drove them to seek outside help to pressure the regimes. These were acceptable practices, since the issue of human rights has ceased to be a domestic matter. However, a problem may arise if these pressures fail to make an impression on oppressive and dictatorial Arab regimes, allowing calls be made by the West to impose democratic change by force.

No suggestion is made that local Arab politico-intellectual currents (whether nationalist, Marxist, or even Islamist) have been imported from the outside. Yet many in the Arab world do, and this is a result of a persecution complex as well as belief in conspiracy theories.

Each of these currents found fertile ground in the Arab world, despite the fact that they originated elsewhere. Yet no one can deny the existence of strong ties between domestic and external factors in all civilizations. Even Islam recognized this. In its early days, Islam stressed its Christian and Jewish roots. Later - in the Abbasid era - it rejoiced in its ties to Hellenic and Hindu cultures. More recently, the West is having an impact and some influence on Islam.

These links were not restricted to philosophical ideas and arguments. External factors and balances of power also had other effects, such as facilitating (or obstructing) the development and success of local politico-intellectual trends.

In the early 20th century, the global atmosphere was conducive to the spread of liberalism. Unfortunately, European colonial domination of the Arab world ultimately caused the failure of the Arab renaissance introduced by Rifaa al-Tahtawi, Sheikh Mohammed Abdu, Qassem Amin and the Wafd Party in Egypt. The result was that the entire Middle East fell into the hands of illiberal nationalist fundamentalism. In the mid-20th century, global circumstances favored the rise of Jamal Abd el-Nasser in Egypt to create the Nasserite experiment in modernism. Despite its undemocratic populism, Nasserism was not a dictatorship. Unfortunately, the Israelis'

---

[506] From the Holy Gospel of Jesus Christ according to St. Mathew, Chapter 10, verses 34

American-supported 1967 war destroyed Nasserism to the benefit of Islamist fundamentalism.

Islamist fundamentalism, supported by most Arab regimes, is applying the seventh century teaching that were needed to organize the Arab of the desert and transfer their behaviors into an organized tribal system to apply the same principle on peoples' life in the twenty-first century. Such a trend made many Arab intellectuals - not American stooges by any means - to call for foreign intervention to change Arab regimes and replace them with governments more responsive to demands for human rights, political participation and fighting corruption.

While some of the blame for this sorry state of affairs rests on the shoulders of these intellectuals who have grown hopeless of their peoples' readiness to instigate change, by far the larger share must be borne by the regimes themselves. It is because of the immovable nature of Arab dictatorships that Arab democrats have had to look outside for help in achieving reform something that will not be long in coming, either. Arab intellectuals began to go back to those movements and individuals in Arab history that saw intellect taking precedence over faith and creativity over obedience.

It is important to review the works of some of those individuals and movements played great roles in Muslim history. The Mu'tazila movement for example had its members sought to give a rational account of Islamic beliefs and held an atomic view of the universe. Some of the great individuals such as Ibn Rushd (Averroes) played a major role in the European renaissance ideas' formation. Ibn Tufail discovered the theory of evolution centuries before Darwin. Ibn Sina (Avicenna) wrote books on medicine and philosophy that continued to be read in the West until the 18th century, and Ibn Khaldoun, that can be called the founder of the principles of civilization in modern sociology can bring a new beginning to the Arab intellects of today.

When a coalition of reactionary clerics and tyrannical rulers, citing external threats and the need to preserve domestic tranquility, conspired to close the door on interpretation, it was that fateful and catastrophic moment in time that took place in the Arab/Muslim world 700 years ago. The most contemporary example took place in Iran when Mr. Hashim Aghajari, a history lecturer university professor and political activist, was sentenced to hang by reactionary clerics, calling themselves judges, after his call for a reform of Iran's state Shi'ite Muslim religion was deemed blasphemous. A professor charged with apostasy and sentenced to death for questioning the right of Muslim clerics to govern Iran in a speech he delivered and in which he called on Iranians not to follow the country's religious leaders blindly like "monkeys." This is what happens when the real political power lies with not elected Islamic conservative clerics and religious fundamentalists, who control the judiciary, security forces and state-owned mass media in a Muslim-ruled country, like Iran.

Is there a difference between returning to the past and that of the Muslim fundamentalist movements that have seized control of Arab and Muslim politics these last 30 years? Yes there is, if the return is a return to the future, using all that is enlightened in Arab/Muslim civilization.

Arab and Muslim intellectuals should recognize that differences of opinion should not lead to bickering, but to dialogue and compromise. They should lead a positive civil war within Muslim civilization to settle the accounts with that clerical-tyrannical coalition that played a major role in stagnating intellect, creativity, and economic and technological progress in the Arab world since the 13th century.

Muslim intellectuals should have the courage to explain the historical events that led to certain discrepancies, for example the ones that encouraged killings and do not seem logical today. They should admit such mistakes as regrettable and should not be taken against contemporary Islam. Muslim intellectuals should reject late Osama Bin Laden who used to encourage them to read "Tafseer Al-Qur'an Al-'Azhim" of Imad-eddin Abi Al-fida Ismaeel Bin Katheer Al-Kurashi Al-Damashki who died in the year 774 Hijriah. [507] Ibn Katheer interpretations are full of attacks against the Christians, the ones who went astray, and Jews, who earned God's Anger, he kept calling Christians and Jews the corrupted and infidels and is the ones who deserve

---

[507] Ibn Katheer, Imad-eddin Abi Al-fida Ismaeel, "Tafseer Al-Qur'an Al-'Azhim", over 4350 pages of interpretation written in seven volumes published by Dar Al-Andalus, Beirut, 1966. The Tafseer is full of talks related to people who heard the Prophet talks with so many interpretations: for example on page 205 as part of his interpretation of verses 77 and 78 from Sura Al-Baqarah – (the Cow) "Know they not that Allah knows what they conceal and what they reveal? And there are among them unlettered people, who know not the Book, but they trust upon false desires and they but guess.". He says that Ibn Jareer that Al-Muthanna told Ibrahim Bin Abd Al-Salam told Saleh Al Kushayri told Ali Ibn Jareer that Hammad Bin Salmat and Abd Al-Hamid Bin Jaafar told Kananat Al-Aldwi heard Uthman Ibn Affan in turn heard the Prophet Muhammad saying "Woe to them for what their hands have written and Woe unto them for that they earn thereby." And said "The woe is a mountain of fire" that fell on the Jews because they perverted the "Torah", they added or revealed what they liked and concealed what they hate and so they concealed the name of Muhammad from the Torah that made Allahs wrath fall on them.

God's wrath.[508] Ibn Katheer also quotes the Prophet warning the believers from the "black dog" because it is the "Shaitan" or "the devil". [509]

Arab intellectuals should go over the writings of a number of Arab thinkers such as Salama Mousa, Ali Abderrazek, Taha Hussein and Shibli Shummayyil to transport the Arab mind from its preoccupation with the superstitions of the past to the rationality and scientific progress of the present. Those thinkers called in the early and mid-20th century for the exclusive adoption of modernity and rationality. But unfortunately, they were unable to penetrate the immovable structure of conservative Arab society. Moreover, many of them failed to base their secular ideas on democratic practice.

It is worth mentioning that the Arab Philosopher, Ibn Rushd, who lived in the twelfth century AD (1126-1198), known by Averroes in the West. Averroes was destined to give the first impulse to a whole intellectual trend in the West by influencing the Islamic thinking through his interpretation of religion. Averroes employed the symbolical and allegorical method to conclude that all the monotheistic religions were true while sharing Aristotle's opinion that, in an eternal world, religions appear and disappear again and again.

Contemporary Arab intellectuals, despite the presence of the vision and will for progress, development, and liberty among Arab intellectuals to interpret religion, have failed to achieve their goals because of their failure to build true democracy. We hope that democracy will prevail, as long as intellectual-political confrontations would not turn violent with those who believe that democracy is anathema to Islam, and that Islam rejects pluralism. It becomes hard to establish a dialogue with those who assume that democracy and the opinions of the majority is not necessarily the right one and believe that only Muslim fundamentalists, the clerics, have the right to run society.

Another example is important to take into consideration the research carried by the recent Arab Development Reports.

The Arab Human Development Reports

The United Nation Development Program (UNDP) and the Arab Fund for Economic and Social Development collaborated together to produce an incredible analysis and research about the situation of the Arabs world, and

---

[508] Ibid. Volume one p. 53 while interpreting the seventh verse of Al-Fatihah "The Way of those on whom You have bestowed Your Grace, not of those who earned Your Anger, nor of those who went astray."

[509] Ibid. Volume One, p. 30

how to improve it. The research has been conducted by Arab researchers and social scientists in an unbiased way, which has been produced in three volumes between 2002 and 2005. [510] Every one of these publications deserves reading thoroughly, not only by every Arab, but also by every person concerned with the Middle East.

According to the report, Arab societies are paralyzed because of the lack of basic freedoms, oppression of women and isolation from new ideas. Arab oil wealth is accompanied by social backwardness. With the possible exception of sub-Saharan Africa, individual income in the Arab world is lowest in the world. Arab productivity is regressing, scientific research is almost nonexistent, and almost half of Arab women are illiterate.

The report implicitly accused Muslim extremists of being a key cause for backwardness and for lack of democracy. It noted that Arab rulers tend to remain in office for life and establish dynasties to carry on after they die. Arab peoples, the report said, are incapable of change.

The UNDP report hung the Arabs' dirty laundry out for the entire world to see. It was a gold mine of information that drew an extremely detrimental picture of the Arab world. Sadly, despite the fact that the team that produced the report was all Arab, all that information was true.

The big question posed by Arab intellectuals now is this: Could fundamentalism have dominated the Middle East for four decades had it not been for Western political support and Gulf oil money?

This question raises another one no less important: Now that Cold War Western political support and Gulf oil funding to these pre-modernist Islamist forces are at an end, who can (will?) fill the politico-intellectual vacuum their failure will leave behind? The direct answer is the forces of democracy and liberalism, of course.

In contrast to what many Orientalists and "clash of civilization" theorists in the West believe, democratic and liberal forces in the Arab world are strong

---

[510] "THE ARAB HUMAN DEVELOPMENT REPORT 2002" is printed by Icons Printing Services in Amman, Jordan under ISBN: 92-1-126147-3. The United Nations Development Program considered the analysis and policy recommendations of this Report do not necessarily reflect the views of the United Nations Development Program, its Executive Board or its Member States. The Report is the work of an independent team of authors sponsored by the Regional Bureau for Arab States, and is available through United Nations Publications Room DC2-853 New York, NY 10017. The first two publications have been published and available in Arabic and English languages, however, the third report should have been released in August, 2004, but it has been held up from distribution, by the Bush Administration, since a portion of it is critical of US and Israeli polices in the Middle East.

enough to make a difference if given a chance. But what "chance" are Arab democrats looking for? For the first time in its 70-year history of engagement in the Middle East, the US might turn away from tyranny and dictatorship and ally itself instead with the democratic and liberal forces of the region.

We say, "Might" because we are afraid that the US would do what it has been used to doing in recent times. US Administration is allowing its narrow immediate interests (guarded by Arab dictatorships) to take precedence over its long-term interests that can only be guaranteed by Arab peoples at peace with themselves, their governments and their alliances.

Such a regressive course of action will be sure to kill off the green shoots of democracy that have begun to sprout all over the Middle East. Yes, the specter of democracy is permeating the Middle East. Given the chance, historic achievements are unleashed. Today, the ball is in Washington's court where they budgeted 29 million dollars to promote democracy in the Middle East and plan to budget 200 billion dollars to wage a war against Iraq that may destroy the heritage and culture of the Arab peoples in the Middle East.

The first Report was not able to investigate deeply the treatment of each of the individual deficits. Therefore, the Regional Bureau for Arab States on the United Nations Development Program decided to produce at least three more annual issues of the AHDR: The AHDR has thus become a series of reports.

The Second AHDR of 2003 that was dedicated to provide in-depth treatment of the Arab knowledge acquisition deficit and concluded with a strategic vision for the establishment of a knowledge-based society.

The Third Arab Human Development Report was due in October 2004 intended to tackle the issue of governance and focus on "Freedom and Good Governance." The Third Report was expected to be the most critical and most sensitive of the trinity of deficits outlined in the First Report to expand the range of freedom and building good governance among the Arab nation. [511]

Ten percent of the report was brutally critical of the invasion of Iraq and the Israeli occupation that the Bush team rejected insisting that language

---

[511] The Arab Human Development Reports (AHDR) series sought to act as a spur to the formation of a strategic vision, to be crystallized by Arab elites through the process of a societal innovation. A serious and objective debate around the substance of this report would pave the way for a process of societal innovation. Rima Huneidi, Regional Bureau Director for Arab States, UNDP, concluded sadly "what Arab constitutions grant, Arab laws frequently curtail. And what laws render legal, actual practice often violates. People are thus besieged in their own country, their takeoff is held back, their development is blocked, and their nation is weakened."

critical of America and Israel be changed. And until it is changed, the Bush folks were apparently ready to see the report delayed or killed altogether. And that they have an ally, the government of Egypt, which is criticized in the report, also doesn't want it out – along with some other Arab regimes.

The AHDR 3 focused on "the acute deficit of freedom and good governance" in the Arab world. It underscored how much Arab peoples crave, and need, freedom and good governance as much any other people.

It was obvious that the source of societal authority is the will of the majority; and the democracy that ensures liberty is the most fertile soil for social progress; and without complete freedom of opinion and debate, the truth cannot emerge.

The third report discussed two factors, which have a far-reaching impact on the major powers towards freedom in the Arab region: the discovery of oil and the establishment of the state of Israel. The Arab despots of the day ruled oppressively, restricting their countries' prospects of transition to democracy, under the pressure of major foreign powers interests in oil and in the support of Israel.

Democracy can harbors flaws if democracy can restrict liberty, then society cannot be considered free. Political society must be protected in the form of a democratic constitution that respects fundamental freedoms, including the right of the minorities.

The report concluded that no Arab thinker today doubts that freedom is a vital and necessary condition for a new Arab renaissance. Freedom is one of the principal human goals and highest human values. It is cherished in itself and sought for its own sake. In short, the individual is free only in a free society within a free nation.

The report also showed that human rights and human development… reinforce each other and their common denominator is human freedom, and at the core of international accords on human rights remains the International Bill on Human Rights. The Arab world remains in need of an Arab Bill of Human Rights.

In spite of the existence of several interpretive texts which assert the congruence between international human rights law and Islamic law (Shari'a), traditional interpretations of Shari'a that stress differences between the two, are used to argue that international human rights laws are not applicable in Arab countries. Therefore, the goals of national liberation and self-determination lead directly to that of liberating Arab territory.

If the Arab people are to have true societies of freedom and good governance, they will need to be socially innovative. Their challenge is to create a viable mode of transition from a situation where liberty is curtailed and oppression the rule to one of freedom and good governance that minimizes social upheavals and human costs. To all those who care about the future of the Arab region, they must strive to avert social conflict and perhaps violence. This challenge concerns, first and foremost, the intellectual and political vanguards of the region.

The third Report also noted that most Arab states political architecture or the executive apparatus today resembles "a 'black hole,' which converts its surrounding social environment into a setting in which nothing moves and from which nothing escapes." Without a majority of people behind them, most of these Arab regimes lack legitimacy, as they resorted to other sources of legitimacy: traditional (religious/tribal), revolutionary (nationalist/liberation), or patriarchal, claiming authority based on the wisdom of the 'family head'. However, the failure to tackle major issues such as the question of Palestine, pan-Arab cooperation, foreign intervention, the advancement of human development and popular representation, drove Arab states into a crisis of legitimacy.

The report's authors concluded with their hope for a broad, peaceful redistribution of power in the Arab world, their fear that nothing will change - which they predicted could lead to "chaotic upheavals" - and their expectation of some externally induced change and muddling through. By 21st century standards, Arab countries have not met the Arab peoples' aspirations for development, security and liberation.

But the important thing about this report is that Arabs are now putting political reform on the Arab agenda. Yes, it's scathing about the Western and Israeli roles in retarding Arab democratization, but it's equally scathing about what Arabs have done to themselves and how they must change - people don't change when you tell them they should, but when they tell themselves they must.

Establishing a society of freedom and good governance requires comprehensive reform of governance at three interactive levels: internal, regional and global. The internal reform requires a structural reform of the state, civil society and the private sector to enhance the principles of sound administration by abolishing the state emergency, ending all forms of discrimination against any minority group and guaranteeing the independence of judiciary.

The report asserted that "structural corruption is part of a systematic state policy" in the Arab world. In this type of corruption, "personal abuse of public office and misuse of public finances are considered normal according to prevailing custom, or even necessary for the regime to endure. It is distinct from conventional corruption where the perpetrator acts behind the back of officialdom, in fear of the law."

The authors maintained "structural corruption is one of the biggest obstacles to reform since it is systematically used to sabotage political and civil activity and creates classes with vested interests in the status quo." In fact the authors link this phenomenon to what is known as 'unspoken corruption' where close supporters are allowed to exploit their positions for unlawful gain and the threat of the enforcement of the law against them secures their absolute loyalty.

Political and legal structures in some Arab states make it difficult to differentiate between corruptions in its conventional form-abuse of political office for personal gain-and inherent failings in the system itself.

Again, dependency on oil sales has also contributed to corruption in many Arab countries as these regimes perpetuate themselves in power "through generous financing of agencies of organized repression and the mass media."

There is nothing short of sweeping political, institutional, administrative and societal reforms that establish representative government accountability, transparency and disclosure at all levels of society, will effectively root out corruption. It is necessary to differentiate between corruption as part of the systematic state policy and corruption as indicative of the failure of the state.

CHAPTER SIXTEEN

"The Dark Arab Spring"

The new term "Arab Spring" was coined by the western governments to describe the most recent revolutionaries who revolted against the regimes in Tunis, Lybia, Yemen, Egypt and Syria. Unfortunately, such revolutionary movements brought distraction to the concept of democracy when the Muslim Brotherhood (the society of Muslim Brothers) took advantage of the chaotic approach that rebellion brought to the Arab scene. Muslim Brotherhood succeeded in taking the opportunity to lead in the above mentioned Arab countries and is still trying to overcome the Syrian regime for over five years of destructive attacks under the banner of rebel brigades displaying al Qaeda-like flags. The conflict in Syria between forces loyal to the Syrian Ba'ath Party government and those seeking to oust it, mostly a Muslim Brotherhood to revenge for the February 1982 an uprising by the Brotherhood took place in the Syrian city of Hamah was crushed by the government of Hafiz al-Assad at a cost of perhaps 25,000 lives, extreme Salafist and Jihadists began on 15 March 2011 with nationwide demonstrations, as part of the wider protest movement that the west called as the "Arab Spring". Instead of springing freedom, equality and democracy, it bounced into extreme dark Islamist anarchy.

Muslim Brotherhood

Origination

The Muslim Brotherhood was founded in March 1928, at Ismailia, Egypt in reaction to Kemal Ataturk's abolition of the caliphate in 1924, after the decline and fading of the Ottoman Empire. Its ultimate aim is to restore the caliphate. Its vehicle for doing so, according to founder Hassan al-Banna

(1906-1949), is a one-party system. Al-Banna envisaged a bottom-up strategy in which people would be Islamized at the local level first. For this purpose, he created his party (the society of Muslim Brothers).

After winning the masses, the Muslim Brotherhood would take total control and to struggle against the British occupation. Al-Banna preached jihad as violent struggle against the occupiers, but targeted the new apostate Egyptian regime once the British left.

Sayyid Qutb [512] became the Muslim Brotherhood's main ideologue after Banna's assassination in 1949. He was radicalized by a trip to the United States, which he found revolting. He merged the teaching of Wahhab and Banna and identified the United States and Britain as the main enemies.

Ideology

The chief ideologue of the Muslim Brotherhood, Sayyid Qutb, wrote that, "Islam chose to unite earth and heaven in a single system." He considered the separate realms of the divine and the human have collapsed into each other, and that it will now be possible, as Qutb said "to abolish all injustice from the earth."

The Muslim Brotherhood is an Islamist religious, political, and social movement. It is considered the largest, best-organized political force in Egypt. Its credo is, "God is our objective; the Qur'an is our constitution, the Prophet is our leader; Jihad is our way; and death for the sake of God is the highest of our aspirations. …and that should be the guidelines for a healthy modern Islamic society". The Muslim Brotherhood is a hard-core cadre party. It takes eight years of training to become a full member.

The current Muslim Brotherhood's leadership concerning its mission and its prospects of changing is expressed by its Deputy Guide, Khairat al-Shater [513], said: "The mission is clear: restoring Islam and its all-encompassing conception; subjugating people to God; instituting the religion of God: the Islamization of life, empowering of God's religion; establishing the Nahda of the Uma [Muslim nation] should be applied on the basis of Islam." As for

---

[512] Sayyid Qutb is an Egyption author, educator, Islamist theorist, poet, and the leading member of the Egyptian Muslim Brotherhood in the 1950s and '60s. In 1966 he was convicted of plotting the assassination of Egyptian president Jamal Abdel Nasser and was executed by hanging

[513] Kharat al-Shater was born on May 4, 1950, in the Nile Delta province of Daqahliya, earned an engineering degree from Alexandria University and a master's in engineering from Mansura University. He joined the Muslim Brotherhood in 1981, after years as a student activist, and was promoted to its executive bureau, known as the Guidance Council, in 1995

change, al-Shater proclaimed that, "no one can come and say: 'let's change the overall mission'... No one can say, 'forget about obedience, discipline and structures'... No. All of these are constants that represent the fundamental framework for our method; the method of the Muslim Brotherhood. It is not open for developing or change..."

Uprising and Falling of Muslim Brotherhood in Egypt

In the 1980s the Muslim Brotherhood experienced a renewal as part of the general upsurge of religious activity in Islamic countries. The Brotherhood's new adherents aimed to reorganize society and government according to Islamic doctrines, and they were vehemently anti-Western. The Brotherhood revived in Egypt and Jordan in the late 1980s, it emerged to compete in legislative elections in those countries.

In Egypt the participation of the Muslim Brotherhood in parliamentary elections there in the 1980s was followed by its boycott of the elections of 1990, when it joined most of the country's opposition in protesting electoral criticisms. Although the group itself remained formally banned, in the 2000 elections Muslim Brotherhood supporters running as independent candidates were able to win 17 seats, making it the largest opposition bloc in the parliament.

In 2005, again running as independents, the Muslim Brotherhood and its supporters captured 88 seats in spite of efforts by President Hosni Mubarak's administration to restrict voting in the group's strongholds. Its unexpected success in 2005 was met with additional restrictions and arrests, and the Muslim Brotherhood opted to boycott the 2008 local elections.

In the 2010 parliamentary elections the Mubarak administration continued to restrict the Muslim Brotherhood by arresting members and barring voters in areas where the organization had strong support. After Mubarak's National Democratic Party won 209 out of 211 seats in the first round of voting, effectively eliminating the Muslim Brotherhood from the parliament, the organization boycotted the second round.

When Tunisians overthrew Zine El Abidine Ben Ali, it helped inspire Egypt's revolt against longtime ruler Hosni Mubarak. In January 2011 a nonreligious Egyptian youth protest movement the Mubarak regime, the Muslim Brotherhood's senior leadership hesitated briefly; then they endorsed the movement and called on its members to participate in demonstrations.

When protests forced Mubarak to step down as president in February 2011, leaving a transitional military administration in control of the country, the Muslim Brotherhood signaled that it intended to begin officially participating in Egyptian politics. The Muslim Brotherhood announced that it would apply to become a recognized political party as soon as constitutional amendments allowing wider political participation were completed but stated that it did not intend to nominate a candidate for the presidential elections.

In May, however, a senior member of the Muslim Brotherhood, Abdel-Moneim Abul-Fotouh, announced his intention to run for president; he was later expelled from the organization. In spite of his expulsion, Abul-Fotouh retained significant support and continued his campaign. Meanwhile, in late April 2011 the Muslim Brotherhood took further steps toward open participation in Egyptian politics, founding a political party called the Freedom and Justice Party and applying for official recognition from the Egyptian interim government.

Leaders of the Freedom and Justice Party stated that the party's policies would be grounded in Islamic principles but that the party, whose members included women and Christians, would be no reconciliation. The party received official recognition in June, allowing it to enter candidates in upcoming elections. The Freedom and Justice Party soon achieved considerable success, winning about 47 percent of seats in elections held between November 2011 and January 2012 for the People's Assembly, the lower house of the Egyptian parliament. The party's secretary-general, Mohammad Sa'ad al-Katatni, was appointed speaker of the Assembly.

The issue of fielding a presidential candidate arose again in March 2012 when the Muslim Brotherhood announced that Khairat al-Shater, a businessman and senior member of the organization, would run for president as the nominee of the Freedom and Justice Party, thus contradicting earlier assurances that the organization would not seek the presidency in 2012.

On 31 March 2012, the Freedom and Justice Party named El-Shater their candidate for the presidential election in May 2012. El-Shater formally resigned from the Brotherhood in order to run for President and to avoid violating the Brotherhood's pledge not to field a candidate. The announcement of Shater's presidential candidacy was a historical first for the 83-year-old group, which originally pledged that none of their members would run for president to calm secular and western governments' fears of a complete Islamist takeover by the group. Earlier in 2012, Khairat El-Shater had denied any intentions for entering the presidential race on 31 March 2012.

The Egyptian Supreme Council of the Armed Forces barred El-Shater from the presidential race on 14 April 2012, stating that he was only released from prison in March 2011, in violation of election rules stating that a candidate has to be released from prison for 6 years before he can become a candidate.

In April 2012 Shater, who had been imprisoned under the Mubarak regime in 2008 for funding the Muslim Brotherhood, was disqualified from running by Egypt's election commission under a rule banning candidates with prior criminal convictions. Mohammad Morsi, the head of the Freedom and Justice Party, entered the race as Shater's replacement.

Morsi won the largest total in the first round of voting in May and defeated Ahmad Shafiq, a former prime minister under Mubarak, in a runoff held on June 16 and 17, 2012. Enthusiasm over Morsi's victory was tempered by the ongoing outcry over the June 14, 2012 ruling by the Egyptian Supreme Constitutional Court calling for the dissolution of the Muslim Brotherhood-led People's Assembly on the grounds that legislative elections held between November 2011 and January 2012 failed to follow procedures requiring that one-third of the seats be reserved for independent candidates. The Muslim Brotherhood also denounced the interim military government's surprise constitutional declaration on June 17, which stripped the presidency of much of its authority. The Muslim Brotherhood candidate Mohammad Morsi was declared winner as the President of Egypt on 24 June 2012.

Mohammad Morsi was ousted by a popular military coup on July 3rd, 2013 after mass protests took place. The liberals, leftists, and youth Egyptian organizations, were dissatisfied as the Brotherhood monopolized state power, and ignored the much needed reforms – reforms that were primary concerns of ordinary Egyptians.

Morsi did not waste time as he appointed fellow Brotherhood members to head key ministries, notwithstanding the criticism by the media as he was cracking down on media and groups that did not share the same political views. He gave Islamists control of key government ministries, including those of education and information. After being ousted, Morsi replaced seventeen provincial governors; replaced seven of them with Muslim Brotherhood members and one with a member of an ex-militant Islamist group, al-Gama'a al-Islamiyaa. Even the army was not safe when he replaced the generals who emerged as the greatest threat to his authority with new generals who would answer to him. Furthermore, he issued a constitutional declaration that gave him full executive power over the state.

Morsi's policies did not look at the interests of the people and the standard of living of the poor; they gave advantage to the leadership of the Muslim Brotherhood, favored billionaires and military leaders - much like during the Mubarak era. The ordinary citizens started questioning the reasons why they started a revolution in the first place. The Egyptians were struggling every single day with a ruined economy and a bankrupt country, plagued with corruption. They suffered of daily blackouts and long queues to get gas. Morsi's governance started resembling the one of Mubarak. But, one year later, most Egyptians hailed the retired field marshal Abdul Fattah al-Sisi as their savior for overthrowing President Mohammed Morsi and the

Muslim Brotherhood. Al-Sisi was elected as the President in May, 2014 with a 97% majority of votes cast.

Uprising of Muslim Brotherhood in Tunisia

Muslim Brotherhood took advantage of the Tunisian people who have risen up against the oppression, injustice, corruption, the government and the family of the ruler and his corrupted assistants for a quarter of a century.

The incidents that happened in Tunisia during December 2010 and January 2011 were a cornerstone for rise of the Brotherhood in the Arab region and the Islamic world.

The Tunisian up rise was a message to the oppressors, corrupt rulers and regimes that nothing lasts forever and nobody is secure at their post. The Muslim Brotherhood society considers itself an integral part participating in building Tunisia on the right tract of Al-Sharia. They took over the chaotic system that could not take serious action to combat the spread corruption and bring the desired reform.

The Tunisia uprising started and suddenly spread across the region seemed to come out of nowhere. The Brotherhood watched from the sidelines before jumping in.

Tunisia was the one country where the Arab Spring had a chance of not becoming a misnomer; crisis has also arrived with a fury. Tens of thousands took to the streets after a leading opposition politician, Chokri Belaid, was murdered. Belaid was a tough critic of Islamists, and many, including those who call themselves "moderate" Islamists, blame them for his death.

The Muslim Brotherhood-inspired the Nahda party, the country's largest, has come under fire, accused of speaking of moderation while siding with more-extremist forces for political reasons and turning a blind eye to violence. The Nahda rejects the accusations, blaming everyone it can think of for the crisis. The Nahda leader Rashid al-Ghannouchi blamed the French model of secularism for the country's problems, adding fuel to public anger by saying most Tunisians oppose "radical secularism." Other Islamists have blamed the media, the old regime and outsiders for their country's problems.

The leader of the Muslim Brotherhood in Tunisia, Rachid Ghannouchi, was cited recently that the Brotherhood has developed a strategy for post-revolutionary Tunis, plus giving full support to the revolution in Libya. He also expressed his prediction that the "Arab Spring" was going to lead to the elimination of foreign aggression in the Muslim Middle East and consider the Muslim Brotherhood omnipresent. He believes in the Muslim Brotherhood motto which includes that the Qur'an is our law; Jihad is our way; Dying in the way of Allah is our highest hope.

Uprising of Muslim Brotherhood in Lybia

In Libya, fighting between forces loyal to Colonel Muammar Gaddafi and those seeking to oust his government was preceded by protests in the eastern city of Benghazi beginning on Tuesday, 15 February 2011, which led to clashes with security forces that fired on the crowd. The protests escalated into a rebellion that spread across the country, with the forces opposing Gaddafi establishing an interim governing body, the National Transitional Council (NTC).

After months of fierce resistance to NTC militia backed by allied NATO forces, Colonel Muammar Gaddafi was captured on October 21, 2011, in his hometown and stronghold of Sirte while trying to escape from encirclement. He was captured alive, but instead of being treated as prisoner of war, interrogated and put on trial, the former ruler of Libya was tortured for several hours and then murdered by a militia mob.

The United States fought diplomatically, militarily and behind the scenes to unseat Gadhafi, with none other than the Muslim Brotherhood poised to take over. The uprising against Muammar Gaddafi eventually ended his 42-year rule.

As Libya emerges from a bloody civil war, many observers believe the next elections could pit religious political groups against secular parties, with better-organized Islamists such as the Brotherhood having a tactical advantage. Libyan Muslim Brotherhood leader Suleiman Abd-el-Kader praised the rebellion and called on Libya's factions to unite and rebuild Libya by every Libyan and by a group or party when he addressed the meeting of about 700 people at a wedding hall in Benghazi, the eastern city where the revolt against Gaddafi began.

Abd-el-Kader remarks appeared to be an expression of support for the idea of a technocratic interim government, which Abdur Rahim El-Keib, the prime minister designate was trying to assemble. He hesitated to draw on whether the Muslim Brotherhood wanted one of its members to be part of the interim cabinet, which was due to organize elections.

According to the Libyans politician Mahmoud Jibril, the head of one of the largest political parties in Libya, the National Forces Alliance, was a high-ranking official with the Gaddafi government and also a leader of the revolutionary Council in 2011, in an interview with Russia Today (RT) [514] "Libya can be used or at least is being seen as an alternative to finance and compensate the lack of assistance that might be coming from Europe and from the US. That's why Libya is a strategic target for too many players in the region and worldwide."

---

[514] Interview with Russia Today (RT) on March 26, 2012.

Jibreel added "Power under theoretical study rests with the legislative body and with the government. But realistically speaking it's the one, who holds the guns, holds the power. So, there is still the cut between real power and official power."

He added: "I think Libya because of this oil was the subject of being targeted by too many countries, because this oil wealth is needed not only for Libya maybe to finance some other projects in the region."

Mahmoud Jibril also said that "he regretted Colonel Gaddafi was not taken alive to face trial, but certain powers that may have wanted him to keep silence due to the secrets he knew."

Wahhabism – Wahhabi Muslim

Muhammad Ibn Abed al-Wahhab, died in 1792, was the first modern Islamic fundamentalist and extremists. Wahhab made the central point of his reform movement the principle that absolutely every idea added to Islam after the third century of the Muslim era (about 950 AD) was false and should be eliminated. Muslims, in order to be true Muslims, must adhere solely and strictly to the original beliefs set forth by Prophet Muhammad. The belief is that the Wahhabi wrongly interpreted and falsely translated away from its true religious message.

Muhammad bin Abed al-Wahhab is the one who paved the road for Abdul Aziz Ibn Saud, the patriarch of the family, to conquer the rest of the [Arabian] Peninsula and to rule. So there is very great cohesiveness between the two.

For more than two centuries, Wahhabism has been Saudi dominant faith forced the Arabs of Najd and Hijaz that were called by the House of Saud, or Saudi Arabia. It is an austere form of Islam that insists on a literal interpretation of the Koran. Strict Wahhabis believe that all those who don't practice their form of Islam are heathens and enemies. Critics say that Wahhabism's rigidity has led it to misinterpret and distort Islam, pointing to extremists such as the late Osama bin Laden, the Taliban, and the "Al-Nusra group". Wahhabism's explosive growth began in the 1970s when Saudi charities started funding Wahhabi schools (madrassas) and mosques from Islamabad to Culver City, California.

From my own experience when I was a bilingual instructor in Aramco Industrial Center, Abqiq, Saudi Arabia, in the late fifties of last century, I consider myself able to say that the religious curriculum in Saudi Arabia teaches that people are basically two sides: Salafist [Wahhabis], who are the winners, the chosen ones, who will go to heaven, and the rest are either "kuffar", who are deniers of God, or "mushriq", putting gods next to God.

Those who are called the Sunni Muslims, for instance, celebrating Prophet Muhammad's birthday, and do some stuff that is not accepted by Salafist are infidels. And all of these moderate Sunni Muslim people are not accepted by Salafist as Muslims.

Austin Cline [515] wrote that: "Too many critics of Islam, including atheists, fail to appreciate just how diverse and varied Islam can be. There are things you can say that apply to all or most Muslims, as is the case with Christianity, but there are many more things which only apply to some or a few Muslims. This is especially true when it comes to Muslim extremism because Wahhabi Islam, the primary religious movement behind extremist Islam, includes beliefs and doctrines not found elsewhere.

It would be a mistake and unethical to criticize all of Islam on the basis of doctrines particular to Wahhabi Muslims. Modern Islamic extremism and terrorism simply cannot be explained or understood without looking at the history and influence of Wahhabi Islam. This means that it's important from an ethical and an academic perspective to understand what Wahhabi Islam teaches, what's so dangerous about it, and why those teachings differ from other branches of Islam."

Muslim Jihadists and Salafist – Al Qaeda and its "Islamic State"

Salafist in Islam use of the word Jihad is to describe three different kinds of struggle:

1. A believer's internal struggle to live out the Muslim faith as well as possible
2. The struggle to build a good Muslim society
3. Holy war: the struggle to defend Islam, with force if necessary

Many modern writers claim that the main meaning of Jihad is the internal spiritual struggle, and this is accepted by many Muslims. While Salafist is a militant group of extremist Sunnis who believe themselves the only correct interpreters of the Qur'an and consider moderate Muslims to be infidels; seek to convert all Muslims and to insure that its own fundamentalist version of Islam will dominate the world.

---

[515] Austine Cline, *"Wahhabism and Wahhabi Islam: How Wahhabi Islam Differs from Sunni - Shia Islam"* - Critics of Islam & Islamic Extremism Must Understand Wahhabi Extremist Beliefs" About.com Guide, www.pbs.org/wgbh/pages/frontline/shows/saudi/

Such new Muslim fundamentalist, Salafist, Jihadist is better known by "Takfeeriyoun" who tolerate the fanatic Muslim only grew strong as they followed to direction of Osama bin Laden's Qaeda to bring the Arab countries to fanatic Muslim rule.

To understand the Jihadists should start with the ideology of Osama bin Laden and the Al-Qaeda organization. According to Peter L. Bergab[516], "Bin Laden came to age as the Muslim world was experiencing an Islamic awakening known as the Sahwa. This awakening came after Egypt, Syria and Jordan had suffered a devastating defeat in the 1967 war with Israel, so exposing the ideological bankruptcy of Arab nationalism/socialism, which had been the dominant intellectual current in the Middle East since the 1950s. And that defeat came a year after the execution of the Egyptian writer Sayyid Qutb, whose writings and 'martyrdom' would play a key role in the burgeoning Islamic movement."

"This period of Islamic awakening peaked in 1979 – the first year of a new century on the Muslim calendar – with four seismic events that would profoundly influence bin Laden and other future members of al Qaeda: the overthrow of the Shah of Iran by the cleric Ayatollah Khomeini, by Saudi militants; Egypt's historic cease-fire agreement with Israel; and finally, the Soviet Union's invasion of Afghanistan. It was a thrilling time to be a deeply committed Muslim, as the two-two-year-old bin Laden already was"

The 9/11 plot against the United States demonstrate the central importance that bin Laden plays in al Qaeda. Now with bin Laden's elimination, new leadership of Jihadists took over mainly the Egyptian Dr. Ayman Zawahiri. Zawahiri became a distinguish leader for the extremist Muslim Brotherhood of Al Qaeda joining him from Egypt, Syria, Jordan, Palestine, Lebanon, Iraq, Sudan, Libya, Tunisia and Algeria and from other Muslim countries such as Afghanistan and Pakistan.

Dr. Ayman al-Zawahiri is al-Qaeda Central's (AQC) chief ideologue, a former surgeon, and the former leader of the Egyptian al-Jihad group. In December 2001, one of his monographs, entitled Knights under the Prophet's Banner, the book was smuggled by an Egyptian Islamist who is a close aide of Al-Zawahiri out of an Afghan cave in the Kandahar region to the border city of Peshawar and then to London where it was published and then serialized partially in al-Sharq al-Awsat, the London-based newspaper connected to the Saudi prince Salman bin 'Abed al-'Aziz al-Saud. Al-Zawahiri recounts the events of the Al-Jihad Organization's early years as he experienced them, beginning with his joining the first Al-Jihad cell in Cairo in 1966, that is,

---

[516] Peter L. Bergan, "The Osama bin Laden I know," FREE PRESS – a division of Simon & Schuster, Inc, New York, 2006, p.1

before he completed his 16th year (Al-Zawahiri was born in 1951) and then recounts subsequent events that shook the world.

The monograph doubles as a memoir of al-Zawahiri's younger days as a radical Islamist activist in his native Egypt and an ideological treatise in which he lays out his political and religious world view, and the role he thinks the "global jihadi movement" that he and Osama bin Laden sought to create with AQC should play in the future.

Al-Zawahiri was arrested in connection with the assassination of former President Anwar al-Sadat and spent three years in jail. In 1985 he left Egypt for Peshawar and there he succeeded in uniting the Afghan Arab fanatic and extremists groups.

Another Jordanian leader Muhannad Al Zarqawi created a "terrorist" organization from followers came from Muslim countries and known as "the Group of Muhannad Abu Mus'ab Al Zarqawi" or "al Tawhid" organization.

Abu Bakr al-Baghdadi, currently at the head of the "Islamic State" is supposed to be born as Awwad Ibrahim Ali al-Badri al-Samarrai in the northern Iraqi town of Samarra in 1971, Baghdadi grew up a Sunni in a devout family. Baghdadi's first appearance on international radars was likely after the 2003 invasion of Iraq, when he was detained in Camp Bucca by U.S. forces. The precise timing and nature of his arrest is unknown, but it is usually dated somewhere between 2004 and 2005, with a release in 2009.

Following his internment, Baghdadi rose through the ranks of Al Qaeda in Iraq (AQI), becoming its leader in 2010 in the wake of United States strikes that wiped out the former chiefs. Baghdadi's elevated status also landed him on the U.S. State Department's terror list, with a $10 million bounty on his head.

AQI went through a series of important changes under Baghdadi, joining the battlefield in Syria's civil war, breaking away from al-Qaeda to become "ISIS" and eventually declaring it had restored a period of historic Islamic rule known as a caliphate, with "Caliph al-Baghdadi" and re-naming itself the "Islamic State".

In Conclusion

Today, the Muslim Brotherhood-who at one point managed to dominate governments have lost its strength in Egypt, Lybia and Tunisia. In Jordan, the Brotherhood's strategy seems also to be failing. In Syria, amid the carnage, the Brotherhood looks militarily effective in destructing Syria's infrastructure, but politically disoriented without hope of success even with the so-called created "Islamic State".

Given that Muslims are now to be found in every corner of the globe, the implication is that the emerging "Islamic State" from "the Islamic State of Iraq and Syria (ISIS)" or "the Islamic State of Iraq and the Levant (ISIL)" is disclaiming all national borders, it wants to create an Islamic world-state, ultimately seeks world domination. "ISIS" strives for a world-wide Caliphate and wants to return to a supposed era of "pure" Islamic rule, the caliphate, when all Muslims were subject to God's laws (*Shari'ah*).

With such global claim, the intolerant and violent extremist groups like "ISIS" and their kin, committing the abhorrent crimes against humanity in the name of Islam, pose an existential challenge not only to Christians, but to all ethnic groups in the world community and especially to Arabs and Muslims. Currently, "ISIS" would like nothing better than to embroil the United States and the American soldiers in a ground war so that it can rally more people to expel the giant United States from invading the Middle East for the "national security of Israel" and the flow of oil under its supervision.

"ISIS" must be defeated before expanding worldwide. As such "Islamic State" has risen to power and prominence recently; hundreds of reports have emerged about the group, often portraying it as a large, somewhat amorphous band of extremists with structures overseeing hundreds of towns, thousands of fighters and millions of dollars in finances.

The world community should be asked to look to the future and imagine the kind of society they want to emerge from the current turmoil. The world community is on a verge of World War III, if diplomacy would fail and allow "ISIS" terrorism to grow worldwide.

If Politics is considered the art of the possible, then looking for a collision or use of violence will not bring stability and perfection, especially after agreeing that the economic crises helped trigger the revolutions; as economic gets worsen criticism increased in accusing the new Islamic governments of focusing more on increasing the Islamist parties' grip on power than on governing in the interest of all their citizens. The decisive solutions never come without "Dialogue".

Dialogue will become the peaceful way relying on the basics of the political game. If dialogue, now and in the future, is followed, the modern Islamic society will become democratic and peaceful without creating a Caliphate state.

The time now for constructive dialogue among conflicting parties and accept that Islam is not the solution; democracy is.

REFERENCES

Abed Al-Razzak Nofal, "Muhammad - Messenger and Prophet".

Abi Jaafar Al-Nahhas, "Al-Nasikh wal Mansukh".

Abu Al-Fida, "History"

Abu An-Nasr, Omar, "Al-Hhadhara Al-Amawiya Al-Arabia fi Dimashk"

Al-Asfahani, "Al-Aghani"

Al-Azraqi, "Akhbar Mecca"

Al-Bukhari, "Sahhih"

Al-Feiruzabadi, "Taj Al-'Arouss"- (the Crown of the Bride)

Al- Kazweeni, "Imtina' Al-Assmaa'"

Al-Mas'udi,"Al-Tanbih wa Al-Ishraf".

Al-Mass'udi, "Muruj Al-Zahab"

Ar-Razi, Imam Abi Al-Fadel Ahmad "Hujaj Al-Qur'an leejamee' Ahl almilal wa ala'dian"

As-Samman, Mohamad, "Muhammad, the Human Prophet"

Al-Shahrastani, "Al-Milal wa Al-Nihal"

Al-Tabari, "Al-Sira"

Al-Tabari, "Tarikh al-Ummam wal Muluk," [History of Nations and Kings], Beirut: Dar al-Fikr, 1987

Al-Ya'kubi, "The History"

Archimandrite Al-Haddad, "Al-Qur'an wa Al-Kitab", Beirut 1982

Archimandrite Yusuf Durrah Al-Haddad, "The Qur'an – a "Nazarene" Call", Beirut, 1986

Arland J. Hulton & Steven A. Haggmark, "The Earliest Christian Heretics – Reading from their opponents," Fortress Press, 1996

Assad Rustum, "History of the Great City of God Antioch".

Az-Zamakhshari's interpretation

Bergan, Peter L. "The Osama bin Laden I know," FREE PRESS – a division of Simon & Schuster, Inc, New York, 2006

Christopher Scarre and Brian Fagan, "Ancient Civilizations", Longman: 1997.

Cyrus H. Gordon, "The Ancient Near East", Norton: 1965

Diodorus

Duchesne, "The Ancient History of the Church"

Ebionite.org website

Effarah, Jamil, "Palestine is not the Promised Land", 2002

Epiphanius, Bishop of Salamis, Refutation of All Hersies – Panarion", translated by Philip R. Amidon, New York, Oxford University Press, 1990.

Epiphanius, "The All-inclusive in History"

Eusebius, "The History of the Church from Christ to Constantine", translated by G.A. Williams, Miniapolis: Augsburg Press, 1975

Farroukh, Omar, "Al-Arab wal Islam", The Arabs and Islam), Beirut

Ferguson, Everett et al., eds., "Monophysitism"" in the Encyclopedia of Early Christianity, New York: Garland, 1970

Ferguson, Everett et al., eds., "Nestorism" in the Encyclopedia of Early Christianity, New York: Garland, 1970

Fliche and Martin, "The History of the Church"

Garraty, John A and Gay Peter, eds., "The Columbia History of the World," New York: Harper & Row, 1972

Giovanni Filorano, "The History of Gnosticism", Blackwell: 1990.

Haykel, Hussein, "Hayat Muhammad" (Life of Muhammad)

Hitti, Philip K., "History of the Arabs from the Earliest Times to the Present," London MacMillan Education, 1970

Hitti, Philip K., "History of the Arabs", Macmillan & Co. Ltd. London, eighth edition, St. Martin's Press, New York, 1964

Hassan Ben Thabet, "Elegy of Prophet Muhammad."

Hermas, "The Shepherd"

Hippolytus, "Refutation of All Heresies"

Hironimus, "Vita Hiharionis XXV".

Ibn Hisham, "Al-Sira Al-Nabawiah", Egypt 1936

Ibn Katheer, Imad-eddin Abi Al-fida Ismaeel, "Tafseer Bin Katheer", published by Dar Al-Andalus, Beirut, 1966

Ibn Khaldun, "History Book", Dar Al-Kitab Al-Lubnani, Volume two, Beirut

Ibn Saad, "Tabakat"

Ibn Saad, "Wafadaat al-Arab".

Irenaeus, "Against The Heresies", translated by Dominic J

Jawad Ali, "History of the Arabs before Islam".

Jerome, "Collection of the Latin Fathers"

Josephus, "The Jewish War".

Julius Scott, "Glimpses of Jewish Christianity from the End of Acts to Justin Martyr", unpublished paper presented at ETS meeting, November 1997.

Justin Martyr, "Dialogue with Trypho the Jew", translated by Thomas B. Falls, New York Christian Heritage, 1999.

Kipfer, Barbara Ann, ed. "Encyclopedia of Archaeology," New York: Kluwer Academic/Plenum, 2000

Mohammad Al-Ghazali, "Fiqeh Al-Sira".

Mohammed 'Izzat Darwazat, "Al-Qur'an Al-Majeed" (The Glorious Qur'an)

Mohammed 'Izzat Darwazat, "'Asr Al-Nabi (Sad) wa Bi'atahu Kabl Al-Bi'that – (The Age of the Prophet and his Environment Before the Revelation")

Mohammed Darwazat "Sira Al-Rassoul – The Life of the Prophet"

Mohammed Hussein Haikal, "The Life of Muhammad".

Mohammed Kurd Ali "Khuttat Al-Shaam"

Mustafa Al-Rafi'I, "Al-Islam Intilak la Jumoud".

Mustapha Al-Sakka, "Al-Sira Al-Nabawiah (the Life History of the Prophecy) of Ibn Hisham", Cairo, 1936.

Origen, "the Collection of the Greek Fathers".

Pheme Perkins, "Gnosticism and the New Testament", Fortress: 1993.

Puin, Gred -R. (1996). *"Observations on Early Qur'an Manuscripts in San'a'"*. In Stefan Wild. *The Qur'an as Text*. Leiden, Netherlands: *E. J. Brill*. Reprinted in *What the Koran Really Says*, ed. Ibn Warraq, Prometheus Books, 2002

Ray A. Pritz, "Nazarene Jewish Christians: From the End of the New Testament Period until its Disappearance in the Fourth Century." 1990.

Rev. Father Shikho, "Divan Al-Samaw'al", 1920

"Revue Biblique" Magazine #476, 1930

Robert M. Grant, "Greek Apologists of the Second Century" Westminster, 1988

Salem, Al-Sayyed Abd el-Aziz, "Tarikh al-Dawlah al-Arabiyyah", [History of the Arab Nation], Beirut: Dar al-Nahdhah al-Arabiyyah, 1986.

Salibi, Kamal "Khafaya Al-Tawrat wa 'Asrar Sha'ab Israel"

Salibi, Kamal "The Bible Came From Arabia", 1986

Shabbir Akhtar, "A Faith For All Seasons", Chicago, Ivan R. Dee Publisher, 1990

Shahid, Irfan "Rome and the Arabs: A Prolegomenon to the Study of Byzantium and the Arabs," Washington D.C.: Dumbarton Oaks, 1984

Simon, Marcel, "Verus Israel", Paris, 1948.

Spenser, Robert, "Did Muhammad Really Exist? An Inquiry into Islam's Obscure Origins," Kindle Edition, Wilmington, Delaware, 2012

Subayhh, Muhammad, "A'an Al-Qur'an" (About the Qur'an)

Tabbarah, Afif Abed Al-Fattah "Rouh Al-Deen Al-Islami" (The Spirit of Islam), 4th ed

The Catholic Encyclopedia, Volume IV, Robert Appleton Company, 1908

The Hebrew Bible, Paralipomenon and the Kings

The Holy Bible, Confraternity and Douay Texts, Rembrandt Edition, Abradale Press Inc., 1959

The Holy Qur'an

The Sira Al-Halabiah, vol.1

The Sira Al-Macciah, published by the Istekamah press in Cairo, 1962

Unger & Rev. John J. Dilllen, Ancient Christina writers 55, New York: Paulist Press, 1992.

Vermes, Geza, "A historian reading of the Gospels," 1981

Walter Wagner, "After the Apostles: Christianity in the Second Century", Fortress: 1994.

Ware, Timothy (Kallistos), The Orthodox Church, Penguin, 1993

William Frend, "The Archaeology of Early Christianity—A History", Fortress: 1996.

World Conference on Religion and Peace, New York, 1999

Yakout, "Mu'jam" (Dictionary)

Zacharie le Rheteur, "Histoire Ecclesiastique VIII".

ABOUT THE AUTHOR

Dr. Jamil Effarah has been a resident of Ventura County, California, since 1978. He is an Arab American from Lebanon, born in Haifa, Palestine. He is married to his cousin Mathilda Effarah and has two sons and six grandchildren.

He obtained a BA degree from the American University of Beirut (AUB), a MEd from Louisiana State University in Baton Rouge (LSU), an MS degree in computer science from University of Southern Louisiana in Lafayette (ULL), an MBA from California Lutheran University in Thousand Oaks (CLU), and a PhD from University of Oregon in Eugene (U of O).

He published his first book in Arabic in 1958, The Political Problems of the Sudan, and an updated second edition in 2000. He established, owned, and directed Kfarshima College in Kfarshima, Lebanon, in 1962.

His dissertation "The Impact of Electronic Data Processing on Business Education in the Secondary Schools of Oregon," is classified at the foundation level of the Mathematics Genealogy Project at North Dakota State University (NDSU) and is being taught as part of the Mathematics Subject Classification: 97—Mathematics Education at the University of North Dakota in Fargo.

Dr. Borg and Dr. Gall quoted Dr. Effarah and added another chapter, "Evaluation Research," in the third edition of their book Educational Research, 1979. Dr. Effarah has originated a baseline to measure the unmet needs.

He has published over one thousand articles in Arabic and English in different newspapers and magazines in United States and in the Middle East.

He published a number of books in English online through the Author House www.AuthorHouse.com. and a number of other published books in English and in Arabic, and more written books are still waiting to be published.